PERSPECTIVES FROM SOCIAL ECONOMICS

Series Editor:
Mark D. White, professor in the Department of Political Science, Economics, and Philosophy at the College of Staten Island/CUNY

The Perspectives from Social Economics series incorporates an explicit ethical component into contemporary economic discussion of important policy and social issues, drawing on the approaches used by social economists around the world. It also allows social economists to develop their own frameworks and paradigms by exploring the philosophy and methodology of social economics in relation to orthodox and other heterodox approaches to economics. By furthering these goals, this series will expose a wider readership to the scholarship produced by social economists, and thereby promote the more inclusive viewpoints, especially as they concern ethical analyses of economic issues and methods.

Published by Palgrave Macmillan

Accepting the Invisible Hand: Market-Based Approaches to Social-Economic Problems
Edited by Mark D. White

Consequences of Economic Downturn: Beyond the Usual Economics
Edited by Martha A. Starr

Alternative Perspectives of a Good Society
Edited by John Marangos

Exchange Entitlement Mapping: Theory and Evidence
By Aurélie Charles

Approximating Prudence: Aristotelian Practical Wisdom and Economic Models of Choice
By Andrew M. Yuengert

Freedom of Contract and Paternalism: Prospects and Limits of an Economic Approach
By Péter Cserne

Toward a Good Society in the Twenty-First Century: Principles and Policies
Edited by Nikolaos Karagiannis and John Marangos

Toward a Good Society in the Twenty-First Century

Principles and Policies

Edited by

Nikolaos Karagiannis and
John Marangos

palgrave
macmillan

TOWARD A GOOD SOCIETY IN THE TWENTY-FIRST CENTURY

First published in 2013 by
PALGRAVE MACMILLAN®
in the United States—a division of St. Martin's Press LLC,
175 Fifth Avenue, New York, NY 10010.

Where this book is distributed in the UK, Europe and the rest of the world, this is by Palgrave Macmillan, a division of Macmillan Publishers Limited, registered in England, company number 785998, of Houndmills, Basingstoke, Hampshire RG21 6XS.

Palgrave Macmillan is the global academic imprint of the above companies and has companies and representatives throughout the world.

ISBN: 978–1–137–27473–1

Library of Congress Cataloging-in-Publication Data

Toward a good society in the twenty-first century : principles and policies / edited by Nikolaos Karagiannis and John Marangos.
pages cm—(Perspectives from social economics.)
Includes index.
ISBN 978–1–137–27473–1 (alk. paper)
1. Social policy. 2. Welfare economics. 3. Welfare state. I. Karagiannis, Nikolaos, 1964– II. Marangos, John, 1962–

HN18.3.T68 2013
306—dc23 2012046504

A catalogue record of the book is available from the British Library.

Design by Newgen Imaging Systems (P) Ltd., Chennai, India.

First edition: May 2013

10 9 8 7 6 5 4 3 2 1

Contents

Tables and Figures

Tables

Figures

Foreword

What constitutes a good society? This is a question that humans have grappled with for ages. The elements thought to make a good society have varied over time. So too has the collection of perspectives regarding those elements. As our interactions have become more global, "society" has become an even larger place. With that expansion comes an increase in the number of opinions, perspectives, and outlooks regarding what is good. Disparate cultural ideas strive for reconciliation or dominance, while local experiences vie for center stage as we seek to define what is good for all.

A common question across time, space, cultures, and ideas is whether perspectives favor the individual or the collective good. Individualism as a fundamental belief gives way to frameworks and doctrines that promulgate the independence of human beings. Within these frameworks, a good society is deemed one where an individual's possibilities are only limited by his or her own lack of focus, initiative, and perseverance. By contrast, the belief in collectivism promotes outlooks grounded in the idea of interrelated destinies. A good society is one that strives to insure that everyone has access to what they need to prosper, and shares in contributing to the goal of equity.

This edited book is born out of the belief that a good society is one that is focused on the collective good. The chapters are grounded in the idea that society pays when it relegates issues such as poverty, crime, hunger, and unemployment to analyses of deficient individuals. The volume suggests that society will fail if it neglects to care for all. The chapters on education and distribution remind us that failure to include everyone in how we define poverty and its impact will lead to social policies that miss the opportunity to cultivate potential contributions from all citizens. Moreover these authors argue that the ultimate price is a society that spends more resources managing underdevelopment (education, employment, health, and the like) than it does developing its full reservoir of talent. In terms of sustainability, the authors propose ideas that help to balance the goals of capitalism with the need to move toward a more environmentally sustainable economic base. These chapters argue that being profitable and being green are not necessarily mutually exclusive concepts and that a marriage between the two provides a healthy economy for today and the future. The pieces on economic development focus on ways to include all people in employment policies. Together these chapters suggest that unemployment and underemployment can be eradicated through policies and programs designed to bring the unemployed and the underemployed more fully into the workforce. The book ends with several chapters focused on developing humans toward a more collective ideology.

Defining a good society in the twenty-first century is a task unlike one at any other time in history. How we choose to reconcile the debate between individual versus collective good has a broader impact than ever before. The impact is not only limited to people and how to best develop human potential but also involves serious questions about the health of the planet. This volume takes a definitive stance on the collective good. The voices within add greatly to what are probably the most important social, cultural, and political debates of our times.

Dr. Brenda A. Allen
Provost and vice chancellor for Academic Affairs
Winston-Salem State University, North Carolina

Preface

In history, a distinction between eras or periods implies a major and fundamental change in the system of institutions governing a society. The twentieth century has seen numerous writings on the role of institutions, and the links connecting state and society. The term "institution" is commonly applied to customs and behavior patterns important to a society, as well as to particular formal organizations of government and public services. As mechanisms of social interaction, institutions are manifest in both formal organizations and in informal social order and organizations—reflecting human psychology, culture, habits, and customs, and encompassing subjective experience of meaningful enactments.

Certainly, in every society, there is some form of government organization that may, or may not, represent the members of the society collectively but indeed plays an important role in the national economy. And, evidently, some institutions work better than others. States not only differ in their institutional design but also in their effectiveness, in their ability to actually govern. Sociopolitical elements, such as political parties, interest groups, social movements, and patron-client relations, which connect citizens to the state, are important because they convey demands to the government. The way in which they are structured—clientelistic or programmatic parties, pluralist or corporatist interest groups—affects which demands get through and which are discouraged, advantaging some groups at the expense of others.

The state and society are connected to each other through political participation. Some countries have "strong, adaptable, coherent political institutions" in which there is high probability that policies will be implemented as the government intended. Other countries suffer from a crisis of governability. The more power is dispersed within the state, the more there are opportunities for special interests to apply pressure upon it. Some states are able to handle the strong influence of political parties and other linkage organizations, while others are overwhelmed by it. The former are called "strong states," which display capacity—ability to pursue national goals and implement demands effectively—and autonomy from social interests, often acting as interest groups. The latter, called "weak states," are captured by narrow interests, are characterized by corruption, and lack the capacity to govern as they cannot translate their authority into policy formulation and execution. Likewise, strong and weak political parties play significant roles in democracies, competing to win elections and form governments, and can be built on patronage and clientelism or public programs. Citizens engage in different forms of political participation depending on the resources they have and the opportunities to deploy them.

In order to distinguish strong from weak states and link them to the concept of good society, we turn to the "Failed State Index 2009," developed by The Fund for Peace in conjunction with the journal *Foreign Policy*. The Failed State Index used 12 indicators, including social factors such as the amount of internal violence, economic parameters such as stability, and political indicators such as the quality of public services, to assess state strength and weakness. States that performed the best on these indicators—what we would call the strongest—were labeled "sustainable." Canada and Australia were members of this select group. The index proceeds down to the next group, which included much of Western Europe and the United States, where state performance was good or "moderate" as the index referred to it. The next group of states, such as Mexico and India, earned a "warning" because there was cause for concern about the quality of these states. The index issued an "alert" to the last and worst performing group of states, which included Somalia and Yemen, because it doubted their continuing viability, or because these states had collapsed entirely.

A good society, we argue, is one that meets the physical needs of its citizens: people should be fed, sheltered, and healthy. Good societies also equip their citizens with skills to make informed decisions regarding their lives and are ones in which people are safe from violence. The quality of the state seems to be linked to the form of government, the extent to which countries have democratic or authoritarian political systems.

To some extent, the formation and mobilization of sociopolitical organizations and institutions have been reduced by technological innovations such as the Internet. Indeed, electronic forms of communication reduce communication, coordination, and information costs, and facilitate group formation and efficiency. The expense of a bureaucracy to carry out basic functions can now be avoided because these tasks can be done cheaply and more quickly through computer-mediated communication. In addition, the Internet has not only facilitated social group formation but has also given impetus to professional advocacy organizations.

All the above theoretical issues are very important in seeking to answer the key question, "Why are some countries better than others at improving their citizens' lives?" and, at the same time, in exploring principles and policies needed to bring about the good society in the twenty-first century. This timely multidisciplinary volume incorporates a wide range of diverse topics and, I am sure, will contribute significantly toward offering sophisticated and suitable answers.

Hon. Dr. Bernard J. Nottage, MP
Minister of National Security and
Leader of Government Business
The Commonwealth of The Bahamas

Introduction

This book, *Toward a Good Society in the Twenty-first Century: Principles and Policies,* is the second volume published by Palgrave Macmillan on the same theme. The first volume, *Alternative Perspectives of a Good Society*, which came out in January 2012, identifies and defines the elements of a good society. The current volume explores the principles and polices needed to bring about the good society and focuses on four broad themes that are deemed important toward achieving a good or better society: quality education and fair distribution; environmentally sustainable prosperity; inclusive economic development and significant job creation; and beneficial civic institutions, and deepening of freedom and time use. All these topics can be highly controversial given the contemporary phenomena of neoliberalism and neoconservativism, and the association of both with right-wing political parties and institutions, especially during the past three decades or so. The same issues however, given the range and magnitude of present socioeconomic problems coupled with numerous neoliberal policy failures worldwide (as ample evidence, available data, and statistical information clearly reveal), call for alternative perspectives on theoretical (philosophical) and policy grounds.

In ordinary parlance, neoliberalism refers to the repudiation of Keynesian economics and policy intervention, and the ascendance of the Chicago school of political economy. In popular usage, neoliberalism is equated with a radically free market doctrine: a range of economic, monetary, and social policies favorable to business and indifferent toward poverty, human distress, social deracination, cultural decimation, long-term resource depletion, and environmental destruction. Consequently, the main task of the book is to provide a milieu of alternative principles and policies toward addressing recent social challenges and multidimensional problems and achieving better or more humane societies. This multidisciplinary edited volume is structured around four parts and offers a collection of essays and contributions by well-respected authors with specialized knowledge and skills on particular issues about a good society.

Part I, titled "Education, Distribution, and Good Society," includes chapters 1, 2, and 3. In the opening chapter, Pearson argues that moral education is clearly a public concern, as the collateral societal consequences and human costs of immoral behavior and incarceration—supported in research, crimes statistics, and school environments—are enormous. According to the author, as the impact of wasted lives, broken and dysfunctional families, maladjusted and troubled children are incalculable as are the adverse social, economic, and political consequences of weakened communities and weakened opportunities for economic mobility, more prisons and other forms of retributive justice systems are not durable solutions to the problem. Being guided by the principles of inclusiveness, modeling, practice, acquisition, and compact (IMPACT), Pearson proposes character development programs, institutionalized moral development interventions by historically black colleges and universities (HBCUs), and competence-building measures for both teachers and students, which, all together, can enhance the good society.

In chapter 2, Williams reminds us that over the past generation, a period of remarkable economic growth and relative prosperity, brought help to many but not all US households. By the evidence given, upward of one-third of the households did not experience a substantial increase in net worth. Further evidence reveals that these households had limited access to the pathways to wealth accumulation, and despite the gains made by them to save regularly and purchase homes, the rising tide of prosperity left many high and dry. Understanding the underlying causes should aid in the creation of effective remedies seeking a more equitable, humane, and functional society. To this end, Williams offers four policy recommendations that can rebalance the twin poles of individual ingenuity and collective responsibility in which the latter is strengthened while the former is more broadly inclusive: (1) funding of individual development accounts, (2) expanding access to post-secondary education, (3) transforming the home mortgage deduction into a mortgage tax credit, and (4) advancing an inheritance tax.

Chapter 3, by Meulders and O'Dorchai, seeks to revisit the existing literature on poverty based on discussion and illustration of the implications of the choice of the measurement unit. The authors present the results of an in-depth analysis at the individual level of the actual income and poverty situation of women and men. Starting out from a conceptual discussion, the chapter illustrates the effects of switching from household income to individual income on the analysis of poverty. Three domains of poverty research are put to the test. First, it is shown how the calculation of poverty rates is affected by the level at which income is assessed (household versus individual level). Second, the literature on the income effects for a couple who are breaking up are put to the individualization test. Finally, the population of working poor is explored from an individual lens rather than applying the standard household-based definition of poverty to workers with a necessarily individual employment status. These results provide ground for numerous policy recommendations that should not be gender-biased but should acknowledge the gender dimension of labor market participation, social inclusion, social protection, and access to social rights.

Part II, titled "Sustainability, Ecology, and Good Society," comprises chapters 4, 5, and 6. In chapter 4, Turnbull identifies a new type of "ecological" capitalism that can simultaneously promote a good society today while achieving environmentally sustainable prosperity. By protecting and nurturing the environment, and especially the nonrenewable resources, ecological capitalism provides a politically attractive way to encourage both depopulation and de-growth to create a virtuous reinforcing process that can not only transform society today but can also establish a good society for future generations. Turnbull anticipates that a sustainable global good life may require a reduction in population as people live longer without the ability to earn a living income. Ecological capitalism widely distributes the ownership of income-producing assets to provide a universal dividend income to replace welfare payments, big governments, and taxes. Ecological property rights increase efficiency and equity by replacing static, exclusive, and perpetual rules of ownership with ones that are dynamic, inclusive, and time limited. A tax strategy is described to provide the incentive for existing owners of firms to voluntarily relinquish their ownership to local stakeholders to localize ownership and control. This enriches democracy and provides communities the power to protect the sustainability of their local environment. Maintenance of ecological ownership for each citizen depends upon their contribution to maintaining ownership values by being a stakeholder such as a resident use of a home, worker, customer, supplier, and so on.

Chapter 5, by Cole and Kepner, explores how green consumers in a capitalist economy are limited in their ability to produce the sustainable economy that being green advocates. The authors then consider questions of how advertising impacts the individual's ability to make environmentally friendly choices, and how government regulations produce (or do not produce) a sustainable economy. In examining what a true green revolution would look like, Cole and Kepner offer concrete recommendations for encouraging the development of green consumers (with less emphasis on the "consumer" and more on the "green") through ethical guidance, government regulations, and the evolution of institutions and social norms.

In chapter 6, Spitz explores the effects that social norms associated with workplace identity and norms associated with national identity exert on sustainability views. Using an original data set collected from US and Australian academics in 2008 and 2009, the author examines whether academics in the field of business tend to value, or not value, specific aspects of sustainability and democratic development consistent with long-term goals of a good society. Compared to ideological orientations held by comparable academics in other fields, business academics in this research are found to be significantly less supportive of sustainable practices. National differences in views about sustainability are also pronounced, with Australian academics valuing sustainability more highly. According to Spitz, the results suggest that a more cosmopolitan approach than "Free Trade" is needed in drafting specific policies to influence or constrain global business activity, if that activity is to lead to a good society for more than business owners and managers themselves.

Part III, titled "Economic Development, Employment, and Good Society," contains chapters 7 and 8. In chapter 7, Powlick analyzes the active involvement of young people in economic development as an important component of a good society by approaching "development" from a human development perspective building on Sen's (1983, 1985) concept of *capabilities*. The author utilizes the mixed-method study from which data involving youth programs in New York State is drawn to support the arguments made. The role of young people as economic actors in the community and the ways youth settings and informal institutions contribute to development through a coevolution of individuals and institutions are extensively discussed, while after-school programs, also called Out-of-School Time or OST programs, are used as an example. Powlick then pays special attention to meaningful participation and participatory structures, and examines how young people are included in development through participation in community change projects and the fostering of agency. By promoting the agency of youth, informal institutions promote long-term development through both individual and institutional channels, providing young people with skills to consciously challenge institutions that influence and potentially limit their lives.

In chapter 8, Murray contrasts the Chicago School of Economics with Lowe's "instrumental method." By isolating the goal of full employment as the macroeconomic objective, the author argues that the promotion of free markets over the past three decades has not achieved, and cannot achieve, this objective. Furthermore, the "unintended consequences" of neoliberalism have not led to advancing social welfare in the United States. Rather, they have led to the deterioration of the working class, an increase in crime, and a deterioration of the psyche of those affected by unemployment. Contrary to neoliberal thought, Murray claims that there must be a clear separation between the macroeconomic goal of full employment and the microeconomic goal of profit generation, as the latter does not promote the former. Consequently, if full employment is to be maintained, it must be an actively pursued policy by the federal government. The chapter ends with a brief discussion of the current Employer of Last Resort (ELR) proposal, which advocates direct government involvement toward the goal of full employment while, at the same time, maintaining the pecuniary interests of capitalists.

Part IV, titled "Civic Institutions, Freedom, Time, and Good Society," contains chapters 9, 10, and 11. In Chapter 9, Bailey, Páez, and Sadri describe good societies as those that exhibit lessened inequality; good governance, prosperity, peace, positivity, passion, and relations among people; and the development of a competitive advantage. These features are typically described in terms that are philosophical, abstract, and long-term or considered as part of addressing specific, short-term social change activities. Their analysis clearly demonstrates the advantages that can be gained by the use of an "honest broker" or provider of data and information as a practical mechanism for creating a good society in the present. According to the authors, Forsyth Futures, a nonprofit organization, is such a provider of community knowledge and plays a role in making such a good society a reality today in Forsyth County, North Carolina.

Chapter 10, by O'Boyle, advances two propositions in support of a personalist reconstruction of the paradigm that informs thinking about economic affairs. In contrast to the oversimplification of the economic agent as *homo economicus* and the use of utility/profit maximization notion of mainstream economics, the author proposes the *acting person* and the "personalist capital" respectively. These two propositions set the foundations for a good society that is built and sustained by the *active* involvement of ordinary human beings in everyday affairs, thus, the origin of the *acting person.* O'Boyle examines how human persons develop as economic agents or acting persons through consumption, work, and leisure while briefly acknowledging the critical role of culture conditions and different modes of human communication.

In the last chapter of the book, Walker outlines a social accounting framework for disposable time. According to the author, much refinement can go into its data handling, such as breaking down the analysis into occupational and industrial classifications, as such refinement might produce a very different trend analysis, and different assumptions could be tested about the macroeconomic effects of work time reduction on consumption and the multipliers that might apply to different scenarios. Throughout the chapter, Walker does not talk about the applicability of this kind of analysis to national income and product accounting but a hint of its applicability could be taken from two of the pillars of his argument and from pioneers of national income accounting, John M. Clark and Edward F. Denison. According to the author, as a community advances, agitation for shorter hours will be constantly breaking out since an outbreak is long overdue.

Our task would have been incomplete if we had not acknowledged those who kindly aided us in completing this book. We thank the contributors for their willingness to participate and to respond to our suggestions, the reviewers who allocated valuable time in providing constructive comments to the authors, as well as the advisers and staff of Palgrave Macmillan who have provided excellent support throughout the preparation of this manuscript. Last, but not the least, we would like to thank our families for their continuous encouragement and support, and our students for the inducements. We owe them more than we can recount.

NIKOLAOS KARAGIANNIS AND JOHN MARANGOS
Winston-Salem, North Carolina, USA and
Rethymno, Crete, Greece
September 2012

Part I

Education, Distribution, and Good Society

Chapter 1

Moral Education and the Good Society: An IMPACT for HBCUs

Denise Pearson

Introduction

My interest in the topic of moral education emerged while pursuing a master's degree in conflict resolution, after completing master's and doctorate degrees in education administration. A close examination of the three programs revealed strong cross-disciplinary connections from my perspective, although only loosely (if at all) associated across the curriculums. Coupled with nearly two decades of higher education experience—including teaching and administration—I have observed the behaviors of stakeholder groups throughout the educational enterprise and at times questioned their individual and collective moral reasoning, including my own. As such, this could not be treated simply as reflective practice, and a deeper study of relationships between these two disciplines continued to evolve. The idea of moral education and the good society is an extension of this pursuit of knowledge and meaning.

An immediate question became, how can you cultivate and sustain the good society in the presence of rising social conflict and educational systems in crisis? The social conflicts at the center of this discussion are not those interpersonal and group situations Coser describes as having the potential to contribute to the maintenance, adjustment, or adaptation of social relationships and structures (1957, 151). The social conflicts at the heart of this argument are those that interfere with individual rights to attain quality education—absent of fear, violence, and hostility in pursuit of one's meaningful life. As a good education is deemed necessary to function freely and effectively in a democratic society, the notion of not addressing harmful relationships and structures has moral implications at its core.

Educators and philosophers differ on the purpose of education in society. Nonetheless, Huitt identifies three main purposes that are widely accepted, which include the development of a purpose for one's life, the development of one's character, and the development of competence (Huitt 2004). Similarly, Walsh claims that the role of education is the development of knowledge and competence, training of ability to think critically, and the development of character (Walsh 1990). At its nucleus, character has been defined as engaging in conduct and words that are morally appropriate, or refraining from inappropriate conduct or words, and consisting of that which can be observed, according to Wynne and Walberg (1984). Pritchard defines character, as reflected in one's actions, as a complex set of relatively persistent qualities of the individual person (1988). It follows naturally that the purpose of all education, including moral and character development, should be reflected in the curriculum, beginning with learning outcomes. The purpose of educational programs is oftentimes carefully crafted in mission, vision, and values statements but falls short of being intentionally reflected in the actual curriculum. This compels some to question if the development of moral character in students is a role schools value and have accepted as a societal mandate.

This essay examines the nexus of education in a democratic society, the notion of the good society, and intentional moral development (educators influence moral development—even if unintentionally). The problem is well documented and the proposition of character education carries little risk but has the potential to offer relief to societal problems that reflect flaws in character development as manifested in our schools and communities.

The issue of morality is wrought with robust controversy. While philosophers, researchers, psychologists, educators, and others have contributed to the debate about the meaning of morality, there is no consensus and the dialogue continues. Are there universal moral codes that apply in all situations, or can we identify and pursue those that will allow citizens to peacefully coexist in a democracy? What is the role of schools in the development of moral character? Who defines what is moral, and how do you protect against imposing one group's values upon another's? Furthermore, what's the difference between moral behavior and convention? Which should be the primary focus of character education? These questions and others will be explored here.

While the debate about morality and education's role in character development continues, discussion about what constitutes appropriate curricular at various stages of the K-16 educational system is also considered. In the end, this essay will focus on character development at the postsecondary level, offering perspectives with possible implications and opportunities for the nation's 103 historically black colleges and universities (HBCUs).

Problem and Thesis

> Facts are stubborn things; and whatever may be our wishes, our inclinations, or the dictates of our passions, they cannot alter the state of facts or evidence. John Adams (In White [2006], 28)

A singular definition of the good society does not exist. However in its simplest terms, the good society allows its members to be good or to do the good. It is a society that values personal development and virtuous behavior by its members. Consequently, the good society is concerned with relationships with other members within the community, however broadly or narrowly defined.

Sociologist Amitai Etzioni's definition of a good society insists on a focus on the term "community," which he defines as consisting of two elements: "A web of affect laden relationships among a group of individuals, relationships that often crisscross and reinforce one another—rather than merely one-on-one or chainlike individual relationships; and a measure of commitment to a set of shared values, norms, and meanings, and a shared history and identity—in short, to a particular culture" (1996, 2).

A broad-brush scan of the environment exposes incidents involving a wide range of harms experienced by community members across the country every year, particularly schools, underscoring the importance and timeliness of this book. Some data is antithetical to the notion of the good society using any definition. For example, the National Center for Education Statistics conducted comprehensive research investigating school crime and safety. The culminating report was divided into five separate and well-defined categories: (1) violent deaths at school, (2) nonfatal student victimization—student reports, (3) violence at schools—public reports, (4) nonfatal teacher victimization at school—teacher reports, and (5) school environment. The report reveals alarming information including statistics that show that in 2001, students between the ages of 12 and 18 were victims of nearly two million nonfatal acts of school violence with the majority (62%) being thefts. A larger number of serious victimizations (rape, sexual assault, robbery, and aggravated assault) occurred away from school in communities.

Schools are not the only source of evidence that compel observers to question assumptions about the good society and moral education. In a study conducted by the National Alliance to End Homelessness, it was noted that the country's homeless population increased by 3 percent between the years 2008 and 2009. The report indicated that while the majority of people classified as homeless received some sort of assistance (e.g., food and temporary shelter), 40 percent of them "lived" in places such as cars and on the street. It is instructive to note that these statistics do not account for the underreporting of homeless youth, evidenced by the fact that 35 percent of communities across the country reported that there were no homeless youth in their community in 2009, suggesting the moral problem of homelessness is considerably more pervasive (National Alliance to End Homelessness 2011). These statistics call into question the social compact of protect and serve held up by law enforcement agencies across the country.

In many communities, the issue of police brutality is a serious and major issue that lends itself to the study of moral character, with implications for the good society. The National Police Misconduct Statistics and Reporting Project reported 5,986 cases of recorded misconduct, which resulted in 382 fatalities and $347,455,000 in settlements and judgments between April 2009 and June 2010. African American communities are the subject of many of these studies (2011).

As a final point to help frame the sense of urgency, I contemplate the issue of domestic violence, which like the aforementioned facts, threatens any common notion of the good society and questions our collective sense of morality. Data obtained from the Domestic Violence Resource Center reports that one in four women have experienced domestic violence in her lifetime. Women of all races are almost equally vulnerable to violence by an intimate partner. Although intimate partner violence reportedly affects people regardless of income, people with an annual income below 25 thousand dollars are at a three times higher risk of intimate partner violence than people with an annual income over 50 thousand dollars (Domestic Violence Resource Center 2012). The positive correlation between education and earnings is widely documented and will be discussed later. The goal here is to again point out the potential role of education in mitigating socials problems that have connections to moral reasoning capacity. The facts are indisputable and they illustrate deterioration of the good society. This would suggest moral and character discrepancies, and schools are positioned to assume a more deliberate role in reversing certain patterns of behavior on behalf of the good society for all citizens.

For centuries, education has played a key role in the development and maintenance of democratic and moral societies. So, why are our social institutions not determinedly seizing this opportunity to affect deep change on behalf of building a moral and just society in the twenty-first century? Are we rejecting the notion that moral education is a public issue with implications in a democracy although data suggests that it is a public issue? Higher levels of education correlate to lower unemployment and poverty rates, which positively impacts tax revenue. Additionally, college graduates are civically engaged at higher levels, they consider others' perspectives more readily, and in general, have healthier lifestyles (Baum and Ma 2007). So, what's the problem and solution? Moral education is no more the panacea than the construction of more jails. However, its transformational potential is more likely than purely retributive approaches to address moral wrongs.

Given current social realities, any serious discussion about the cultivation and maintenance of the good society is considered incomplete in the absence of a critical examination of education in a democratic society and its role in the creation and sustainability of any such society. Furthermore, as the quality and effectiveness of American educational systems continue to be contemplated, stakeholders should be compelled to consider the issue of morality—morality of students, teachers, parents, and contiguous communities. The current state of society discussed thus far endangers the good society, and public schools are squandering in large numbers the opportunity to contribute to its realization. This lack of action and neglect is in itself immoral and calls into question our collective character as a society. Meanwhile, schools are not safe, students' physical and psychological safety is questionable, and teaching and learning are diminished. In essence, students' ability to develop into contributing citizens of a democratic society, and personal and communal freedoms are compromised—that's the essence of *the problem*.

This essay attempts to construct an argument for a moral education renaissance to promote a durable good society. The timing is ripe for such advocacy when you consider the facts. The *thesis* is many of the problems that challenge the realization and sustainability of the good society are in part the result of our institutions' (particularly schools') failure to act on the realization that our interdependent lives are shaped by educational policies and the degree to which we as a democratic society can shape these policies for the better. Instead of cultivating a sense of common purpose and community, we continue to adopt extreme positions of individualism and act primarily out of self-interest. This is reflected in the resistance to moral and character development as a core learning outcome in K-16 education. Nonetheless, the good society without developing members of good character is hard to conceive.

Opposition to the notion of moral education should be expected and welcomed in a diverse and democratic society. Many educators, policy makers, and others see moral education as covertly bringing in religion through the back door, threatening the separation of church and state. Some educators are reluctant to embrace character education because they don't see it as a mandate to deal with issues of morality or character, which is supported by the fact that there are only a few teacher education programs that deal directly and substantially with the subject.

Morality

The study of morals concerns the whole character, and the whole character is indistinguishable from the individual in all their actions and expressions. The moral and the social quality of individuals are not separate from each other, and the school should exist as an extension of the community where social perceptions and interests can be developed. As such, the learning in school, including moral and character development, should be continued outside of the school. A narrow non-communal view of morals may be responsible for the failure to recognize that all the aims and values that are desirable in education are themselves moral.

The Stanford Encyclopedia of Philosophy provides a historical account of important developments in philosophical perspectives about moral character. Much attention is given to the views of Plato, Aristotle, and Karl Marx, with Marx accepting Aristotle's perception that virtue and good character are based on one's sense of self-esteem and self-confidence. Plato believed that a person's soul is divided into three parts of desire: the rational (logical reasoning), the appetitive (instinctive desire), and the spirited (inner nature) (The Stanford Encyclopedia of Philosophy).

Swiss psychologist Jean Piaget posited a theory of moral development during the early twentieth century. The theory was conceptualized similar to his earlier four-stage theory of cognitive development (sensorimotor, preoperational, concrete operational, and formal operational), which children progressed through at approximate ages. The three-stage model of moral development is summarized in Table 1.1 (Piaget 1965).

Table 1.1 Moral development and relationship to Piaget's cognitive development theory

Moral Development	Relationship to Piaget's Cognitive Development Theory
Stage 1. Pre-moral: Birth–5 years of age. Children do not understand the concept of rules or morality.	Overlaps with sensorimotor and preoperational stages.
Stage 2. Moral realism: 5–9 years of age. Children understand the concept of rules but see them as external and absolute. Rules are obeyed because they exist, and children evaluate wrongdoing in terms of its consequences, as opposed to the intentions of the offender.	Corresponds to the preoperational and concrete operational stages.
Stage 3. Moral relativity: Begins at about 7 years of age so it overlaps with moral realism stage. Children reaching this stage recognize that rules are not fixed and can be changed by mutual consent. At this stage they begin to develop their own internal sense of morality.	

American educator and philosopher John Dewey was among the first to distinguish between the inner and outer dimensions of morality. When theorizing about morality and its focus on behavior, Dewey recognized the dichotomy that existed between the inner and outer dimensions—between the mind and activity—nearly a century ago. He asserted that "the conscious deliberating and desiring precede overt action and except where there is a disciplined disposition, the tendency is for the imagination to run loose. Instead of its objects being checked by conditions with reference to their practicability in execution, they are allowed to develop because of the immediate emotional satisfaction which they yield" (349). Morality, from his perspective, did not comprise of the inner workings of the individual—inside one's consciousness; rather, it was about one's actions. Behavioral outcomes are what matter, as they were considered by Dewey to be the sole measure of morality. To him, the rise of conscious purpose, conscious desire, and deliberate reflection are cultivated through moral education (Dewey 1916).

Although the inner self guides the outer self and the internal mind naturally drives the external actions, according to Dewey, "in morals it takes the form of a sharp demarcation of the motive of action from its consequences and of character from conduct. Motive and character are regarded as something purely 'inner,' existing exclusively in consciousness, while consequences and conduct are regarded as outside the mind; conduct having to do simply with the movements which carry out motives; consequences with what happens as a result. Different schools identify morality with either the inner state or the outer act and results, each in separation from each other" (Dewey 1916, 347). The tendency to associate the inner with the spiritual, and thus religion, poses a challenge for some educators and educational policy makers, which had in the past resulted in near complete abandonment of moral development curriculum.

Commonly held notions of morality and character include the *personal dimensions* of integrity, responsibility, honesty, and self-discipline, and the *social dimensions* of goodwill, care, politeness, responsibility, and trustworthiness. When defined in terms of justice and rights, morality can exist as one's perceptions, cognitive deliberations, and behaviors relating to the well-being, rights, and fair treatment of people. Moral behavior, it follows, consists of those interpersonal behaviors that are held to be right or wrong independent of governing social rules or laws and are maintained as universally required (Turiel 1983).

Evaluation of one particular school-based program suggests a positive correlation between a structured and intentional character development program and decrease in lateness and suspension, drug usage, and bullying as well as increase in standardized test scores and self-confidence in relation to higher education potential (Hoedel 2003). Another related research project investigating the impact of moral education on moral judgments was conducted in the mid-1980s. Using the Defining Issues Test (DIT), the researchers concluded modest but definite effects of the moral education intervention. Programming with adults (24 years of age and older) seemed to produce larger effect sizes although the researchers offered explanations for the trends. Interventions lasting longer than 12 weeks had no more impact than interventions lasting between 3 and 12 weeks, although interventions lasting less than 3 weeks were evaluated as ineffective when measured using the DIT (Schlaefli, Rest, and Thoma 1985).

As with all intellectual quests for truth, debate persists over assumptions about morality and moral character. The situational nature of morality is often at the root of these debates, consisting of three central claims. The *non-robustness claim,* which states that moral character traits are not consistent across a wide spectrum of trait-relevant situations, and that whatever moral character traits an individual has are situational in nature. The *consistency claim,* which says that while a person's moral character traits are relatively stable over time, they should be understood as consistency of situation-specific traits rather than robust traits. The *fragmentation claim*, which asserts that there may be considerable disunity in a person's moral character (Tempe 2007). This is an important debate but should not occur at the expense of advancing the moral education discussion as there is ample evidence to support the need to bring back this aspect of public education.

When contemplating the meaning of moral behavior, it's instructive to contrast it with the concept of convention. Conventions are posited to be established by social systems (e.g., dress codes, how people should address one another, and dining etiquette) and are considered correct or incorrect forms of conduct based on a shared system of meaning, culture, or social interaction. Conventions are relevant to the discussion of morality as they function to coordinate social interaction and interaction within social systems (Nucci 1989). Public schools are major social systems in America with profound influence on the input and output of resources (human and monetary).

Moral Education

To educate a man in mind and not in morals is to educate a menace to society.

The case for moral education is supported by the report, *A Nation at Risk*, which recognizes that education "goes well beyond matters such as industry and commerce... [to include] the intellectual, moral, and spiritual strengths of our people which knit together the very fabric of our society" (National Commission on Excellence in Education 1983, 7). Gutmann asserts that education with moral purposes has the capacity to strengthen the nation as it cultivates morals in its citizens, while having a direct impact on communities striving to build the good society. As a nation, we can choose to avoid political controversies including moral education, however, "we cannot make good educational policy by avoiding political controversy; nor can we make principled educational policy without exposing our principles and investigating their implications" (Gutmann 1987).

Several factors influence moral and character development including heredity, early childhood experience, modeling by important adults (e.g., parents, teachers, community leaders) and older youth, peer influence, general physical and social environment, communication media, teaching in schools and other institutions, and specific situations and roles that elicit corresponding behavior. The concept of character can imply a variety of attributes including the existence of or lack of virtues such as integrity, courage, fortitude, and loyalty, or of good behaviors, or habits. Moral character primarily refers to the assemblage of qualities that distinguish one individual from another—although at a cultural level, the set of moral behaviors to which a social group adheres can be said to unite and define it culturally as distinct from others (Campbell and Bond 1982).

In the context of moral education and policy implications, nonetheless, there is some level of agreement about certain types of behavior that are considered immoral and reflective of poor character including theft, slander, vandalism, violence, and bullying. However, the notion of moral education in school is challenged when the acquiring of knowledge and the development of understanding are conceptualized as having nothing to do with character. When schools link knowledge acquisition with student action, its social significance will be realized as the curriculum can serve as a medium of development of personal and community values.

Moral education has a long history in this country and can be traced back to colonial times when moral education was taken for granted and formal schooling had a distinctly moral emphasis. Throughout this period, leaders saw government as a moral covenant amongst its citizens. Also during the nineteenth century, schooling was promoted for secular and moral purposes, with Horace Mann emerging as a champion of common schools and an advocate for moral education. He saw public schools as the ethical transformer of society—a place where morality would be developed. However, religious diversity became a problem as each faith wanted moral education to be rooted in its respective religious doctrine. The twentieth century witnessed growing reaction against organized religion and schools began to ignore the moral dimension of education. Subsequently, during the last quarter of the twentieth century, as schools attempted to ignore the moral dimensions of education, three things happened: standardized test scores began to decline, discipline and behavior problems increased, and voices were raised accusing schools of teaching secular humanism. At the same time, educators were asked to address moral concerns of students using values clarification and cognitive developmental approaches to moral education (Ryan 2012).

Values clarification was said to be upheld by little theory other than the assumption that students needed practice choosing among moral alternatives, and that teachers should be facilitators of the clarification process rather than indoctrinators of moral ideas or values choices.

This approach was criticized because of claims that it promoted moral relativism amongst students. Moral relativism asserts that moral judgments are not right or wrong, good or bad; they are only relative to some particular perspective, and no perspective is uniquely superior to all others. Moral relativism has been associated with other claims about morality, particularly the argument that dissimilar cultures can exhibit different moral values. Advocates of moral relativism assert the absence of universal moral values shared by every human society and insist that we should refrain from passing moral judgments on beliefs and practices characteristic of cultures other than our own (Westacott 2012). These positions are pertinent to the discussion but should be measured carefully in the debate over the relevance of character education as there is persistent evidence of teacher neutrality and hesitance to intentionally address the moral domain of education in the midst of escalating immoral behavior in schools.

Cognitive developmental moral education built on the work of Jean Piaget (1964) and Lawrence Kolhberg (1984). Kolhberg theorized six stages of moral development, each representing a distinct way in which individuals contemplate moral situations or problems. The sequential, three-level, six-stage model is illustrated in Table 1.2.

Application of this model allows teachers to engage students in discussions of moral issues and dilemmas, facilitating developmentally appropriate opportunities to build moral character while simultaneously considering the whole versus the self in search of common interests and purposes. Students of good moral character think right and do right according to universal values that define the qualities of a good person—trustworthiness, respect, responsibility, fairness, caring, and citizenship. Teachers' role as character developers is to guide students' thoughts, words, and actions toward these characteristics, which the majority of people share regardless of differences and culture.

Since the 1930s, American education has increasingly turned away from character education as a primary focus of education, although educators have cited the matter as important and necessary as students (and in some cases teachers) are showing evidence of a deficit in moral reasoning. Fortunately, there appears to be a modest shift in the general lack of interest in character education, and school districts across the country are adopting values-based curriculum toward moral and character development. These programs aim to develop a wide range of generally accepted positive character traits including responsibility, compassion, self-control, perseverance, integrity, and responsibility (Power, Higgins, and Kohlberg 1989).

Table 1.2 Kolhberg's moral development

Level one: Pre-conventional morality	
Stage 1	*Obedience and punishment orientation.* Egocentric deference to superior power or prestige, or a trouble-avoiding mindset. Objective responsibility.
Stage 2	*Naively egotistic orientation.* Right action is instrumentally satisfying the self's needs and occasionally other's. Naïve egalitarianism and orientation to exchange and reciprocity.
Level two: Conventional morality	
Stage 3	*Good-boy orientation.* Orientation to approval and to pleasing and helping others. Conformity to stereotypical images of majority or natural role behavior, and judgment of intentions.
Stage 4	*Authority and social-order-maintaining orientation.* Orientation to "doing duty" and to showing respect for authority and maintaining the given social order for its own sake. Regard for earned reputations of others.
Level three: Post-conventional morality	
Stage 5	*Contractual legalistic orientation.* Recognition of an arbitrary element or starting point in rules and expectations for the sake of agreement. Duty defined in terms of contract, general avoidance of violation of the will or right of others, and majority will and welfare.
Stage 6	*Conscience or principle orientation.* Orientation not only to actually ordained social rules but to principles of moral choice. Orientation to conscience as a directing agent and to mutual respect.

Source: Lawrence Kohlberg, "Moral Education in the Schools: A Development View," *The School Review* 74, no. 1 (1966): 1–30.

To complement character development programming, schools are also instituting restorative justice programs (primarily reactive) as an alternative means of addressing behavior identified to be lacking in moral fortitude. In essence, restorative justice principles acknowledge the importance of relationships, build systems that address harm in ways that strengthen relationships, focus on the harm and not solely on the broken rule, give voice to persons harmed, engage in collaborative problem solving, empower change and growth, and develop personal responsibility.

Restorative justice is a sharp contrast to traditional approaches to antisocial behavior, which are retributive and aim to be unpleasant and punitive. Retributive approaches to discipline in schools have intentional consequences that are decided and enforced by authority figures and thus eliminate the opportunity for students to take responsibility for their choices. Restorative justice programs promote moral development as the emphasis is on discipline (vs. punishment), violation of relationships (vs. violation of rules/laws), and personal responsibility and reparation (vs. retribution). Restorative justice in schools further advances moral development as it aims to build relationships between offenders and their victims including the school community (capacity for compassion, empathy, and duty is enlarged). As students take responsibility for their action and making things right is the primary focus, restorative justice approaches have the potential to interrupt the cycle of immoral behavior as harm is repaired by the offender himself.

Moral education is understandably viewed by some as having religious overtones. However, character (education), with its Greek translation meaning to engrave, is appearing more acceptable and is in the best interests of the individual and society. Although it is widely accepted that parents are responsible for early moral and character development, schools have a role to play as well as the development of morals and character has ecological dimensions. The internal focus on character education can have both religious and civic purposes, but for opponents of the idea, the focus can be strictly civic (external), dealing exclusively with the formation of the good citizen.

Fixing the Roof at HBCUs through IMPACT

There are obvious and significant bright spots in American society, especially within its educational systems, so as John F. Kennedy has been quoted as saying, "The time to repair the roof is when the sun is shining." HBCUs are a celebrated and proud part of American higher education and have a history of responding to moral challenges, particularly as it relates to educational access and addressing the needs of the whole student, regardless of their background—particularly African American citizens. The Higher Education Act of 1965 defines an HBCU as "any historically black college or university that was established prior to 1964, whose principal mission was, and is, the education of black Americans. There are 103 HBCUs in the 50 states and the District of Columbia. Most are located in the South and near areas with relatively low levels of economic well-being.

HBCUs have a legacy of admitting students to their institutions who would not be welcomed at other colleges and universities. Many of these institutions continue to accept students who are first generation college attendees. Furthermore, it is not uncommon for these same students to come from challenging environments plagued by violence, crime, poor schools, and poverty. In spite of perceived achievement barriers, these historical institutions continue to enroll and attain unusual effort from and make winners out of students—including the seemingly ordinary. They have advanced the discussion of moral ecology—intentionally or unintentionally—through the offering of curriculum and academic environments that nurture the whole student. Today, HBCUs are well positioned to lead a renaissance of moral education in America.

Although some would argue that society has realized significant progress in the realm of race relations in America, HBCUs continue to play a significant societal role with moral implications. According to the National Science Foundation's analysis of the National Center for Education Statistics (NCES), HBCUs conferred 23.6 percent of bachelor's degrees earned by blacks in 2001. The contribution was even greater in the physical, mathematical, biological, and agricultural sciences, where HBCUs accounted for over 40 percent of bachelor's degrees earned by blacks. Moreover, HBCUs conferred 13.1 percent and 10.6 percent of master's and doctoral degrees earned by blacks, respectively (Hill and Johnson 2004). These numbers may have considerable moral implications given the fact that HBCUs account for only 3 percent of the nation's institutions of higher education.

North Carolina is home to more HBCUs (11) than any other state. An examination of their mission statements suggests a commitment to moral and character education. Defining messages include: Winston-Salem State University—"As a comprehensive, historically Black constituent institution of the University of North Carolina, Winston-Salem State University contributes to the social, cultural, intellectual and economic growth of the region, North Carolina and beyond"; North Carolina Central University—"Prepare students academically and professionally to become leaders prepared to advance the consciousness of social responsibility in a diverse, global society"; Livingston College—"Increase their awareness and appreciation of other cultures, and prepare them to become well-adjusted individuals in a global society"; Johnson C. Smith University—"We provide an environment where students can explore and grow—intellectually, physically, socially, culturally, and spiritually"; and Shaw University—"Additionally, the University stresses character development, which includes religious, cultural, social, and ethical values. Ultimately, Shaw University endeavors to graduate students with demonstrated competencies in their chosen fields of study."

The IMPACT Curriculum

The cultivation of character and competence increases one's chances for success. Graduates who are capable and proficient in the liberal arts as well as other fields of study are better equipped to make a contribution to society and to their professions when exercised with moral behavior. When students enter higher education, they are still engaged in the process of character development—the thoughts, actions, and values they enter with will not be the same as those with which they depart. Here lies a moral opportunity for colleges and universities to make an impact on the development of students' character. This character becomes who they really are, what they will do as adult citizens; it becomes the byproduct of an accumulation of thoughts, values, words, and actions developed over the course of four, five, and, sometimes, six years of undergraduate study. Simply stated but nonetheless profound, they become the people that will determine our destiny as a society.

To take the position that their character is fully developed when they enter higher education is not supported by the research. As research does suggest ongoing self-creation and concern for moral values and principles beyond high school, the value of moral character development in colleges and universities is implicated and there are three general frameworks to consider: (1) distinctive programming (institution-wide and standalone programs outside of academic disciplines), (2) discipline specific (occurring in certain academic disciplines such as philosophy or ethics), and (3) programming across the curriculum (an integrated approach).

Character education should not be treated as a discrete subject and efforts should be made to integrate it across the curriculum and mirror other cross-disciplinary initiatives such as reading and writing. It complements other "universal" learning outcomes including critical thinking, communication, and global awareness. Intentionally, and across the curriculum, educators can speak and model character characterizing words such as responsibility, respect, honesty, perseverance, civility, and integrity in addition to others that may have cultural relevance. An integrated curriculum would serve as a unifying compact among schools, between students and faculty—one that would impact the ecology of character development.

An IMPACT curriculum is represented by the tenets of inclusiveness, modeling, practice, acquisition, compact, and transparency and promotes good habits, civic virtues, and community harmony. A focus on *inclusiveness* involves creating academic environments that are respectful and welcoming of different perspectives and learning styles. Inclusive learning environments require character educators to have an understanding and sensitivity to students with diverse opinions, even those not considered to be in the mainstream. Incorporating *modeling* into the curriculum requires faculty to display those behaviors, attitudes, and vocabularies that facilitate character development without engaging in dogmatic practices. Behaviors and attitudes that are disrespectful, unfair, and discriminatory are counterproductive to moral and character development. The use of modeling can also take the form of using groups and individuals who epitomize virtues of good character. Character education includes providing students with the opportunity to *practice* character building in a safe environment, employing high impact practices advocated by the Association of American Colleges and Universities including internships, undergraduate research, service/community-based learning, and diversity/global learning (2008). This is complemented by case studies, simulations, and other opportunities to confront moral dilemmas. Incorporating practice opportunities using current events and moral dilemmas promotes constructive dialogue and requires feedback from educators and students. The intended outcome is character reflection, development, and transformation. The *acquisition* component of the curriculum emphasizes the importance of acquiring the prerequisite knowledge and skills to enhance moral reasoning capabilities, which transcend disciplines and include critical thinking, critical reading, critical listening, and oral and written communication.

HBCUs have an unparalleled *compact* with the African American community, which should extend to their moral development. This legacy compact, as expressed in mission, vision, and values statements, should have a reciprocal component assigning responsibility to students and faculty to realize a moral academic community. New student orientation, new faculty orientation, convocations, and graduations are the obvious forums to anchor a compact. *Transparency* must underpin the curriculum to guard against claims of covert intentions. Students and faculty should be in accord with the character development mission and values of the institution. The transparency approach supports the objectives of Inclusiveness, Modeling, Practice, Acquisition, and Compact. Student and faculty exposure and understanding of the goals of an *IMPACTful* curriculum can serve to advance moral reasoning and thus the good society. Dialogues around transparency are important before, during, and after the recruitment of students and faculty, particularly given the controversial nature of the concept of moral and character education in higher education.

Concluding Remarks

Moral education is clearly a public concern, and the societal consequences of immoral behavior are clearly supported in research, crimes statistics, and school environments. However constructing more prisons and other forms of retributive justice systems are not durable solutions to the problem. More than two million people are incarcerated in America; the country incarcerates a higher percentage of its people than any other country. According to the US Department of Justice, as of June 2008, state and federal correctional authorities had jurisdiction or legal authority over more than 1.6 million prisoners and more than 780,000 prisoners were held in the custody of local jails (2009).

The collateral societal consequences and human costs of incarceration are enormous. The impact of wasted lives, broken and dysfunctional families, and maladjusted and troubled children are incalculable as are the adverse social, economic, and political consequences of weakened communities and weakened opportunities for economic mobility. Although African Americans account for only 12 percent of the US population, they account for 37 percent of the prison population. African American males were incarcerated at 6.6 times the rate of white males. One in 21 black males was incarcerated compared to one in 138 white males (US Department of Justice 2009).

Regardless of one's perspective on the role of education in a democracy, arguing about whether or not to provide character education to citizens is counterproductive as there are universal concepts of right and wrong that are largely absent from existing public education curriculum. By sharing authority with family and community, theory-based character development programs offer encouragement as an intervention for manifestations of moral decline, particularly in schools. A role for HBCUs in institutionalizing moral development interventions is strongly suggested if we are truly committed to the advancement of the good society, as reflected in our educational policies and programs.

HBCUs have historically functioned as the foci of a collective moral response to systems of educational inequality in America. Today they are positioned to lead a renaissance to reverse the country's state of extreme individualism and moral decay undermining the good society. HBCUs can create safe spaces for students to practice democracy, further explore the concept of civic responsibility, and build capacity for moral reasoning. Furthermore, when students are engaged in opportunities to think about themselves as part of a whole, they broaden their interests and expand their commitment to search for a common purpose and mutually beneficial solutions to problems.

Competence is limited in the absence of character. Students need to build capacity to live in harmony with others because regardless of how you define the good society and community, they are meager concepts when critical masses of its members think and behave without character. Capacity building begins with examination of teacher education programs and educational policies, which should be a mirror of a commitment to character development. Character development is a developmental process that does not cease after graduation from high school. Not claiming exclusivity, HBCUs are well-positioned to facilitate opportunities for personal discovery, competence building, and character transformation—once again making an impact on students and enhancing the good society.

References

Association of American Colleges and Universities. 2008. *High Impact Educational Practices.* http://www.aacu.org/leap/hip.cfm. Accessed May 25, 2012.

Baum, S., and J. Ma. 2007. *Education Pays: The Benefits of Higher Education for Individuals and Society.* Trends in Higher Education Series. Washington, DC: College Board.

Campbell, V., and R. Bond. 1982. "Evaluation of a Character Education Curriculum." In *Education for Values,* edited by D. McClelland. NewYork: Irving Publishers. As described in Huitt, 2004. http://www.edpsycinteractive.org/topics/morchr/morchr.html. Accessed March 10, 2012.

Coser, L. 1957. *The Functions of Social Conflict.* NY: Macmillan.

Dewey, J. 1916. *Democracy and Education.* NY: Free Press/Macmillan.

Domestic Violence Resource Center. 2012. http://www.dvrc.org. Accessed May 5.

Etzioni, A. 1996. *The New Golden Rule.* NY: Basic Books.

Gutmann, A. 1987. *Democratic Education.* Princeton, NJ: Princeton University Press.

Hill, S. T., and J. M. Johnson. 2004. "Science and Engineering Degrees by Race/Ethnicity of Recipients." In U.S. Department of Education (2006), *Economic Impact of the Nation's Historically Black Colleges and Universities.*

Hoedel, J. 2003. "Character Development & Leadership: Skills That Last a Lifetime." www.characterandleadership.com. Accessed May 20, 2012.

Huitt, W. 2004. Moral and Character Development. *Educational Psychology Interactive.* http://chiron.valdosta.edu/whuitt/col/morchr/morchr.html. Accessed May 10, 2012.

Kohlberg, Lawrence. 1984. *Essays on Moral Development:* Vol. 2, *The Psychology of Moral Development.* San Francisco: Harper and Row.

National Alliance to End Homelessness. 2011. "State of Homelessness in America 2011." http://www.endhomelessness.org/content/article/detail/3668. Accessed May 25, 2012.

National Commission on Excellence in Education. 1983. "A Nation at Risk: The Imperative for Educational Reform." Washington, DC: U.S. Government Printing Office, April.

National Police Misconduct Statistics and Reporting Project. 2011. "Police Misconduct." www.policebrutality.info/2011/04/police-brutality-statistics.html. Accessed June 8, 2012

Nucci, I., ed. 1989. *Moral Development and Character Education: A Dialogue.* Berkeley, CA: McCutchan.

Piaget, J. 1965. *The Moral Judgment of the Child.* New York: Free Press.

Power, F. C., A. Higgins, and L. Kohlberg. 1989. *Kohlberg's Approach to Moral Education.* New York: Columbia University Press.

Pritchard, I. 1988. "Character Education: Research Prospects and Problems." *American Journal of Education* 96 (4): 469–495.

Ryan, K. 2012. "Moral Education: A Brief History of Moral Education, the Return of Character Education, Current Approaches to Moral Education." http://education.stateuniversity.com/pages/2246/moral-education.html.

Schlaefli, A., J. R. Rest, and S. J. Thoma. 1985. "Does Moral Education Improve Moral Judgment? A Meta-Analysis of Intervention Studies Using the Defining Issues Test." *American Educational Research Association* 55 (3): 319–352.

The Stanford Encyclopedia of Philosophy. http://plato.stanford.edu/entries/moral-character/. Accessed May 5, 2012.

Tempe, K. 2007. "Moral Character." Internet Encyclopedia of Philosophy. http://www.iep.utm.edu/moral-ch. Accessed May 5, 2012.

Turiel, E. 1983. *The Development of Social Knowledge: Morality and Convention.* New York: Cambridge University Press.

US Department of Justice. 2009. "Growth in Prison and Jail Populations Slowing: 16 States Report Declines in the Number of Prisons." www.ojp.usdoj.goc/bjs. Accessed June 8, 2012.

Walsh, K. 1990. "The Three Dimensions of Education." In Huitt 2004. http://www.edpsycinteractive.org/topics/morchr/morchr.html. Accessed March 10, 2012

Westacott, E. 2012. "Moral Relativism." Internet Encyclopedia of Philosophy. www.iep.utm.edu/moral-re.

White, B., ed. 2006. *Classic Wisdom for the Good Life.* Nashville, TN: Thomas Nelson.

Wynne, E., and H. Walberg., eds. 1984. *Developing Character: Transmitting Knowledge.* Posen, IL: Association of Research Libraries.

Chapter 2

What Does the Rising Tide Bring?

Robert B. Williams

Introduction

Since coined by President Kennedy in 1963, economic growth has been likened to "a rising tide that lifts all boats" (Kennedy, 1963), thereby evoking a picturesque harbor where yachts and skiffs alike rise with the incoming tide. Yet, the importance of this clever aphorism goes beyond its pithy and vivid depiction. Within neoclassical economics, economic growth represents the surest means to alleviate poverty. According to this view, sustained economic growth offers new opportunities to entrepreneurs and business owners as they respond to the surging demand by hiring new employees. During prolonged expansions, these employment gains can extend through all neighborhoods, even reaching those last to be hired. The resultant expansion of incomes from rising profits and payrolls underwrite further spending that fosters additional production and employment in a self-sustaining manner. Rising incomes permit households to accumulate wealth as each works toward its version of the American Dream. Indeed, economic growth can yield a surge of opportunities that extends material prosperity through all parts of our communities. It can bring opportunity and lift the hopes of those who are often neglected and left stranded.

In the natural world, coastal ecosystems are among nature's most productive habitats (Vernberg and Vernberg 2001, 36) as the tidal flows bring rich nutrients to the resident plants. Nonetheless, even in coastal areas, protected from the full force of ocean waves, life in estuaries can be harsh indeed. On the surface, tidal flows appear calm and incremental while below strong currents pull in different directions. To withstand this violent ebb and flow, resident flora must adapt by anchoring themselves strongly to the rocks or sediments or simply by bouncing with the shifting currents (Broaden and Seed 1985, 36). Safely tethered, they still must bend to abrupt and substantial changes. Just as the incoming tide can bring sustenance and succor to stranded plants and animals, it yields to an equally strong reverse current that removes such aid. This ebb and flow produces substantial shifts in temperature, adding further stress. Fluctuating water flows causes salinity levels to oscillate, creating hardship for all including the most resilient plants and animals. In addition, the water turbulence can stir bottom sediments that increase turbidity, reduce light, and foul animal filtration systems. Only selected plants and animals, highly adaptable to these difficult conditions, thrive in these tidal areas. As such, coastal estuaries can function as highly productive habitats, though the diversity of their biotic community is quite narrow (McLusky and Elliott 2004, 22). In the natural world, the rising tide does not bring relief to all residents but only to those that are highly adapted to take advantage of its turbulent opportunities.

Which of these views of tidal action best reflect the impact of economic growth on our society? To what extent does a period of sustained economic growth bring opportunity and improvement broadly shared across all communities as JFK's imagery evokes? Or to what extent do the disquietudes that accompany a dynamic, growing economy offer disparate opportunities to different households, leaving some stranded and unprotected from the reverse tides that inevitably occur? To answer these questions, I intend to examine the impact of the economy on US households over the period 1989–2007. During this period, the US economy experienced its longest economic expansion in history while suffering only two mild recessions (NBER 2010).[1] During this period, real GDP averaged a robust 3.0 percent annual growth, unemployment rates fluctuated across low to tolerable ranges, and inflation remained mild and stable. Even, real average hourly earnings rose during this period after suffering declines in previous decades. As this period represents the US economy arguably at its "best," it offers a credible case study to examine the pervasiveness of economic growth's benefits.

The chosen period is desirable for a second reason. Since 1989, the Federal Reserve has regularly questioned US households on matters of household finance in their Survey of Consumer Finances (SCF).[2] These surveys ask detailed questions regarding household assets and debt as well as gifts and inheritances, and they query households on their attitude toward saving and credit. Both the range and detail of these questions produce an unmatched illumination of household wealth, a topic that historically has remained hidden. In addition, the survey combines sampling techniques to achieve a truly representative sample of household wealth. Although the SCF queries different households with each wave rather than follow the same households through time, a comparison of the 1989 to the 2007 survey allows us to assess how well the relative prosperity of this period has translated into rising net worth broadly shared. Like measures of household income, household wealth gives us a measure of household well-being and the ability of households to participate in the rising tide of prosperity. Yet, better than income, household wealth gives a truer measure of any household's capacity to withstand and survive the inevitable reversals in economic fortunes.

Indeed, the selected period offered an additional curiosity. The bulk of the household surveys were conducted from May to December of the survey year. As such, the 2007 survey assessed the household balance sheets at the point of economic "high tide." During this period, GDP was still growing, the unemployment had inched only up to 5 percent, and the stock markets had yet to suffer their dramatic decline. Per se, we can evaluate not only the consequences of an extended period of economic growth but also the relative strength of US households just prior to the collapse. The very conditions and circumstances that created the material prosperity of this period also contributed to the causes that led to the subsequent financial collapse. The optimism and exuberance that led to rising stock prices, housing prices, and novel financial instruments also permitted the excessive risk-taking and intemperance that produced the collapse. Like the tidal systems off our coasts, the very same forces that buoy our economic fortunes also contribute to their decline. By itself, the years from 1989 to 2007 allows us not only to examine a period of unusual growth and prosperity but also to examine the status of households at the very precipice of the ensuing economic fall.

Household Wealth and Economic Resiliency

Though neoclassical economics argues that economic growth offers the most reliable and effective means to raise households out of poverty, ecological economics has challenged this view. The fruits of growth are shared selectively, not universally. Impoverished households neglected in the past will likely experience similar disregard in the future. Even if economic growth improves the fortunes of all, ecological economics argues it cannot last. Specific thresholds on finite nonrenewable resources, limited reproduction rates of renewable resources, and the waste absorption capacity of natural systems all impose binding constraints on further economic growth. Daly (1973) and others (Ayres 1996; Wackernagel and Rees 1996; Constanza et al. 1997) argue that the neoclassical growth models view nature as simply a provider of resources that are substitutable with either capital or labor. This assumption of substitutability portrays nature as an elastic and largely infinite provider of needed goods and services, thereby suggesting economic growth is a permanent feature of our modern, technological economies. Yet, many, if not most, essential services from nature appear more complementary than substitutable with capital and labor. In this case, continued growth will exacerbate shortages in essential ecological services, leading to higher costs. As these higher costs translate into higher food, water, utility prices, to name but a few, their effect will disproportionately affect the poor, thereby deepening their poverty, rather than alleviating it. According to this view, future growth will impose higher costs and generate less inclusive benefits, leaving more boats stranded and mired in poverty.

Using natural models as a basis of understanding economic phenomena is useful, but only if one uses these models accurately and wholly. The rising tide metaphor serves as a case in point. In the natural world, a rising tide is always followed by a falling tide. Similarly, our economic history reflects periods of economic expansion subsequently followed by periods of decline and deprivation. To focus only on the rising tide and its benevolence and to neglect the subsequent contraction is indeed a folly. Simply thriving during the good times can offer only temporary solace. Recognizing that our world is subject to dynamic and reversible forces means we must consider a more complex view of what it takes to thrive. Resilience offers such a perspective.

In arguments that sound remarkably familiar to Joseph Schumpeter's concept of creative destruction, ecologists (Holling and Meffe 1996; Reice 2001) argue that natural disturbances like fire, flood, drought, and pestilence are not only inevitable but also essential to the ongoing health of natural systems. Though these disturbances can wreak much damage and harm, they also provide opportunities for new growth and increased biodiversity that ultimately improve ecosystem's health and functioning. Resilient ecosystems can temper the damage wrought by these disturbances as well as heal and regenerate in their wake. Resilient systems are less prone to suffer a significant and long-term loss in ecological functioning. While much remains largely unknown about what gives natural systems their resiliency, research indicates the importance of having healthy biotic residents, diverse communities of flora and fauna, and multiple and redundant pathways for varied ecological interactions (Peterson, Allen, and Holling 1998).

Similarly, resilient economies are those that can endure and regenerate themselves in the aftermath of a variety of natural and human caused disturbances, including floods, hurricanes, earthquakes, and financial tsunamis. While one can argue whether these disturbances are ultimately beneficial to functioning market economies, they are inevitable. Many of the same factors that encourage resiliency in natural systems do the same for our economic systems. Economies that have decentralized networks, including communication, transportation, and energy, will likely suffer less damage and recover more quickly. Local and regional economies that exhibit increased diversity of industry and commerce will endure less economic disruption as some sectors actually expand during the downturn. Economies populated by protected and affluent households are less vulnerable to the ravages of particular disturbances and have greater resources to respond and regroup in their wake. One need only compare the fates of different New Orleans neighborhoods, whether wealthy or not, in the face of the disaster visited by Hurricane Katrina and the ensuing response.

To be sure, the concept of economic resiliency extends beyond what this analysis can examine. Instead, I intend to focus on the status of US households at the end of a long period of unusually good economic growth, just prior to the onset of the Great Recession. Given the remarkable economic growth during the chosen period, it offers a convincing test case of which view of economic growth the available evidence best supports, neoclassical or ecological economics. Rather than gauge household well-being using the more traditional income measures, I examine to what extent this period generated rising household wealth across all spectrums of US society. Household wealth, or net worth, offers the most comprehensive measure of household capacity, particularly in times of stress. Increased household wealth, particularly when spread across a broader set of assets, offers less exposure to any given calamity. Having wealth to draw upon means households can endure more easily the ravages of the disturbance and it provides the financial means to initiate recovery from any injury or damage. To the extent that an increasing proportion of households have title to some moderate threshold of wealth, one can plausibly argue that economic resiliency is advanced.

Household Wealth Accumulation

Households accumulate wealth in three ways, through unspent current income, through appreciation of household assets, and through family gifts and inheritances. Undoubtedly, household saving of current income offers the most broadly shared means of wealth accumulation. From such savings, households can purchase cars to commute to work, homes, and other properties as well as stocks, bonds, and a variety of real and financial assets. Most forms of household wealth appreciate over time, thereby complementing household saving in boosting household wealth directly. Family gifts and inheritances to offspring can both initiate and support these avenues of wealth accumulation. Family resources that finance college and other professional education provide the prospect of increased household income. Unsurprisingly, household saving is strongly related to household income. Further, family gifts can fund the purchase of homes, businesses, and other high return assets that accelerate wealth accumulation. Family wealth protects younger households from having to support parents and grandparents in their declining years. Such outlays make current saving much more difficult thereby hampering this means of wealth accumulation. In these ways, each pathway to wealth accumulation support and complement the others.

Further, each avenue of wealth accumulation is subject to a self-reinforcing feedback loop. Households capable of saving out of current income can invest in income generating assets, thereby raising future income. Higher household income makes saving even easier, thereby creating an upward spiral of income and saving through time. Further, higher household income can generate improved credit scores and lower interest rates, providing a further boost to saving. The asset appreciation pathway functions in a similar manner once a threshold is reached. Many household purchase cars as their initial primary asset; this asset itself depreciates over time even though it may raise employment income. Once households accumulate additional assets like homes and stocks, they can benefit from the price appreciation that these assets provide. As these investments are subject to the risk return trade-off, households willing and able to invest in riskier assets are likely to experience higher rates of appreciation. Since wealthier households can better tolerate increased risk, they are likely to experience increased opportunities for wealth appreciation. The inheritance track can function in a comparable way across generations. Parents of means can offer their children a variety of gifts including money, real estate, businesses, and the financing of higher education. By making use of these advantages, their children can parlay these gifts into higher incomes and larger nest eggs, permitting them to take advantage of other pathways. Further, they have the opportunity to pass along to their offspring similar and even greater gifts. As such, each of these three pathways to household wealth accumulation can spiral without limit even as they reinforce and complement each other.

Periods of substantial economic growth can support each of these avenues for household wealth. Lower unemployment rates, higher salaries and wages, and rising business profit should expand household income across the socioeconomic continuum. Rising incomes should expand the opportunity for saving in more households as well as augment the flow among those households already accustomed to saving. Periods of prosperity yield increased asset appreciation as real estate prices, stock values, and business assets rise with the economic tides. As households accumulate wealth, they can assist their offspring more generously and require less help in times of crisis. As such, the rising tide of material prosperity can yield broadly shared advances in household wealth.

Evidence from the SCF

To illuminate the long shrouded mysteries surrounding household wealth, the SCF extensively queries households regarding their household assets, debt, inheritance, and giving patterns as well as their opinions on a variety of financial matters. The survey randomly samples several thousand households and adds a selected oversample to ensure adequate representation of extremely wealthy households. Household weights are assigned to each respondent to make the sample reflective of the broader population of US households. Though the survey includes different households in each sample, the extensiveness of the survey questions as well as the sampling methodology makes the SCF peerless in its examination of household wealth in the United States. Regrettably, the SCF survey is a single wave survey, which limits the kinds of longitudinal analysis one can undertake.

As suggested in Table 2.1, there exist some remarkable trends in the distribution of household wealth over the past generation. Strictly speaking, the wave of economic growth during this period has lifted nearly all households. From the tenth percentile of households through the top, the evidence suggests that most households experienced at least some gain in real net worth. Remarkably, there appears a rather uniform improvement in fortunes (about 50 percent) across the wealth spectrum, suggesting that wealth accumulation during

Table 2.1 Household net worth at selected percentiles

Net worth percentiles	Median net worth ($))		Percentage change (%)	Difference from median ($)	
	1989	2007		1989	2007
Fifth	-1,426	-4,600	-225	80,392	125,030
Tenth	0	30	na	78,965	120,400
Twentieth	3,692	7,300	98	75,274	113,130
Thirtieth	17,434	26,500	52	61,531	93,930
Fortieth	43,141	64,680	50	35,825	55,750
Fiftieth	78,965	120,430	53	0	0
Sixtieth	130,194	197,700	52	51,228	77,270
Seventieth	196,323	300,000	53	117,357	179,570
Eightieth	317,304	496,900	57	238,339	376,470
Ninetieth	617,493	908,400	47	538,528	787,970
Ninety-fifth	1,163,438	1,890,000	62	1,084,472	1,769,570
Ninety-ninth	3,894,620	8,327,000	114	3,815,655	8,206,570

Source: Author's computations from the 1989 and 2007 Survey of Consumer Finances.

this period was largely evenhanded.[3] However, analyzing the changes based on absolute gains offers a different perspective. Only those households at the thirtieth percentile and above arguably experienced significant gains in their net worth. Below the thirtieth percentile, the gains were increasingly modest, while underneath the tenth percentile, households experienced an absolute decline in their net worth as they found themselves deeper in debt. The disparate outcomes are best illustrated by the differences in each groups median net worth from the population median. Over the period, the differences in absolute net worth relative to the population median net worth rose substantially. In particular, these figures indicate that wealth-poor households are increasingly left behind; for many, their net worth is largely unaffected by the economic prosperity of the period. To understand more fully how these differences occurred, I compare the bottom wealth quintile of households with their better-endowed neighbors on a variety of measures.

As household net worth is the difference between household assets and debt, one can sift through the evidence to discover how the period of economic growth affected different households. From 1989 to 2007, virtually all households experienced an increase in household assets as increasing numbers of households gained possession of vehicles, homes, other real estate, and a bevy of financial investments. Table 2.2 illustrates the increased possession of selected assets by households of different wealth status. Interestingly, the bottom wealth

Table 2.2 Asset ownership by net worth quintiles

Wealth quintile	Percentage of households who own							
	Cars (%)		Real estate (%)		Retirement assets (%)		Stocks (%)	
	1989	2007	1989	2007	1989	2007	1989	2007
Bottom	54	64	4	10	5	17	2	5
Second	84	91	41	48	23	40	8	9
Middle	92	93	84	86	37	55	15	17
Fourth	95	93	95	94	51	70	23	31
Top	95	94	96	97	69	82	51	57

Source: Author's computations from the 1989 and 2007 Survey of Consumer Finances.

quintile experienced significant gains in asset ownership among each asset class, with the largest gains occurring in increased ownership of retirement accounts and vehicles. These advances suggest recognition among the least affluent of the importance of asset ownership. Yet, these figures somewhat exaggerate their improvement over the period. Among all households in the bottom wealth quintile, median household assets increased by just over $3,000, with nearly $2,000 of this increase due to increased median ownership of cars and related vehicles. Though car ownership is frequently essential to expanding employment prospects, it represents an investment in a depreciating asset unlike virtually all other household assets. Since most of their modest assets are by necessity tied up in their cars, they are largely unable to experience the financial windfalls of appreciating assets.

The purchase of household assets, particularly cars and real estate,[4] usually means assuming more debt. Table 2.3 shows the pattern of debt found among the different wealth quintiles. No surprise, a larger proportion of households regardless of wealth assumed some form of debt over the period. In all categories, save one, the bottom wealth quintile experienced the lowest rate of assumed debt. While wealthier households reduced their reliance upon installment debt, households in the bottom wealth quintile increased theirs modestly over the period. Two factors likely explain this difference. Due to their lower rate of homeownership, less wealthy households have less access to mortgages and home equity lines to finance their purchases. Not only do these forms of secured debt carry lower interest rates, but they also retain their tax preferential treatment under the Tax Reform Act of 1986 whereas installment credit does not. Largely precluded from this preferred form of debt, many households from the bottom wealth

Table 2.3 Debt assumption by net worth quintiles

	Percentage of households who have							
	Any debt (%)		Mortgage debt (%)		Credit card debt (%)		Installment debt (%)	
Wealth quintile	1989	2007	1989	2007	1989	2007	1989	2007
Bottom	61	67	5	9	28	38	49	54
Second	74	80	28	41	44	51	57	52
Middle	79	83	54	66	49	54	57	49
Fourth	74	79	56	64	49	52	49	46
Top	73	76	54	63	29	46	36	33

Source: Author's computations from the 1989 and 2007 Survey of Consumer Finances.

quintile relied on installment loans to pay for college and other major purchases. Indeed, among the bottom wealth quintile, percentage of total installment debt used to finance education-related expenses rose from 33 percent in 1989 to over 50 percent in 2007, by far the largest margin. As Table 2.3 illustrates, there is little evidence that irresponsibility with credit can explain satisfactorily the lack of progress made by the least wealthy among us.

To understand the disparate effects of the rising tide, we should not only examine aggregate assets and debt but must also consider the circumstances that face different households as they work to accumulate wealth. Table 2.4 illustrates key factors that influence household saving. Strikingly, the bottom wealth quintile experienced the greatest gains in median household income during the period; even their absolute gain in median income exceeded the absolute gains of the next two wealth groups. This pattern is replicated when one considers the gains in households that report saving on a regular basis. Here again, households in the bottom quintile reported among the highest jumps in savings behavior. No doubt the decline in interest rates during the period, whether mortgages, car loans, or installment debt, effectively stretched household incomes further and made saving easier. Yet, the fruits of lower interest rates are not uniformly available. Whether borrowing to finance a car, home, or education, less wealthy households face higher interest costs, particularly recently.[5] Their limited access to homeownership skews this disadvantage even further as renters must rely upon unsecured installment credit rather than lower interest and secured debt such as home equity. As such, the disparities in interest costs are reflected by the differences not only within each credit category but also across the categories. In recognizing

Table 2.4 Household income, saving, and credit costs by net worth quintiles

Wealth quintile	Real median income ($ 2007) 1989	Real median income ($ 2007) 2007	Regularly saves (%) 1989	Regularly saves (%) 2007	Mortgage rate (avg.) (%) 1989	Mortgage rate (avg.) (%) 2007	Car loan rate (avg.) (%) 1989	Car loan rate (avg.) (%) 2007	Installment loan (avg.) (%) 1989	Installment loan (avg.) (%) 2007
Bottom	15,753	21,596	17	27	12.1	7.4	10.8	9.2	8.6	13.6
Second	33,257	35,993	31	34	10.3	6.8	11.3	8.3	9.1	12.8
Middle	43,760	48,333	37	41	9.8	6.5	11.5	7.2	9.1	8.2
Fourth	56,012	63,965	43	50	9.4	6.1	11.0	5.9	10.0	5.8
Top	96,270	111,064	43	59	8.8	5.9	10.6	5.8	8.8	3.9

Source: Author's computations from the 1989 and 2007 Survey of Consumer Finances.

these interest rate disparities, the substantial increase in regular saving among the least wealthy becomes even more impressive.

Declining credit costs not only stretch household incomes, but they also facilitate the purchase of various household assets. Lower interest rates effectively reduce the cost of cars and homes, thereby permitting more households to gain from their ownership. In addition, cheaper credit allows households greater opportunities to purchase real estate, stocks, and other appreciating assets. Once again, the least wealthy are at a disadvantage as their lower home and business ownership rates suggest in Table 2.5. Even as these households are able to accumulate a down payment for a home, they face higher mortgage rates when shopping for credit. Due to these steeper rates, they "qualify" for fewer and cheaper homes than do their wealthier counterparts with a similar down payment. Facing fewer choices, they experience less price appreciation from home ownership as Table 2.5 clearly illustrates. Higher credit costs hinder less-wealthy home buyers from buying houses and neighborhoods that carry a higher price, which often are likely to further appreciate in price. Some of this disparity is due to wealthier home owners spending more money on home improvements; yet this evidence corroborates what others have found regarding different rates of home appreciation (Flippen 2004; Coate and Schwester 2008). Similarly, less wealthy households experience much lower rates of business ownership, and the value of their businesses is much less, indicating a reduced potential for future appreciation. Understandably, their meager net worth makes less wealthy households more averse to risk-taking than their wealthier counterparts, creating an additional barrier to accumulating wealth. Further, as the gap in net worth among the wealth quintiles increases, so does the gap in risk taking.

Table 2.5 Selected asset ownership and risk tolerance by net worth quintiles

Wealth quintiles	Homeowners (%)		Median annual appreciation (%)		Business ownership (%)		Median value of the business ($)		Unwilling risk-taker (%)	
	1989	2007	1989	2007	1989	2007	1989	2007	1989	2007
Bottom	4	9	0	1.8	2	2	100	0	61	61
Second	36	44	3.4	3.7	6	5	2,000	11,000	54	50
Middle	78	82	5.4	4.8	9	11	5,000	17,000	54	46
Fourth	87	92	6.2	5.3	15	15	45,000	54,000	43	32
Top	87	94	7.0	6.3	36	35	185,000	370,606	33	20

Source: Author's computations from the 1989 and 2007 Survey of Consumer Finances.

Table 2.6 Family inheritances, past and expected, by net worth quintiles

Wealth quintiles	Inheritance (%)		Median inheritance ($)		Expect inherit (%)		Median expecting ($)	
	1989	2007	1989	2007	1989	2007	1989	2007
Bottom	5	7	5,034	7,500	12	8	45,305	75,000
Second	15	14	10,118	20,000	16	13	144,305	85,000
Middle	23	21	20,136	30,000	21	13	73,831	116,000
Fourth	33	25	25,170	70,000	20	15	117,458	189,000
Top	42	38	65,441	123,000	23	17	174,509	300,000

Source: Author's computations from the 1989 and 2007 Survey of Consumer Finances.

Curiously, during this period of expanding net worth, respondents reported a decline in the incidence of family inheritances. As illustrated in Table 2.6, nearly all quintile groups in 2007 indicated a decline in receiving past gifts as well as a falling expectation of getting a future gift. Though these declines are not statistically significant, they do suggest that the spread of major, family gifts and inheritance may be narrowing. At the same time, the median gifts, both past and expected, rose for nearly all of the quintile groups, even when adjusted for inflation. This shifting pattern of intergenerational giving reflects both the rise in household wealth over the past generation as well as its increased concentration.

The pattern of family giving and inheritances across the different wealth groups is hardly surprising. Not only are households in the wealthier quintiles two to five times as likely to have received a family inheritance, but also their median gifts are many times larger than what a typical bottom-quintile household receives. Regarding expectations of future gifts, the disparities among the wealth groups are narrower. Households from the wealthiest quintile are only twice as likely to expect future gifts, though they do hold much rosier views of how large the bequests will be. The younger median age of household respondents in the bottom quintile can explain some of these differences. While their younger age may lower the likelihood of receiving past gifts, it should raise the prospect of future inheritances. To those fortunate to receive such a gift, its expected size is sufficient to raise the recipient household beyond their current wealth quintile.

Although family inheritances, both received and expected, account for the bulk of family giving, it does not measure what these households *give* to other family members. Fortunately, the SCF asks the households how much they gave in the prior year as well as to whom. Given this information, one can assess the level of "beneficiary" giving—aid to future generation members—versus the level of "distressed" giving—assistance to one's own or prior generations. Certainly, different circumstances and motives drive gifts given to one's children as opposed to those given to one's parents. No doubt, family resources play a substantial role in the case of distressed giving. A summary of family giving is provided in Table 2.7. Among all households that offered support to family members in the prior year, household wealth played only a moderate role in determining median level support. In 2007, the least wealthy households offered about one-fourth the typical assistance of that was offered by the wealthiest households, a surprisingly modest difference. Similarly, household wealth has little impact on the percentage of households that offered "distressed" assistance to parents, grandparents, or other aging family members. In contrast, household wealth does affect significantly the likelihood that households offered "beneficiary" support to their offspring in the past year. Households from the top two wealth quintiles are two to three times more likely to offer gifts to offspring than are the less wealthy households. This suggests that the bottom wealth quintiles expend a majority of their largesse supporting their aging family members, leaving a much smaller portion to their offspring. In comparison, the wealthiest households expend a fifth of their support as "distressed" help, leaving the bulk of their giving to their offspring. In this way, we can see how the present patterns of giving can influence future household wealth through the disposition of intergenerational transfers.

Perhaps the rising wealth disparities illustrated by the evidence are due to substantially different household attitudes toward saving,

Table 2.7 Household giving patterns by net worth quintiles

Wealth quintiles	Median family support ($)		"Distressed" giving rate (%)		"Beneficiary" giving rate (%)		"Distressed" out of total giving (%)	
	1989	2007	1989	2007	1989	2007	1989	2007
Bottom	1,007	1,500	4	5	2	5	68	52
Second	1,007	2,000	5	6	4	5	39	56
Middle	1,678	3,500	8	7	6	8	52	31
Fourth	3,356	4,000	4	8	7	10	20	26
Top	6,712	6,300	7	9	16	16	16	19

Source: Author's computations from the 1989 and 2007 Survey of Consumer Finances.

Table 2.8 Attitudes toward credit and legacy by net worth quintiles

Wealth quintile	Favorable view of credit (0=no, 0.5=mixed, 1=yes)		OK to borrow for education (%)		OK to borrow to buy jewelry (%)		Importance in leaving legacy (%)	
	1989	2007	1989	2007	1989	2007	1989	2007
Bottom	0.61	0.49	81	84	7	5	54	55
Second	0.60	0.47	84	84	5	7	54	55
Middle	0.55	0.47	79	82	5	4	53	51
Fourth	0.52	0.46	84	83	5	4	49	51
Top	0.49	0.45	80	82	5	4	50	57

Source: Author's computations from the 1989 and 2007 Survey of Consumer Finances.

credit, and leaving a legacy. As already noted in Table 2.4, the percentage of households that regularly report saving rises with household net worth. Similarly, the percentage of households that regularly pay off their credit card balances also rises with household wealth. Perhaps, these differences in savings behavior are not simply due to differences in household income but rather due to disparate postures toward credit. A difficult issue to untangle, certainly; nonetheless the SCF sheds some light. As Table 2.8 illustrates, household wealth has little impact on attitudes toward the use of credit, whether in general or for specific purposes. Over the period, there is a modest decline in the perceived value of credit; yet, the views across the wealth groups are remarkably similar. Most households approve of using credit for educational expenses just as most disapprove using credit to buy jewelry. In neither case does wealth status have an impact. Further, there exists remarkably little difference in household opinions on the importance of leaving a legacy. The SCF survey offers little evidence to suggest that disparate attitudes toward credit or leaving a legacy explain differences in household savings rates.

Policy Recommendations

Even during this period of strong economic growth, the rising tide of prosperity did not lift all households in a substantial way. Despite substantial gains among the least wealthy in their household income, savings behavior, ownership of vehicles, homes, and retirement assets, this group was unable to make significant gains in their net worth. There is no evidence that their misfortune is simply the result of dysfunctional attitudes that may perpetuate their condition. Instead, it appears that systemic barriers made it more difficult for many households to access the usual means of accumulating wealth. For less wealthy households, lower incomes and higher credit costs produce higher barriers to regular household saving. Without an adequate source of savings, these households cannot acquire houses and other properties that will appreciate. Further, historic wealth patterns mean that relatively few households can expect an inheritance to supplement their own efforts. In each case, the evidence indicates the systemic barriers are getting larger and more significant.

Understanding these underlying causes should aid in the creation of effective remedies seeking a more equitable, humane, and functional society. To this end, I offer four policy recommendations that should mitigate the current advantages, now held by wealthier households, by making the wealth pathways more accessible to wealth-poor households. Implementing these structural changes requires some financial cost. Yet, we live in an era of Tea Party radicals holding hostage to nominal decisions like raising the debt ceiling; the political restraints on increased government spending are firmly entrenched, even if the economic and financial conditions suggest a much more flexible stance. As such, any set of proposals must reflect these political realities by meeting the test of budgetary neutrality. Further, the proffered proposals should offer a political attraction that resonates with mainstream political values. I believe the proposals offered below meet both of these tests.

Funding Individual Development Accounts

To encourage household saving, federal and state governments offer a variety of tax exclusions and credits as they offer preferential treatment to employer retirement plans, IRAs, 401Ks, and Keogh plans. The Office of Management and Budget estimates that these tax expenditures will cost over $120 billion in 2010 (OMB 2009, Table 19.1). Since most wealth-poor households earn incomes that generate little or no federal and state income taxes, these tax preferences offer them little incentive to save. Instead, many public policy experts argue for the expansion of individual development accounts (IDAs). Though varied in practice, these IDAs offer qualified individuals matching funds for every dollar deposited in them. The specific match of funds ranges from one to three dollars per dollar deposited. In virtually all cases, restrictions limit the use of these matching funds, usually toward the down payment for a home, money for college tuition, capital for a new business, or retirement income. In many cases, recipients must participate in credit counseling and financial management classes prior to the release of the matching funds. Participation is generally limited to individuals with moderate or lower incomes.

While IDA programs have shown significant capacity to encourage household saving, partial funding for these programs leaves most eligible households unable to participate. To redress this disparity, we should implement full funding for federally sponsored IDA programs. Two pieces of proposed federal legislation provide the starting point to eliminate this gap. The Savings for Working Families Act (S.985/H.R.2277) would create a federal government match of one dollar for each deposited dollar, up to $500 per year for four years. Making this match open to any individual between the ages of 18 and 65 years old with limited income (defined as federal adjusted gross income of $20,000 for individuals, $30,000 for heads of households, and $40,000 for married couples) would allow 2.7 million potential beneficiaries (CFED 2009). At this level of limited generosity, the program would cost about $400 million annually, far below the aid that wealthier households get. To help parents save for their children's future, the ASPIRE Act (H.R. 4682/S. 3577) provides similar assistance. According to this plan, each child born receives a one-time contribution of $500. Families earning less than the national median income would receive additional one-dollar matches for each dollar saved up to $500 annually for each child. This benefit would continue until the child reaches 18 years of age. Withdrawals of these matching funds could start only at the age of 18 for postsecondary education and at 25 for either a home purchase or the start of retirement savings. The annual estimated cost of this program is $3.8 billion (New America Foundation 2009) thereby raising the cost of both savings programs to $4.2 billion annually.

Expanding Access to Postsecondary Education

No doubt, making IDAs accessible to more wealth-poor households will encourage increased household saving; however, raising their incomes will generate more immediate and discernible results. While incomes are subject to a variety of factors, one change is likely to generate substantial improvements. Extensive evidence demonstrates the value of a college education in raising future earnings. In 2007, the typical (median) college graduate earned just above $62,000, almost twice the median earnings for those with a high school diploma (US Census Bureau 2010, Table 686). Even some college, short of any degree, offers substantial improvements in annual earnings. Further, this college "salary premium" has been growing in recent decades. According to the College Board (2007, 45), a college education can add $280,000 over the course of a typical work life, even when accounting for tuition repayment and the "lost wages" that occur during the college years. In addition, the authors show that college graduates are much more likely to find jobs that offer health insurance and pension benefits than high school graduates. With these benefits, college-educated heads of households can increase their household saving and finance their wealth-building strategies.

Still, the high cost of college severely limits access to a college education. Not only does college education result in tuition and related expenses but also living expenses and, often most importantly, a substantial reduction in current earnings. Among those unmarried, 18 to 24-year olds with a high school diploma, 85 percent of those whose family incomes were among the highest quartile were enrolled in college. The college participation rate for those from families among the bottom quartile was only 57 percent (Maag and Fitzpatrick 2004, 5). Even when controlled for achievement test scores, family socioeconomic status substantially influences college enrollment rates (Baum 2004, 38). The Advisory Committee on Student Financial Assistance (2002, 28) predicted that over the ensuing decade over 4 million college-ready high school graduates would not enroll in four-year colleges and two million would not enroll in any college, largely for financial reasons. The escalating costs of a college education are reducing access to matriculation among qualified students from families of modest means.

As in the prior discussion on household savings, past federal aid to students have focused on tax deductions like the Coverdell Education Savings Account and Hope Scholarships. Though important programs, they offer scant value to low-income households. Far more important to these households is the Pell Grant program that offers educational grants to eligible individuals and families. Unlike other college aid programs, Pell Grants target qualified students with the greatest need. In 2008–2009 over 61 percent of the Pell Grant recipients came from households of $30,000 annual income or less (College Board 2010, 23). Recent funding increases have raised the top grant currently to $5,550 in the current year and doubled the number of recipients over the past decade. Yet, the value of these grants have lagged over the years compared to need and cost. Today, this maximum grant only covers 34 percent of the average tuition, room, and board fees of a four-year public college and only 15 percent of the cost of a four-year private college (College Board 2010, 22). Thirty years ago, the maximum Pell Grants covered 77 percent of four-year public college costs and 36 percent of private college costs (King 2003, 4).

To ensure adequate access to college for all qualified persons, Congress should authorize and fund a doubling of current Pell Grants.[6] Such a doubling of the program grants would increase the program costs by about $30 billion annually. In addition, the federal government should end the restrictions against using the funds to cover room and board expenses. These changes would mean that individuals from low-income families could meet two-thirds of their out-of-pocket expenses at the typical, four-year public university. Either modest family resources or other funding sources could fill the gap in these cases. To prevent future erosion of the Pell Grants, the maximum grant should rise according to the Higher Education Price Index, one that better measures the impact of inflation among higher education institutions. Even with this increase in help, lower-income families will still need to overcome the hurdle of "lost earnings" that usually accompany the decision to enroll full-time.

Targeting the Home Mortgage Deduction

Besides simply saving out of current income, households build their wealth by investing in assets that appreciate over time. Encouraging homeownership throughout our communities is both a time-honored and effective means of advancing household wealth. Currently, we expend nearly $150 billion annually through tax deductions given to homeowners (OMB 2009, Table 19.1); these generous tax deductions have no doubt contributed to expanded homeownership rates that reached 69 percent in 2004. However, the vast bulk of this generous tax deduction goes to our wealthiest households since the value of the deduction increases with the size of one's mortgage, the number of homes owned and mortgaged, and the height of one's tax bracket. Over 80 percent of the mortgage interest deduction and local property tax deduction goes to the highest-earning households while only 0.3 percent goes to the lowest-earning households (Carruso, Steuerle, and Bell 2005, 25). Although the mortgage deduction generously rewards homeownership, its offers only modest help to those seeking to become first-time homeowners.

With some rather simple changes to the mortgage deduction, we can redirect assistance to those who need it most. First, without raiding the taxpayer's pocket, we could replace our current mortgage interest deduction with a refundable federal tax credit equal to 1.03 percent of the value of the primary residence up to $100,000 (Carruso, Steuerle, and Bell 2005). This change would offer several benefits. Tying the credit to the home's price rather than outstanding mortgage reduces federal encouragement of mortgage debt. Unlike tax deductions, refundable tax credits effectively assist all taxpayers. In this case, all homeowners would receive a tax credit, capped at $1,030, thereby targeting the help.

According to estimates, this change would halve the share of tax benefits going to the highest-income households (from 82 percent to 42 percent) while raising the share to the lowest-earning households to nearly 8 percent (Carruso, Steuerle, and Bell 2005, 27). This share undoubtedly would rise over time as more households become homeowners. One could make the tax credit more generous without need for a tax increase simply by ending the tax credit after 20 years, whether consecutive or not. As older households generally have increased personal wealth, they would have less need for such benefits. Further, the exclusion on capital gains when homes are sold would remain in force and continue to benefit these older homeowners.

Making these changes in the home mortgage deduction would expand homeownership but will not likely reach all households with the means for owning a home. Many families make rental payments that are comparable to locally prevailing mortgage payments. Tax credits offer needed help, but they require substantial patience as it often takes a year before one receives the credit, a period beyond the financial means of many households. Further, the requirement of a down payment deters other potential homebuyers. Yet, these barriers are scalable with the help of amply funded IDAs previously discussed. Further, local, state, and federal governments can implement modest, revolving-loan funds that would assist lower-income households in getting these needed funds. As the loans are repaid, these funds can assist new homebuyers in their quest for homeownership.

In targeting our homeownership tax incentives, we can improve access to homeownership without increasing the burden on the federal treasury. In doing so, we have the capacity to dramatically redirect wealth generation within our society. Given the usual rise in property values over time, extending homeownership to all who are interested offers an effective way to broaden prosperity throughout communities. Rising home equity would provide each household with a financial cushion in the face of unforeseen challenges. Further, these programs need not carry the problems associated with the sub-prime loans made in recent years, which led to higher foreclosure rates.

Advancing an Inheritance Tax

For nearly a century, the federal government has taxed intergenerational transfers of wealth to limit the prevailing concentrations of wealth that mark our society. Known to its detractors as the "death tax" and to others as the "voluntary tax," it represents a nominally progressive tax that is avoidable through a variety of tax schemes and philanthropy. Under current law, most estates pass from one generation to the next without taxation. Only estates that are valued above a certain threshold ($5 million in 2011) are subject to any tax at all, meaning that all but 2 percent of the estates go untaxed. While estates are nominally subject to a 35 percent tax rate, most private wealth transfers across generations largely unimpeded. Never much of a revenue source for the federal government, this tax raised about $22 billion annually through much of the past decade.

Several changes to our wealth transfer tax system can make it more effective at reducing wealth disparities and raising additional revenues. We should transform our estate and gift taxes into an inheritance tax system. Currently, the deceased nominally pays the estate tax; under an inheritance tax, the beneficiary pays any levy. Assuming progressive tax rates, this change encourages a wider dispersion of estates to more recipients to limit tax liability. Increased dispersion limits the concentration of wealth and expands access to this wealth pathway. Further, the recipient's circumstances determine the tax levy. For example, inherited wealth beyond some threshold amount would be taxed at the recipient's income tax bracket plus 20 percent, causing higher-income recipients as well as the benefactors of more generous gifts to pay higher levies. The 20 percent premium reflects the "unearned" nature of these gifts as distinguished from income earned at work. Closure of tax loopholes can ensure that all wealth transferred from one generation to the next is subject to the tax, over some threshold limit. For example, a current threshold of $250,000 would enable any offspring the opportunity to go to the college of their choice and have enough remaining to put a down payment on a median-priced home. Any gifts or inheritances below that level, over the course of one's lifetime, would be exempt from any tax; all amounts above that level would be subject to the tax. In this way, each parent can ensure their children have the means toward a generous stake in life. Wealthy parents certainly could provide more, but the supplement would be subject to the inheritance tax.

Clearly, the discussion of any tax increase in our current political environment generates little traction. Yet, this proposal has some unique elements. First, it does not restrict the ability of most parents who have the means to offer substantial help to their children; it permits a substantial financial transfer tax-free. Second, only a small number of taxpayers would actually pay the tax as the vast majority of households never receive such a generous gift. Admittedly, this small group of potential taxpayers represents substantial political power in their right; yet, the existence of noblesse oblige among some of this group would undercut this clout. Lastly, this tax would easily raise the revenues needed to pay for the programs already mentioned. Over the past decade, estates have averaged around $125 billion annually. With an effective tax levy that would approach 50 percent, the additional funds raised could easily fund the IDA programs and Pell Grant increases already discussed. While parents could still target the majority of their estates to their offspring, the remainder would serve as a covenant from one generation to the next, ensuring that the opportunities realized in one generation are broadly shared with the next.

Conclusion

Over the past generation, a period of remarkable economic growth and relative prosperity brought help to many, but not to all US households. By the evidence given, upward of one-third of the households did not experience a substantial increase in net worth. Despite the gains made by these households to save regularly and purchase homes, the rising tide of prosperity left many households high and dry. Further evidence demonstrates how these stranded households had limited access to the three pathways to wealth accumulation. While any household is free to save, low and moderate-income households have the burden of modest incomes and higher debt costs that challenge their capacity to save regularly. Without adequate savings, they cannot invest in homes, real estate, stocks, and other assets that appreciate over time. In addition, these households rarely receive substantial gifts from family members that might bankroll their wealth creation efforts. Instead, they are more frequently expected to help their own parents at the expense of assisting their children. Not even the sustained economic prosperity experienced during this period was sufficient to offset these disadvantages. Even before the savage financial riptides of the past several years, roughly one-third of households were largely isolated from the wealth gains of the period.

Implementing these public policy recommendations can remedy the wealth disparities. Passage and ample funding of the IDA programs can offer modest-income households attractive financial incentives to save regularly, giving them the kind of help their wealthier neighbors already receive. The availability of generously funded IDAs will simply level the playing ground for all households to engage in saving. Yet, elevating household income represents the most direct way to increase household saving. By raising the Pell Grant awards, we can make a college education much more accessible to all eligible students, regardless of family background. Even at these higher-award levels, the Pell Grants will not cover the full cost of college. Household savings from an IDA can fill some of this gap. With a college diploma and without the burden of college loans, these individuals can expect to earn significant increases in household income. Targeting the home mortgage deduction will help these same individuals as they purchase their first house. In doing so, they can experience the capital gains that generate most of the wealth creation realized by their more affluent neighbors.

As we enter an era of increased budgetary restraint, it is essential to identify specific means of paying for new policy initiatives. While these proposed policies will cost taxpayer dollars, they can be easily funded by the proposed revamping of the inheritance and gift tax. Such a tax modification could easily raise $40 billion annually, enough to cover the policy proposals discussed above. As a funding source for these wealth-creation programs, the revamped inheritance tax could serve as an intergenerational covenant in which the good fortunes on one generation support the initial efforts of the next. While affluent families could still pass along enough to their heirs to provide them with a strong start in life, their taxes would also help their neighbors. Taken together, these policies would increase access to each of the wealth-building pathways as they promote increased household saving, higher household incomes, expanded asset ownership, and eventually broader participation in the sharing of household wealth within and beyond familial bounds. Over time, more households would find themselves able to take advantage of the rising tides of future economic expansions.

There is little evidence that we can count on economic growth to provide a fully inclusive prosperity as argued by neoclassical economics. Worse, one wonders how such growth can continue in a world of unforgiving ecological limits as indicated by climate change, water shortages, and resource depletion. Yet, we need not recoil from this prospect. Implementing the policy changes discussed in this chapter can offer a hopeful alternative. By increasing access among all households to the different wealth pathways, these policies can unleash a somewhat untapped resource. Creative and energetic children from economically disadvantaged households will find increased opportunities to develop their latent potential. By leveling the playing field, more households will effectively maneuver the wealth-accumulation pathways. By increasing their household wealth, more of our neighbors, communities, and regional economies will have greater resiliency to weather the inevitable riptides of the future. By creating the covenant between one generation and the next, we can foster a greater sense of community and shared experience across our land. With these changes, we can rebalance the twin poles of individual ingenuity and collective responsibility in which the latter is strengthened while the former is more broadly inclusive.

Notes

1. The NBER does date the start of the Great Recession in December 2007, at the very end of this period.
2. Though these surveys do date back to 1983, the 1989 survey represents the start of a relatively consistent survey methodology thought today.
3. There are notable exceptions at the very bottom and at the very top of the household wealth spectrum. I want to express my appreciation to researchers at the Levy Institute for making apparent this anomaly among the very wealthy.
4. This includes residential and commercial real estate as well as ownership of principal home, except for mobile homes that do not generally appreciate in value (Jewel 2002).
5. In 1989, the pattern of auto loans was counterintuitive as less wealthy households paid lower rates than some wealthier households did. One possible explanation is that the higher rates reflected the longer loan terms extended to these wealthier households. In any event, this anomaly disappears in 2007.
6. Even restoring the maximum grant to 68% of public college tuition cost overstates the program's generosity. As few recipients receive the full funding level, most households will continue to bear the majority of college costs.*

References

Advisory Committee on Student Financial Assistance. 2002. *Empty Promises: The Myth of College Access in America.* Washington, DC: Advisory Committee on Student Financial Assistance.

Ayres, R. 1996. "Limits to Growth Paradigm." *Ecological Economics* 19: 117–134.

Baum, S. 2004. *Student Financial Aid Policies: Do They Promote Universal Education?* New York: Ford Policy Forum.

Carruso, A., C. E. Steuerle, and E. Bell. 2005. "Making Tax Incentives for Homeownership More Equitable and Efficient." Tax Policy Center Discussion Paper No. 21, Washington, DC: Urban Institute.

Coate, D., and R. Schwester. 2008. "Black-White Appreciation of Owner-Occupied Homes in Upper Income Suburban Integrated Communities: The Cases of Maplewood and Montclair, New Jersey." Working Paper #2008–001, Newark, NJ: Rutgers University.

College Board. 2007. *Education Pays, 2007.* Washington, DC: College Board.

College Board. 2010. *Trends in Student Aid, 2010.* Washington, DC: College Board.

Constanza, R., J. Cumberland, H. Daly, R. Goodland, and R. Norgaard. 1997. *An Introduction to Ecological Economics.* Boca Raton, FL: St. Lucie.

CFED. 2009. "Savings for Working Families Act." Corporation for Enterprise Development Website. http://cfed.org/assets/documents/SWFA/IDA_One_Pager_5_12_09.pdf. Accessed January 11, 2011.

Daly, H., ed. 1973. *Toward a Steady-State Economy.* San Francisco: W. H. Freeman.

Flippen, C. 2004. "Unequal Returns to Housing Investments? A Study of Real Housing Appreciation among Black, White, and Hispanic Households." *Social Forces* 82 (4): 1523–1551.

Holling, C. S., and G. Meffe. 1996. "Command and Control and the Pathology of Natural Resource Management." *Conservation Biology* 10: 328–337.

Jewel, K. 2002. *Appreciation in Manufactured Housing: A Fresh Look at the Debate and the Data.* Consumers Union Website. http://www.nw.org/network/comstrat/manufhsg/documents/appinmhhousing_000.pdf. Accessed January 17, 2011.

Kennedy, John F. 1963. "Remarks in Heber Springs, Arkansas, at the Dedication of Greers Ferry Dam.," October 3, Online by Gerhard Peters and John T. Woolley, *The American Presidency Project.* http://www.presidency.ucsb.edu/ws/?pid=9455. Accessed January 18, 2013.

King, J. 2003. *2003 Status Report on the Pell Grant Program.* Washington, DC: American Council on Education.

Maag, E., and K. Fitzpatrick. 2004. *Federal Financial Aid for Higher Education: Programs and Prospects,* Washington, DC: Urban Institute.

McLusky, D., and M. Elliott. 2004. *The Estuarine Ecosystem: Ecology, Threats, and Management.* 3rd ed. Oxford, UK: Oxford University Press.

NBER. 2010. "US Business Cycle Expansions and Contractions." NBER Website. http://www.nber.org/cycles. Accessed January 13, 2011.

New America Foundation. 2009. "The ASPIRE Act of 2009." New America Foundation Website. http://www.newamerica.net/publications/policy/aspire_act_2009. Accessed January 20, 2011.

OMB. 2009. *Analytical Perspectives: Budget of the US Government Fiscal Year 2010.* Washington, DC: US Government Printing Office.

Peterson, G., C. Allen, and C. S. Holling. 1998. "Ecological Resilience, Biodiversity, and Scale." *Ecosystems* 1: 6–18.

Reice, S. 2001. *The Silver Lining: The Benefits of Natural Disasters*, Princeton, NJ: Princeton University Press.

US Census Bureau. 2010. *The 2010 Statistical Abstract*, Washington, DC: US Census Bureau.

Vernberg, F. John, and Winona B. Vernberg. 2001. *The Coastal Zone: Past, Present, and Future.* Columbia: University of South Carolina Press.

Wackernagel, M., and W. Rees. 1996. *Our Ecological Footprint: Reducing Human Impact on the Earth.* Gabriola Island, British Colombia: New Society.

Chapter 3

Divided We Stand, United We Fall—A Good Society Needs an Individual Poverty Measure*

Danièle Meulders and Síle O'Dorchai

Introduction

The aim of this chapter is to revisit the existing literature on poverty, based on a discussion and illustration of the implications of the choice of the measurement unit. One of the first considerations of any researcher interested in examining poverty is the unit of measurement or unit of analysis.

Traditional poverty research was built around the convenient device of the "household utility function," as developed in Becker's early work (1974, 1981). Poverty measures were thus based on the resources of family units that are assumed to share these equally between their members. The poverty rate is traditionally estimated on the basis of a clear hypothesis that, however much individual members of a household contribute, they pool and fully share all of their income. According to this approach, a person belonging to a poor household is poor, however much he or she earns personally.

The validity of this hypothesis, a legacy of the neoclassical approach whereby the household was viewed as a black box behaving "as one man," altruistically maximizing the homogeneous utility of the household, urgently needs questioning not in the least because when the household serves as the unit of analysis in poverty research, women's poverty is severely understated (Folbre 1986; Kabeer 1994; Woolley and Marshall 1994; Nelson 1996). A good society is one where policies are correctly targeted to have the most positive effect possible. In order for policies toward women at risk of poverty to be effective, they need to be based on a correct assessment of their situation relative to men's.

This chapter presents the results of an in-depth analysis at the individual level of the actual income situation and poverty of women and men. Starting out from a conceptual discussion, this chapter will illustrate the effects of switching from household income to individual income on the analysis of poverty. Three domains of poverty research are put to the test. First, it is shown how the calculation of poverty rates is affected by the level at which income is assessed (household versus individual level). Second, the literature on the income effects for a couple who are breaking up are put to the individualization test. Finally, the population of working poor is explored from an individual lens rather than applying the standard household-based definition of poverty to workers with a necessarily individual employment status. These three case studies summarize three more substantive research analyses that have been published or have been submitted for publication to various journals.[1]

Review of the Literature

Poverty research has a long-standing history. Although alternative methods exist, income measures remain the most widespread tool to measure poverty and inequality (Briar 2000). However, the gender sensitivity of income measures varies widely and, given the absence of large-scale data collections on personal incomes of partnered women, this leads to women's poverty being systematically understated.

In traditional poverty research based on Becker's notion of the "household utility function," (Becker 1974, 1981), the assumption that family units share their resources equitably between their members implied that each family member had the same poverty status. Adoption of the household as the unit of analysis thus became standard practice although some studies, mainly in British literature, applied a narrower unit in terms of blood or marital relationship, or of dependence (Atkinson and Micklewright 1992).

Over the years both feminist and mainstream economists have expressed increasing dissatisfaction with some of the poverty measures in common use. Much of the mainstream criticism of poverty measures has focused on the resource side, contending, for example, that in-kind benefits such as housing or other subsidies should be counted as income. Feminist economists have stressed the inadequacy of the poverty thresholds (Ruggles 1990; Renwick and Bergmann 1993). In addition, many feminist economists contend that the poverty of women may be understated when it is assumed that income is shared equally within families (Folbre 1986; Kabeer 1994; Woolley and Marshall 1994; Nelson 1996).

In the empirical economic literature, a shift is observed from the family unit as the basis of models of household behavior (rejection of Becker's unitary approach) toward the individuals composing the household. Non-unitary (cooperative/collective or noncooperative/strategic) models of household behavior explicitly suppose that households consist of a number of different members with preferences that are different from each other (Chiappori 1988, 1997; Browning et al. 1994; Purkayastha 1999; Lundberg, Pollak, and Wales 1997; Fortin and Lacroix 1997; Manser and Brown 1980; Horney and McElroy 1988). There is also substantial sociological evidence that access to resources within families is unequal (Graham 1987). This shift in approach has particularly strong consequences for the analysis of poverty.

The gendered nature of poverty is not a new concept. Although originally mainly American, research on the feminization of poverty spread to the rest of the developed world over time (Goldberg and Kremen 1990; Casper, McLanahan, and Garfinkel 1994; Pressman 2002). In this literature, the issue at stake is the disproportionate number of poor households that are female headed or the disproportionate number of women in poor households. However, it is household income that serves as the basis to determine the individual poverty status. In an important contribution, Phipps and Burton (1995) showed that making different assumptions about the extent of income pooling and the existence of "public goods" within families leads to large differences in the measured amount of individual poverty in Canada. Similar studies covering the UK or Canada were carried out by Borooah and McKee (1994) and Davies and Joshi (1994). Findlay and Wright (1996) also showed with data from the United States and Italy that if intra-household inequality exists, poverty among women is likely to be seriously underestimated.

Various studies have attempted to examine how resources and expenditures are managed within households, looking at the power relations between partners, their methods of decision-making, and the taxation and benefit systems (Pahl 1989; Woolley and Marshall 1994). Others have sought to identify the rules on sharing by disaggregating household expenditure according to the goods and services procured (Browning et al. 1994). Others still have quantified the degree of income sharing within households and its sensitivity to changes in the taxation and benefit systems (Lundberg, Pollak, and Wales 1997).

We have developed a new methodology to analyze poverty at the individual rather than at the household level based on the resources of each individual, whatever the characteristics of the household in which he/she lives.[2] This presupposed measuring inequalities between individual incomes of men and women. We also carried out a statistical and econometric study of these income disparities in order to propose indicators for monitoring purposes. Other attempts to individualize measurements of poverty have focused solely on individuals living alone or else have considered only individual incomes, ignoring income that is pooled within the household (Daly and Rake 2002).

Besides the fact that women's poverty is understated when intra-household income pooling and sharing is assumed, another argument in favor of using purely individual income rather than equivalized household income in poverty analysis is that what is measured, at least in Europe, is not someone's actual poverty status but the poverty risk or the at-risk-of-poverty rate.[3] Since the 1960s there has been a drastic increase in divorce rates in Europe. In 1960, there were two to three divorces per 1,000 married couples. By 2002, this rate had more than tripled, with over seven annual divorces per 1,000 married couples (González and Viitanen 2009). This has generated a great deal of attention from researchers and policy-makers. Many worry about the negative economic consequences of divorce for women and children.

Opting for an individual rather than a household approach also has important policy implications. Targeted policies aimed at improving the welfare of particular household members are effective only when the assumption of full income pooling and sharing within households fails to hold true.

Individualizing the measure of the poverty risk thus offers an important alternative perspective with a huge potential toward improving our societies.

Presentation of Data and Methodology

To illustrate to what point poverty measures are sensitive to the choice of the unit of reference, this chapter presents three case studies.

In the first case study, cross-sectional EU-SILC (European Statistics on Income and Living Conditions) 2006 data are used to show the difference between poverty rates measured on the basis of household or individual income. The EU-SILC are the reference source of statistics on income and social exclusion in the European

Union (EU). This dataset covers only private households, not collective households or people in institutions. Also persons without a fixed place of residence are left out. We consider all adults above 24 years of age as well as individuals between 18 and 24 years of age who are active in the labor market (i.e., employed or actively looking for a job). In order to compute a net income for each individual person in the sample, the tax burden was assessed through a comparison of the gross and net amounts of all income components. In the EU-SILC 2006, this was not possible in all countries. The final sample thus consists of 133,071 individuals spread over nine countries (Austria, Belgium, Spain, France, Ireland, Luxembourg, Poland, Sweden, and the United Kingdom). The reader can find a detailed description of the methodology of the first stage of this research relative to the computation of individual net incomes in Meulders et al. (2011, 376). Individualizing income implied that certain household-level income categories needed to be shared between the household members. To do so we worked according to a number of hypotheses that are also fully described in Meulders et al. (2011, 376). In short, family- and child-related allowances are equally shared between the parents while other household-level income categories such as housing allowances are shared equally among the adults in the household.

In the second case study, the impact of partnership dissolution is studied in terms of its implications on individual net income (measuring variations in individual incomes before and after the breakup) and confronted with the rest of the literature that compares an equivalized household income prior to separation (adopting an assumption of shared income within households) with an individual income after the event. The analysis uses longitudinal data from the EU-SILC for 18 European countries (Finland, Hungary, Iceland, Lithuania, the Netherlands, Norway, Slovakia, the United Kingdom, Austria, Belgium, Cyprus, the Czech Republic, Estonia, Spain, Luxembourg, Poland, Sweden, and Slovenia) covering the period 2004–2007. As in the first case study, our sample contains only adults, defined as persons above 24 years of age or between 18 and 24 years of age if they are economically active (i.e., persons of this age group who are not living with their parents, or if they are, they are working or available for work and actively looking for a job). Our sample is composed of adults living as a couple in the course of the year *t* (2004 or 2005) but without a partner the following year, that is, *t*+1 (2005 or 2006). Widows and widowers are excluded from our sample. Among these individuals who are breaking up, we have retained only those for whom all the necessary variables are still available in *t*+2 (2006 or 2007). We assume the data for the year *t* to represent the individuals' situation prior to the breakup and those relative to the year *t*+2, their situation after the breakup (a similar methodology was applied by Smock [1994]; Uunk [2004]; Poortman [2000]). We thus analyze the short-term impact on income. Although this may not be the best measure of income variation following a breakup, we assume short-term change to approximate longer-term change (Duncan and Hoffman 1985). Our final sample comprises 543 women and 480 men in 18 different countries, that is, a total of 1,023 divorced or separated adults.

As the change in income over the period considered is at least in part due to changes in the price level, the post-breakup income is deflated. When a couple breaks up, it is likely that there will be an effect not only on the ex-partners' incomes but also on their cost of living, especially for the one who gets custody of the children. To account for this we have computed variations not only in individual incomes before and after the breakup but also in equivalized individual incomes. The equivalized individual income was obtained by applying an equivalence scale to adjust individual income for the number of children a person has in charge. The income of an adult was divided by 1 + 0.3 for each child of whom he or she has the sole custody and by 1 + 0.15 for each child of whom he or she has shared custody (with another adult).

In the third case study, the working poor population is analyzed in eight EU countries (Austria, Belgium, Spain, France, Ireland, Luxembourg, Poland, and the United Kingdom) using the 2007 wave of the EU-SILC. The working poor are at the crossroads of an individual employment status and a household-based poverty measure. In this case study, the emphasis is on the impact on the rate of working poor because of changing the unit of analysis from the household to the individual, comparing the proportions of working poor between the European definition of working poverty and a fully individualized definition. According to the European definition, the working poor are all full-time or part-time employees/self-employed workers aged 15–64 who live in a household with an equivalized household disposable income below 60 percent of the median of this income in the country whereas according to the fully individualized definition, the working poor are all full-time or part-time employees/self-employed workers aged 15–64 with an individual net income below 60 percent of the median of this income in the country.

Case Study 1: Individual Poverty or Financial Dependence

The European "at-risk-of-poverty rate" is defined as the percentage of persons belonging to households whose disposable adult equivalent income is less than 60 percent of the national median equivalent income. This rate of poverty risk therefore implies the clear assumption that the incomes of members of a household are pooled and shared in full. Given that it is the risk of poverty that is measured, that an equal division of income within the household is in fact an abstract notion, not a real-life fact, and that the two-person household with or without children is progressively losing ground as the reference model, a household-level analysis of poverty may not be the most appropriate. Based on the European definition and on the individual incomes we calculated, we coined the term "financial dependence": people in a situation of financial dependence are those whose individual net incomes are less than 60 percent of the individual median income. The notion of financial dependence in fact represents the poverty risk run by persons having to meet their needs out of their own income without assistance from anyone else. Our hypothesis is that individuals are protected from the risk of poverty solely by the income that they themselves possess. The key difference between this and the European poverty rate is that we do not consider the household as a unit where sharing occurs; we consider every individual separately, irrespective of the household to which they belong, and we examine the individual income of each person.

The differences are substantial in the case of women, and the level of financial dependence is much higher than the rate of poverty risk. Conversely, men's level of financial dependence is relatively similar to their rate of poverty risk.

Figure 3.1 shows that in all of the countries studied, apart from Poland, the level of financial dependence among women is at least twice as high as their rate of poverty risk. This indicates that many women would find themselves in poverty if they were unable to avail themselves of part of the income of another member of the household.

These findings bear out those of Daly and Rake (2002): "Measuring household income and calculating poverty rates at the household level implies that incomes are shared equally within households. Where such sharing does not occur, it is women who are most likely to be affected, since they command lower incomes on average. Hence, this

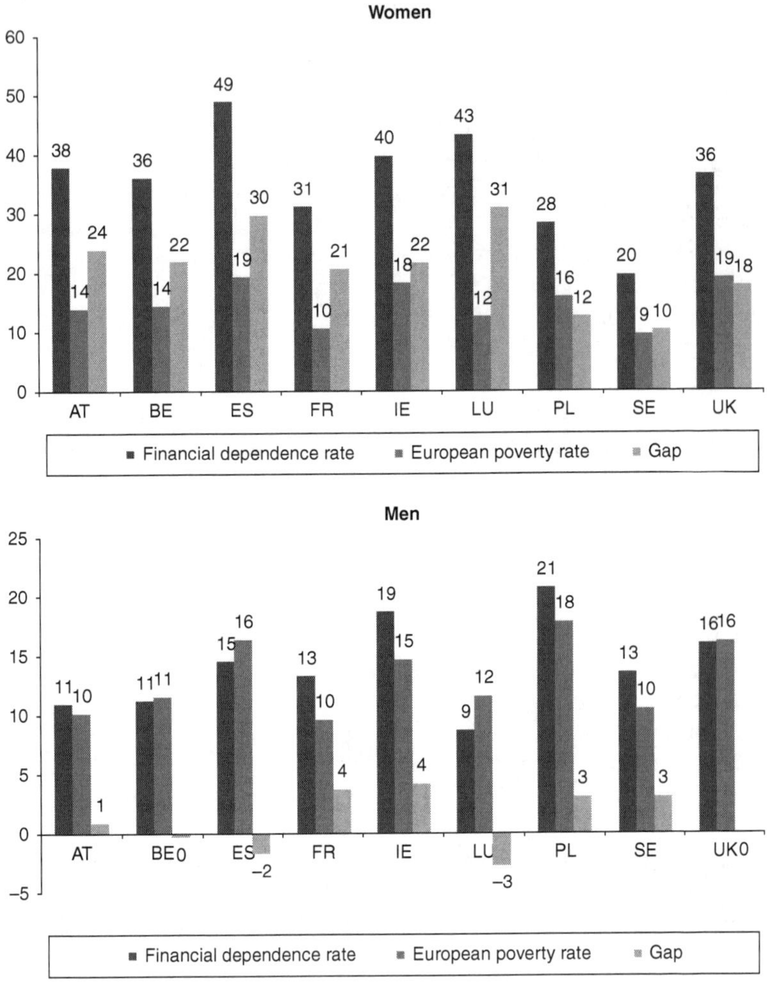

Figure 3.1 Comparison of financial dependence levels and European at-risk-of-poverty rates.

Source: EU-SILC 2006.

methodological practice tends to overstate women's access to income (and understate their poverty rates)" (3 [appendix]). A good society being one with effective social policies, we believe that a thorough questioning of the sharing assumption would greatly contribute to improving existing welfare state provisions.

Case Study 2: Effects of a Breakup

The society we live in is marked by increasing divorce rates and changing models of household structure. It is crucial for a good society to correctly assess the economic effects of these transformations for each of the parties involved.

In the literature, there is a widespread belief that divorce produces negative economic consequences, especially for women, whose economic situation is assumed to deteriorate sharply following a breakup (Burkhauser et al. 1991; Smock 1994; Jarvis and Jenkins 1999; Poortman 2000; Andreß et al. 2003; Manting and Bouman 2006). The extent of this deterioration varies widely from country to country, depending on the methods and the timescale employed in the study: the effects are most marked in the short term. As far as men are concerned, these studies reveal a status quo or a lower level of deterioration than that observed for women.

Nevertheless, we also find that most divorce proceedings are instigated by women (Brinig and Allen 2000). This contradiction between the desire to divorce and the traumatic consequences of a divorce can be explained in several ways. First, women may underestimate the future economic consequences of a breakup. Second, there are many reasons why people divorce, and financial losses may be offset by other benefits: greater independence, life satisfaction, and so on. A third reason might lie in the way that the financial effects are measured: incorrect measurement of the effects of a divorce on the partners' income, resulting in the financial loss being overstated, especially for women. As Smock, Manning, and Gupta (1999, 794) indicate: "Women experiencing separation or divorce typically undergo marked declines in family income and in measures of economic well-being that take account of family size."

The latter explanation is a matter of concern to us, as a review of the literature relating to this topic produces an initial finding: the majority of studies that try to measure the effects of breakups on couples' incomes work on the clear hypothesis that incomes are shared among household members prior to the breakup, and thus compare a total household income shared among its members with each member's presumed individual income following the breakup. For example, a woman with an income of 5,000 euros living with a man who earns 10,000 euros is notionally credited, when the modified OECD (Organisation for Economic Co-operation and Development) equivalence scale is applied,[4] with an income of 10,000 euros before the breakup and an income of 5,000 euros after the divorce, that is, a loss of 5,000 euros or 50 percent. Yet based on our hypotheses (we reject the assumption that the household income is shared among its members, and we consider only the personal incomes of individuals, i.e., those possessed by them alone as a result of their work, any state benefits they may receive, and their income from immovable and movable property—whatever the nature of their lifestyle and the household to which they belong), the woman's income would be 5,000 euros in both cases, and consequently, she would not be losing anything.

This hypothesis of sharing adopted by authors clearly explains the disastrous results observed for women who, prior to separation or divorce, possessed a more or less substantial share of their partner's income but no longer possess this afterward.

Our study of the effects of a couple's breaking up on the individual incomes of women and men, based on longitudinal data from the 2004–2007 European SILC for 18 countries, shows that following a breakup the median of men's net individual income is roughly unchanged whereas that of women increases by as much as 37 percent (Table 3.1). This difference is slightly less pronounced when we look at the evolution of mean income: men's average net individual income increases by 9 percent following a breakup, whereas for women, this figure rises to 32 percent (Table 3.1). Our results contradict the rest of the literature, which generally reports negative economic consequences resulting from a breakup, especially for women. This can be explained by the hypothesis that resources within households are fully shared, which is adopted in most income and poverty studies but is rejected in our analysis. Despite the substantial rise in women's net individual income highlighted by our results in the event of a breakup, their average income remains lower than men's.

As part of the increase in individual income of women and men following a breakup may be due to changes in the price level over the period considered, we deflated post-breakup income using average annual variation rates in the harmonized consumer price index in the 18 countries in our sample. Table 3.2 summarizes the results.

Women's individual income still increases much more than men's but the income effect of the breakup is nevertheless tempered. When inflation is controlled, women's median individual income increases by 29 percent (instead of 37%), and men's, decreases by 7 percent (instead of remaining unchanged). The effect of correcting for inflation is similar on mean income variations. For women, the mean individual income increases by 23 percent following a breakup (compared with 32% when inflation is not accounted for), and for men, the mean individual income rises by 2 percent (instead of 9%).

Table 3.1 Variation in median and mean individual net income in the event of the couple breaking up

	Median individual net income at *t* or before the breakup	Median individual net income at *t*+2 or after the breakup	Variation in median net individual income between *t* and *t*+2 (%)
Women	10,200	13,955	+36.81
Men	17,816	17,830	+0.08
	Mean individual net income at *t* or before the break-up	**Mean individual net income at *t*+2 or after the breakup**	**Variation in mean net individual income between *t* and *t*+2 (%)**
Women	12,175	16,105	+32.28
Men	18,036	19,739	+9.44

Source: EU-SILC, longitudinal data 2004–2007.

Table 3.2 Variation in median and mean individual net income in the event of the couple breaking up accounting for inflation

	Median individual net income at *t* or before the breakup	Median deflated individual net income at *t*+2 or after the breakup	Variation in median net individual income between *t* and *t*+2 (%)
Women	10,200	13,160	+29.02
Men	17,816	16,649	−6.55
	Mean individual net income at *t* or before the breakup	**Mean deflated individual net income at *t*+2 or after the breakup**	**Variation in mean net individual income between *t* and *t*+2 (%)**
Women	12,175	14,989	+23.11
Men	18,036	18,330	+1.63

Source: EU-SILC, longitudinal data 2004–2007.

One may argue that not only income is affected by partnership dissolution but also the cost of living, especially when custody of children is not shared between parents but assigned to either one of them. Comparing equivalised individual incomes (which adjust individual income for the number of children a person has in charge) before and after the break-up allows to account for this. Recall that the income of an adult was divided by 1 + 0.3 for each child of whom he or she has the sole custody and by 1 + 0.15 for each child of whom he or she has shared custody (with another adult). Table 3.3 presents the results. For women, accounting for the number of children hardly affects the increase in their median individual income

Table 3.3 Variation in median and mean individual net income in the event of the couple breaking up accounting for inflation and family size

	Median equivalent individual net income at *t* or before the breakup	Median deflated equivalent individual net income at *t*+2 or after the breakup	Variation in median net equivalent individual income between *t* and *t*+2 (%)
Women	8,850	11,964	+35.19
Men	16,096	15,369	−4.52
	Mean equivalent individual net income at *t* or before the breakup	Mean deflated equivalent individual net income at *t*+2 or after the breakup	Variation in mean net equivalent individual income between *t* and *t*+2 (%)
Women	10,984	12,842	+16.92
Men	16,538	17,416	+5.31

Source: EU-SILC, longitudinal data 2004–2007.

whereas it noticeably reduces their mean income increase from 32 percent (Table 3.1) to 17 percent (Table 3.3). For men, their median and mean income variations are affected to a similar extent: accounting for the number of children cuts their income increase by roughly 5 percentage points.

The rise in women's net average income following a breakup is primarily due to state benefits. The income women possess on account of their economic activity seems to be relatively little affected by the breakup (cf. Table 3.4).

We took Uunk's study (2004) as our starting point, but unlike him, we worked on individual incomes to estimate an econometric model that would enable us to identify the individual and macroeconomic variables influencing the variation in net individual income where a couple breaks up.[5] At the level of individual characteristics, we show that the income received prior to the breakup exerts a negative influence on the rise in income following the breakup, and consequently, the rise in income brought about by the breakup is less marked for an individual with a high income before the breakup. Age exerts a positive influence on the variation in income as a proxy for occupational experience. Following the breakup, individuals with higher education see their income rise to a greater extent than do the less-educated individuals. A high level of educational attainment enables women who were not working before the breakup to return to the labor market more easily following this event. The breakup produces a rise in

Table 3.4 Components of mean individual net income of men and women before and after a breakup

	t	t+2
Women		
Earned income	12,676	13,338
Wealth	74	–142
State benefits	3,374	7,091
Inter-household transfers	30	380
Taxes	3,980	4,562
Total individual net income	12,175	16,105
Men		
Earned income	19,335	21,683
Wealth	-93	–203
State benefits	5,524	6,282
Inter-household transfers	–49	–416
Taxes	6,682	7,608
Total individual net income	18,036	19,739

Source: EU-SILC, longitudinal data 2004–2007.

net individual income, which is all the more significant in that the event prompts the person to (re)enter the labor market.

As far as macroeconomic variables are concerned, an increase in the number of places available with public childcare facilities exerts a positive influence on the variation in income in the event of a breakup. Public childcare therefore appears to be a key policy to enable women, and especially single mothers, to combine their family and work-related responsibilities. Interpreting the estimated impact of the type of welfare state on the economic consequences of a breakup proved complicated. This finding underlines the need to adopt a very critical approach to dealing with welfare state classifications of the type produced by Esping-Andersen (1990, 1999).

Case Study 3: The Working Poor

Since the 1970s, the emphasis on policies to boost competitiveness among firms in order to increase labor supply and the emphasis on flexibilization, deregulation, and casualization in European labor markets have generated a new form of poverty also affecting workers. Since the introduction of the European Employment Strategy in 1997 and the launch of the Lisbon strategy in 2000, working poverty has gained a more prominent place in the European debate. Indeed, in the framework of the European process toward social inclusion and social protection, and the European Employment Strategy, the EU adopted a new social indicator in 2003, the "in-work at-risk-of-poverty rate" which considers the working poor as all full-time or part-time employees/self-employed workers living in poor households.

This indicator has been amply analyzed and criticized ever since (Lelièvre, Marlier, and Pétour 2004; Ponthieux 2009; Cazenave 2006). First, the European approach ignores that the working poor are at the heart of a conceptual problem as employment is an individual state whereas poverty is usually defined at the level of the household.

Second, the European at-risk-of-poverty rate implies the clear assumption that the incomes of members of a household are pooled and shared in full. However, an equal division of income within the household seems an abstract notion rather than a real-life fact. Two generations of studies have tested this assumption. The first studies testing the income pooling assumption were hindered by the endogenous nature of the intra-household income distribution. The most obvious example is that of earned income, the level and distribution of which depend on all household members' labor supply. These studies have nevertheless generally rejected the assumption of income pooling within households (Thomas 1990; Phipps and Burton 1998; Bourguignon et al. 1993). More recently, studies have evaluated the degree of income pooling within households through an analysis of the quasi-experimental variation in the distribution of income within households as a result of changes in the policy context (e.g., Attanasio and Lechene 2002; Lundberg, Pollak, and Wales 1997; Ward-Batts 2008). They all reject the income pooling assumption.

Finally, the income pooling and sharing assumption particularly hinders the correct assessment of women's poverty situation. Women often live with men whose income lifts them above the poverty threshold, while men often live with women who are less economically active (Ponthieux 2009). This might be the reason why women do not tend to be overrepresented among the working poor in EU-level studies.

An alternative approach is upheld in our research and by a few others (e.g., Ponthieux 2009; Smock 1994). This approach allows overcoming the three main difficulties that are raised by the European Commission's definition of the working poor. Using an individual measure of income to determine the poverty status avoids the conceptual problem that employment is an individual state whereas the poverty risk is usually determined through a household approach. It further allows going without an income pooling assumption and as such contributes to a more correct identification and understanding of the working poor, especially of its female population.

In the present analysis, we have opted for a definition of the poverty risk at the individual level. The working poor, according to our definition, are thus those full-time or part-time employees/self-employed workers aged between 15 and 64 years of age whose total individual net disposable income is below 60 percent of the median total individual net disposable income in the country of residence.

Based on this individual definition, we assessed the size and characteristics of the working poor population in 8 European Union countries in 2007.By analyzing the link between work and the risk of poverty at the individual level, we distinguish between poverty due to low earnings and poverty due to having a large family as a way of separating labor market factors from household factors (Rowntree 2000; Ponthieux 2010). The EU household-based definition of the poverty risk actually measures the proportion of workers who are poor because they have too many other household members relying on their income. On the contrary, when the poverty risk is computed on the basis of individual income, what is measured is the proportion of workers who, because of their employment conditions, earn a wage that is insufficient to stay out of poverty. In a good society, employment acts as a protective mechanism against the poverty risk. For some people, employment cannot fulfill this role (temporary jobs, part-time work, and so forth). This is a major challenge for labor market policies. However, in order to correctly guide labor market policies, the population of working poor needs to be evaluated on correct grounds, that is, on the ground of their employment situation and not on the ground of the type of family to which they belong. In a good society, the analysis of working poverty should thus assess the individual income of every worker rather than fallaciously attribute them with an equivalized share of their household's income.

Table 3.5 shows the impact of changing the unit of analysis from the household to the individual on the rate of working poor. It compares the proportions of working poor between the European Commission's definition of working poverty and our definition. The difference between the two measures illustrates the impact of the household structure.

A first finding is that with the European definition, the proportion of poor male workers exceeds that of poor female workers in all countries but Belgium. When individual income is used to evaluate the poverty risk, the inverse holds true; the proportion of poor

Table 3.5 Comparison of rates of working poor using individual or equivalized household income to measure poverty

	EC definition			Our definition		
	Men	Women	Ratio	Men	Women	Ratio
AT	7.37	6.43	0.9	6.92	19.94	2.9
BE	4.37	4.40	1.0	3.70	10.49	2.8
ES	10.51	7.92	0.8	6.74	14.86	2.2
FR	7.83	7.04	0.9	4.72	14.04	3.0
IE	5.31	5.12	1.0	5.20	10.60	2.0
LU	8.17	7.97	1.0	3.36	16.25	4.8
PL	11.95	10.02	0.8	8.99	14.37	1.6
UK	8.68	8.06	0.9	8.09	22.82	2.8

Source: EU-SILC 2007.

female workers largely exceeds that of poor male workers in all countries. This illustrates the impact of women's overrepresentation in part-time low-paid jobs, a fact that is hidden by the assumption of intra-household income pooling and sharing as it is upheld in the European definition of the in-work at-risk-of-poverty rate.

A second finding is that the move from the European household-based definition to the individual definition reduces the proportion of male working poor, but it substantially increases the proportion of female working poor. The decrease in the proportion of male working poor results from the fact that most households are still headed by men. When they no longer need to share their income with other dependent members in their household, their income appears to be more than sufficient to protect them against the risk of poverty. On the contrary, the European definition appears to severely understate female workers' at-risk-of-poverty rate. As long as female workers can depend on supplements from their household's income, they manage much better to stay out of poverty than when they have to survive on their personal income only.

A third finding results from the previous two: the relative share of women with respect to men in the category of the working poor increases enormously when the European definition is traded in for an individual measure of poverty.

Conclusion

Traditionally poverty has been studied assuming that, regardless their personal contribution to household income, each household member receives an equal share of total household income. As a result, a person is poor when the household he or she lives in is poor.

The absence of large-scale data collections on personal incomes of partnered women, especially when unemployed or inactive (e.g., European Labour Force Survey, Luxembourg Income Study) at least partly explains why the assumption of income pooling and sharing within households has hardly ever been questioned.

The fact that the principal databases do not contain any individual data that can be used to study resources and consumption reflects a particular—and partial—vision of society equating to the unitary model. This outmoded view likewise becomes apparent when we note that social entitlements are not always assigned on an individual basis, as is the case in Belgium; it is also evident from the way in which the indicators for policy monitoring are calculated. As Briar (2000) puts it,

> Ways of conceptualising and measuring poverty, inequality and well-being are political and contestable, and thus are subject to constant reinterpretation and change. Indices and concepts, to a considerable extent, reflect the values of the people responsible for framing them. Concepts and measures potentially can be framed in ways that expose the poverty of disadvantaged groups, such as women, and that act as a basis for action to improve the situation of these groups. However, the choice of concepts and measures also can be used by governments to present the results of their policies in a more favourable light, or to restrict demands for assistance. (12)

It is therefore politicians who are accountable, and this has far-reaching implications. How can gender inequality be combated effectively unless these forms of inequality are measured in the light of individual incomes? How can poverty among women be combated if it is hidden by being buried within the household? Indeed, the policy implications are very different according to whether an individual or a household approach is opted for. With the traditional household-based definition, the fight against poverty should be driven by birth-control policies that have nothing to do with the organization of the labor market. Having few children should be promoted as a means to protect oneself against poverty. On the contrary, with an individual measure, poverty should be combated through employment and wage policies. Stable, high-quality, and well-paid employment should be promoted as the main mechanism of social redistribution and the most effective protection against poverty. Moreover, targeted policies aimed at improving the welfare of particular household members are effective only when the assumption of full income pooling and sharing within households fails to hold true.

Therefore, if a good society is to promote economic independence and resilience to better respond to and recover from inevitable mayhem, then it should enable individuals in this sense rather than make them dependent on the households of which they are a part. This chapter presented the results of an in-depth analysis at the individual level of the actual income situation and poverty of women and men. Starting out from a conceptual discussion, this chapter has illustrated the effects of switching from household income to individual income on the analysis of poverty.

First, it showed how the calculation of poverty rates is affected by the level at which income is assessed (household versus individual level). The differences are substantial in the case of women. In all of the countries studied, apart from Poland, the level of financial dependence among women is at least twice as high as their rate of poverty risk. This indicates that many women would find themselves in poverty if they were unable to avail themselves of part of the income of another member of the household. Conversely, men's level of financial dependence is relatively similar to their rate of poverty risk.

Second, the income effects for a couple who are breaking up were evaluated through a comparison of their individual incomes before and after the event. Results showed that following a breakup, men's average net individual income increases by 9 percent whereas for women this figure rises to 32 percent. Deflating post-breakup income to account for inflation tempers the income increase: women's mean individual income increases by 23 percent following a breakup (compared with 32% when inflation is not accounted for) while men's mean individual income rises by 2 percent (instead of 9%). Finally, in response to the argument that partnership dissolution not only affects income but also the cost of living, especially when custody of children is not shared between the parents but assigned to either one of them, variations in equivalized individual incomes were also computed. Equivalized individual income was obtained by applying an equivalence scale to adjust individual income for the number of children a person has in charge. For women, accounting for the number of children further reduced their average income increase to 17 percent. In this configuration, men's average income was estimated to increase by 5 percent.

Although the literature generally puts forth negative economic effects associated with a breakup, especially for women, the rejection of the assumption of fully pooled and shared income within households in the present study explains the positive economic consequences we find to come with a breakup. However, even though women's income increases more than men's in the event of a breakup, it remains lower.

The rise in women's net average income following a breakup is primarily due to state benefits. The income women possess on account of their economic activity seems to be relatively less affected by the breakup.

The population of working poor was explored from an individual lens. Two major findings were set forth by this analysis.

First, with the European household-based definition of working poverty, in all countries but Belgium, the working poor are more likely to be men. The opposite is found under the individual definition: in all countries, working poverty affects more female than male workers because of the feminization of part-time and low-paid employment.

Second, trading in the European definition for a measure of the poverty risk based on individual income reduces the proportion of male working poor but it substantially increases the proprotion of female working poor. In other words, the income pooling assumption that underlies the European definition results in an overstatement of male workers' at-risk-of-poverty rate and in a huge understatement of female workers' risk.

A third finding follows automatically: the relative share of women in the category of working poor increases enormously when the European definition is replaced by an individual measure of poverty.

These results provide ground for numerous policy recommendations.

One initial reform would be to develop databases that make it possible to identify precisely what is produced and consumed by each individual member of a household: that is, to no longer hide behind the household but to examine how it functions. Such data are crucial in order to identify the exact makeup of inequality and its effects. Formulating theories on the basis of nonexistent data is the best way of designing ineffective policies.

Once individual data are collected, it will also be necessary to revisit the inequality and poverty indicators, and to challenge at long last the clear hypothesis that resources are shared equally between members of a household. At the European level, the common indicators geared to monitoring the process of social protection and social inclusion ought to be supplemented by indicators based on individual incomes: the rates of poverty and income inequality presented are calculated without taking individual incomes into account, relying on the clear hypothesis that resources are shared fully by couples.

Inasmuch as the effects of national policies on social integration, pensions, and health care are measured on the basis of these indicators, it should be understood that indicators that are skewed from a gender perspective could cause governments to neglect the inequality between women and men that they mask. Policies could prove inappropriate for promoting women's employment and social inclusion, given that their specific situation is not correctly reflected by the indicators used.

Even after the databases have been redesigned, and the indicators calculated and monitored, there will still be a need to revisit the social security systems operating in Europe in order to ensure individual social entitlements for everyone irrespective of gender and the type of household to which individuals belong. All too often, taxation systems and social benefits are still predicated on the traditional formula of the male breadwinner meeting the needs of his family.

Notes

* This article was realized in the framework of the research project "Belgian Gender and Income Analysis" (BGIA), financed by the Belgian Politique Scientifique Fédérale, at the request of the Institute for the Equality of Women and Men (IEFH) and the Direction Générale des Statistiques et de l'Information Economique (DGSIE).

1. D. Meulders and S. O'Dorchai, "Revisiting Poverty Measures towards Individualisation," *Journal of Income Distribution* 20, no. 3–4 (2011): 55–82; D. Meulders and S. O'Dorchai, "a Re-Evaluation of the Short-Term Financial Income Consequences of Marital Separation: Individualising Concepts and Definitions," *Feminist Economics* (forthcoming); D. Meulders and S. O'Dorchai, Who Are the Working Poor in Europe: The Importance of Concepts and Definitions (unpublished).
2. The BGIA project, "Genre et revenu: Analyse et développement d'indicateurs—Belgian Gender and Income Analysis (BGIA)," was a joint research effort by Belgium's Politique Scientifique Fédérale, the Institut pour l'égalité des femmes et des hommes, the Direction générale des Statistiques et de l'Information Economique, and the Département d'Economie Appliquée de l'Université Libre de Bruxelles (DULBEA)
3. Note that contrary to the absolute poverty line applied in the United States, the official measurement method adopted in the EU is based on a relative definition of the poverty risk.
4. This scale assigns a value of 1 to the household head, 0.5 to each additional adult member, and 0.3 to each child.
5. The detailed results of these probit estimations are available from the authors upon request.

References

Andreß, H. -J., B. Borgloh, M. Gullner, and K. Wilking. 2003. *Wenn aus Liebe rote Zahlen werden. Uber die wirtschaftlichen Folgen von Trennung und Scheidung* [When love becomes being in the red. About the economic consequences of separation and divorce]. Wiesbaden (DE): Westdeutscher Verlag.

Atkinson, A., and J. Micklewright. 1992. *Economic Transformation in Eastern Europe and the Distribution of Income.* Cambridge: Cambridge University Press.

Attanasio, O., and V. Lechene. 2002. "Tests of Income Pooling in Household Decisions." *Review of Economic Dynamics* 5 (4): 720–748.

Becker, G. S. 1974. "On the Relevance of the New Economics of the Family." *American Economic Review* 64 (2): 317–319.

———. 1981. *A Treatise on the Family.* Cambridge: Harvard University Press.

Borooah, V. K., and P. M. McKee. 1994. "Intra-household income transfers and implications for poverty and inequality in the UK." In *Taxation, Poverty and Income Distribution*, edited by J. Creedy. London: Edward Elgar, 69–86.

Bourguignon, F., M. Browning, P. -A. Chiappori, and V. Lechene. 1993. "Intra Household Allocation of Consumption: A Model and Some Evidence from French Data." *Annales d'Economie et de Statistique* 29: 137–156.

Briar, C. 2000. "In Search of Gender-Sensitive Concepts and Measures of Poverty, Inequality and Well-Being." *Social Policy Journal of New Zealand* 14: 17–29.

Brinig, M. F., and D. W. Allen. 2000. "These Boots Are Made for Walking: Why Most Divorce Filers Are Women." *American Law and Economics Review* 2: 126–169.

Browning, M., F. Bourguignon, P. -A. Chiappori, and Lechene. 1994. "Income and Outcomes: A Structural Model of Intra-Household Allocation." *Journal of Political Economy* 102: 1067–1096.

Burkhauser, R., G. Duncan, R. Hauser, and R. Berntsen. 1991. "Wife or Frau, Women Do Worse: A Comparison of Men and Women in the United States and Germany after Marital Dissolution." *Demography* 28 (3): 353–360.

Casper, L. M., S. S. McLanahan, and I. Garfinkel. 1994. "The Gender-Poverty Gap: What We Can Learn from Other Countries." *American Sociological Review* 59 (4): 594–605

Cazenave, M. -C. 2006. "Les travailleurs pauvres dans les pays développés: Acquis et controverses." Report of Les Travaux de l'Observatoire national de la pauvreté et de l'exclusion sociale 2005–2006, Paris: La Documentation Française, 199–225.

Chiappori, P. -A. 1988. "Rational Household Labor Supply." *Econometrica* 56: 63–89.

———. 1997. "Introducing Household Production in Collective Models of Labor Supply." *Journal of Political Economy* 105: 191–209.

Daly, M., and K. Rake. 2002. "Gender, Household and Individual Income in France, Germany, Italy, the Netherlands, Sweden, the usa and the uk." Luxembourg Income Study working paper series, 332, p. 26 + appendix.

Davies, H., and H. Joshi. 1994. "Sex, Sharing and the Distribution of Income." *Journal of Social Policy* 23 (3): 301–340.

Duncan, G. J., and S. D. Hoffman. 1985. "a Reconsideration of the Economic Consequences of Marital Dissolution." *Demography* 22: 485–497.

Esping-Andersen, G. 1990. *The Three Worlds of Welfare Capitalism*. Oxford: Polity.

———. 1999. *Social Foundations of Post-Industrial Economies*. Oxford: Oxford University Press.

Findlay, J., and R. E. Wright. 1996. "Gender, Poverty and the Intra-Household Allocation of Resources." *Review of Income and Wealth* 42 (3): 335–351.

Folbre, N. 1986. "Hearts and Spades: Paradigms of Household Economics." *World Development* 14 (2): 245–255.

Fortin, B., and G. Lacroix. 1997. "A Test of the Unitary and Collective Models of Household Labour Supply." *Economic Journal* 107: 933–955.

Goldberg, G. S., and E. Kremen. 1990. *The Feminization of Poverty: Only in America?* New York: Praeger.

González, L., and T. Viitanen. 2009. "The Effect of Divorce Laws on Divorce Rates in Europe." *European Economic Review* 53 (2): 127–138.

Graham, H. 1987. "Women's Poverty and Caring." In *Women and Poverty in Britain*, edited by C. Glendinning and J. Millar. Hemel Hempstead: Harvester Wheatsheaf, 221–240.

Horney, M. J., and M. B. McElroy. 1988. "The Household Allocation Problem: Empirical Results from a Bargaining Model." *Research in Population Economics* 6: 679–694.

Kabeer, N. 1994. *Reversed Realities: Gender Hierarchies in Development Thought*. London: Verso.

Jarvis, S., and S. Jenkins. 1999. "Marital Splits and Income Changes: Evidence from the British Household Panel Survey." *Population Studies* 53 (2): 237–254.

Lelièvre, M., E. Marlier, and P. Pétour. 2004. "Un nouvel indicateur européen: Les travailleurs pauvres. " In *Les indicateurs dans l'Union européenne : Avancement et perspectives*. Dossiers Solidarité et Santé de la DREES, 2, avril-juin.

Lundberg, S., R. A. Pollak, and T. J. Wales. 1997. "Do Husbands and Wives Pool Their Resources? Evidence from the u.k. Child Benefit." *Journal of Human Resources* 22: 463–480.

Manser, M., and M. Brown. 1980. "Marriage and Household Decision Theory—A Bargaining Analysis." *International Economic Review* 21: 21–34.

Manting, D., and A. Bouman. 2006. "Short and Long-Term Economic Consequences of Union Dissolution of Marital and Consensual Unions. The Example of the Netherlands." *European Sociological Review* 22 (4): 413–429.

Meulders, D., S. O'Dorchai, R. Plasman, and F. Rycx. 2011. *Gender and Income—Analysis and Development of Indicators*. Brussels: Institute for the Equality of Women and Men.

Nelson, J. 1996. *Feminism, Objectivity, and Economics*. London and New York: Routledge.

Pahl, J. 1989. *Money and Marriage*. Basingstoke: Macmillan.

Phipps, S. A., and P. S. Burton. 1995. "Sharing within Families: Implications for the Measurement of Poverty among Individuals in Canada." *Canadian Journal of Economics* 28 (1): 177–204.

———. 1998. "What's Mine Is Yours? The Influence of Male and Female Incomes on Patterns of Household Expenditure." *Economica* 65: 599 613.

Ponthieux, S. 2009. *The Working Poor as a Statistical Category—Methodological Difficulties and Exploration of a Notion of Poverty in Earned Income*. Paris: INSEE.

———. 2010. "In-Work Poverty in the eu." *Eurostat Methodologies and Working Papers* [online]. http://epp.eurostat.ec.europa.eu/cache/ITY_OFFPUB/KS-RA-10–015/EN/KS-RA-10–015-EN.PDF. Accessed March 3, 2011.

Poortman, A. 2000. "Sex Differences in the Economic Consequences of Separation: a Panel Study of The Netherlands." *European Sociological Review* 16 (4): 367–383.

Pressman, S. 2002. "Explaining the Gender Poverty Gap in Developed and Transitional Economies." *Journal of Economic Issues* 36 (1): 17–40.

Purkayastha, D. 1999. "Patriarchal Monopoly and Economic Development." *Feminist Economics* 5 (2): 61–78.

Renwick, T., and B. R. Bergmann. 1993. "a Budget-Based Definition of Poverty." *Journal of Human Resources* 28: 1–24.

Rowntree, B. S. 2000. *Poverty: a Study of Town Life*. Bristol: Policy.

Ruggles, P. 1990. *Drawing the Line: Alternative Poverty Measures and Their Implications for Public Policy*. Washington, DC: Urban Institute Press.

Smock, P. 1994. "Gender and the Short-Run Economic Consequences of Marital Disruption." *Social Forces* 73 (1): 243–262.

Smock, P., W. Manning, and S. Gupta. 1999. "The Effects of Marriage and Divorce on Women's Economic Well-Being." *American Sociological Review* 64 (6): 794–812.

Thomas, D. 1990. "Intra-Household Resource Allocation: An Inferential Approach." *Journal of Human Resources* 25 (4): 635–664.

Uunk, W. 2004. "The Economic Consequences of Divorce for Women in the European Union: The Impact of Welfare State Arrangements." *European Journal of Population* 20 (3): 251–285.

Ward-Batts, J. 2008. "Out of the Wallet and into the Purse: Using Micro Data to Test Income Pooling." *Journal of Human Resources* 43 (2): 325–351.

Woolley, F., and J. Marshall. 1994. "Measuring Inequality within the Household." *Review of Income and Wealth* 40 (4): 415–431.

Part II

Sustainability, Ecology, and Good Society

Chapter 4

Achieving Environmentally Sustainable Prosperity

Shann Turnbull

Why Do We Need a New Type of Market Economy?

The contribution of this chapter is to explain how to achieve a universally prosperous environmentally sustainable global good society. This objective is incompatible with traditional economic policies dependent on full employment and ideologies based on uninhibited use of nonrenewable resources or the various descriptions of a "good society" articulated by Berliner (1999). Politically attractive incentives of smaller taxes and other policies are identified as a way of changing the way an economy operates so that prosperity can be increased even with a declining and aging population. Localizing the ownership and control of the means of production and exchange with individuals creates a way to establish a universal minimum social dividend to replace the need for full employment, welfare, pensions, and big government. Local democracy becomes enriched with the power to nurture its host environment. The introduction of ecological forms of cost-carrying money redeemable into local services of nature allows market forces to encourage production techniques that reduce their environmental impact. Increased life expectancy with depopulation is already occurring in 20 countries and this is expected to spread globally in the current century. This phenomenon with current environmental pressures creates an imperative for achieving environmentally sustainable prosperity sooner rather than later.

The changes required to achieve sustainable prosperity as shown in Table 4.4 are not as great as the societal changes that have occurred over the last millennium. However, there is an imperative to achieve changes in a very much shorter time. Increased life expectancy with depopulation is already occurring and the United Nations expects that this will spread globally in the current century.

The imperative for designing an economic system to achieve prosperity without growth sooner than later arises from:

1. the need to protect and nurture the environment to sustain humanity on the planet and
2. coping for the first time with declining populations in advanced economies.

Berliner did not consider either of these concerns in his book *The Economics of a Good Society*. Nor did he consider the possibility of creating a novel type of economic system as proposed in this chapter. Likewise he did not consider the objective, let alone the imperative, of "achieving environmentally sustainable prosperity." Sustainability of society was not discussed and "protecting the environment" was considered only as an issue for "liberals" not "conservatives" or "socialists." Nor did Berliner consider that a good society could be achieved by an "agrarian" or "undeveloped" economy. This is not necessarily so for a country like Bhutan, which places happiness before growth. The proposals in this chapter include the topics neglected by Berliner.

Berliner states that a good society "depends upon your values." He then compares the values of conservatives, liberals, and socialists based only on existing systems of capitalism and socialism. This chapter describes the creation of a new type of "ecological" capitalism outlined in Table 4.4. Ecological capitalism is created by the introduction of ecological ownership and control rights to realty, firms, and money. This provides the means to increase the efficiency, equity, and environmental sustainability of capitalism. This chapter describes how ecological property rights provide a way to increase the efficiency of a market economy directly and also indirectly by reducing the size of taxes, government, and welfare as sought by conservatives described by Berliner. At the same time, greater equity is achieved while providing all citizens income security as sought by liberals and socialists described by Berliner. In addition, this chapter takes into account economic and environmental sustainability that Berliner neglected.

In short, a good society in this chapter extends the concerns identified by Berliner while enhancing elements of the diverse concerns of conservatives, liberals, and socialists. In particular a good society is one that provides income security to all citizens so that they can obtain fulfillment in work and/or leisure on basis that protects and furthers the natural environment for future generations. This will require achieving prosperity without growth as the populations of nations decline.

Twenty countries now have negative or zero population growth before immigration with only one country, Austria, achieving net positive growth through migration. The Ukraine expects to suffer a 28 percent decrease in its population from 2006 to 2050 with a 22 percent decrease in Russia and Belarus and a 21 percent decrease in Japan. Even strong economic countries like Germany are suffering a declining population. There are now 70 countries with their fertility rate at or below the replacement rate. “The move to replacement-level fertility is one of the most dramatic social changes in history” (*The Economist* 2009b). While this is easing the environmental impact of humanity it also introduces economic and social problems.

With such large reduction in populations, there could soon arise problems in having excess infrastructure and facilities like water catchments, sewerage facilities, power generators, hospitals, schools, shops, sports grounds, entertainment centers, churches, and so on. Depopulations in some urban centers could result in many facilities not paying their way with the need for decommissioning. Ghost suburbs could develop with substantial falls in real estate values. Depopulation could also lead to many privatized public facilities becoming uneconomic and/or redundant leading them into bankruptcy.

As noted by Reddaway (1939, 60), a declining population reduces demand for goods and services as well as for new and replacement investment. For these reasons, unemployment can be expected to increase just because the population declines. Reddaway proposed that the State becomes responsible for providing unemployment income. However since his book was written over 70 years ago, the problem of citizens living longer well past their retirement age is now making impact. An increasing proportion of the population is requiring income support. This in turn jeopardizes the living standards for those employed from the need to increase their tax burden to support growing unemployment, those too old to work and their growing medical costs. To mitigate the problem some countries are increasing the retirement age.

Increases in life expectancy have been on a straight line for the last 160 years (Weiner 2010). In being interviewed on his book, Weiner (2011) stated: “You get an increase in life expectancy around the world in every country that has the benefit of modern medicine.” The increase has been so predicable to date that “it looks as if every day we live, we’re granted another five hours, somewhere down the road.” Life expectancy is being increased by science and medicine so "we're constantly gaining time even as we use it up, consume it by living."

According to the United Nations (2003, 5), "Life expectancy is projected to increase steadily in all countries after 2050. No limit is set on the increase of life expectancy." The UN report went on to state that "the world's dependency ratio rises from 0.7 in 2000 to 1.1 in 2300, implying that by that time there will be more than one 'dependent' per person of working age," the working age being defined as being between 15 and 60.

However, even with the benefit of current science and medicine, increase in life expectancy is not changing the rate we age. So the quality of life continues to decrease with age as reported by Milne. He (2010, 5) found that there was no change in the rate of aging in a Swedish study that went back to 1751. This means that as populations increase their life expectancy, the need for income support for medical care and income support will escalate.

The tax burden on those employed will spread globally as more nations increase their living standards to provide life extending health care and improved education. Improved education of women allows them to control their fertility. The incentive to produce fewer children increases when families have access to income support when the parents become too old to work (*The Economist* 2009b). In this way increased living standards provide both the incentive and means to reduce the birth rate to accelerate global depopulation.

A squeeze will be created on government budgets as more and more medical care and income support is required to support Increaded number of citizens incapable of earning an income. Many existing pension plans are insufficiently funded to provide for their beneficiaries as they live longer.

The United Nations (2001) identified a short solution for these problems for some nations through migration. But as declining birth rate spreads to more nations this option may soon diminish. The culture of the countries that are expected to maintain population growth from the year 2000 to 2100 might give rise to inhibitions in seeking immigrants from them. "Just three—Niger, Uganda and Yemen—are expected to account for over half of the positive contribution to population growth at that time" (United Nations 2003, 3).

The United Nations (2003, 2) report identified three possible scenarios of global populations over the next two hundred years. According to the medium scenario, world population rises from 6.1 billion persons in 2000 to a maximum of 9.2 billion persons in 2075 and declines thereafter to reach 8.3 billion in 2175. By 2050, India is expected to have surpassed China in population size and will remain as the most populous country in the world thereafter. However, between 2000 and 2100, the three most populous countries are expected to account for a declining share of the world population, passing from 43 percent in 2000 to 34 percent in 2100. China and India alone are projected to account for nearly 48 percent of the population losses projected to occur in 2100.

Some commentators consider that the root cause of many concerns over the sustainability of human society arise because there is "plague of people on the planet."[1] The need to "abandon affluence and growth" has been proposed for over a quarter of a century (Trainer 1985). Trainer (2010a) advocates "de-growth" with a simpler lifestyle to reduce the pressures creating climate change, extinctions of fauna and flora, pollution, and loss of nonrenewable resources.

"The new economy" proposed by Trainer (2010b) has many features in common with the "Future society" outlined in the last column of Table 4.4. "Ted" Trainer and I share concerns over the inefficiencies, and injustices, inherent in capitalism detailed in the next section and the problems that arise from over reliance on market mechanisms. Also shared is the objective of a society composed of locally controlled largely self-sufficient, self-reliant, and self-financing democratically governed communities that can minimize the need for markets by relying more on other coordinating mechanism such as families, associations, and networks. It is a vision that goes beyond the concerns of many environmental writers (Berger 2010; Gummer and Goldsmith 2007; Jackson 2010) and economists (Daly 1991, 1996).

One fundamental difference with that of Trainer (2010b) in this chapter is his assumption that to initiate change there is a need for an "enormous" change in the values held by people. The approach taken in this chapter is that "the greatest benefits that may arise from the new rules for owning property may be the modifications they may initiate in man's values and behaviour patterns" (Turnbull 1975, 4). This aspect is discussed in the section "Ecological Corporations" with the proposals for changing the economy through self-interest and market forces.

Since writing my 1975 book, *Democratising the Wealth of Nations*, I have developed a literature developing, refining, and explaining its proposals for introducing on a voluntary basis a new system of property rights through tax concessions. By necessity this literature also became concerned with reforming the theories and practices of capitalism. This led me to complete a PhD in 2000, the same year when two of my academic articles were republished with the seminal contributions of leading scholars in Tricker (2000). This chapter draws upon these and many of my writings since my first refereed article was published in 1973. What is new in this chapter is how *Democratising the Wealth of Nations* can also answer the question raised by Jackson (2010) on how to achieve "prosperity without growth" and fill gaps left by Berliner (1999) in identifying a good society.

The next section identifies the need to reform capitalism to make it more efficient for achieving an environmentally sustainable society. Reformed capitalism also distributes prosperity more equitably to promote a good society. The section "Making Capitalism Efficient, Equitable, and Sustainable" describes political attractive techniques for introducing what is described as "ecological" capitalism. A vision of a sustainable society is presented with concluding remarks in the section "Building Sustainable Communities."

Why Do We Need a New Type of Capitalism?

This section identifies how the existing static, exclusive, and perpetual rules for owning and controlling money, corporations, and realty are inefficient and inequitable. To ameliorate these shortcomings, different rules are proposed. These are described as "ecological" because they mimic the character of living things by being dynamic, inclusive, and time limited.

Ancient ways for owning money described below need to be reinstated because modern money can misallocate resources. Money has also become a major driver in generating wealth inequality and the over expansion of the financial sector described as "financialization" (Palley 2007). Likewise, the property rights of corporations allow investors to be overpaid with "surplus profits" in a way that is not reported by accountants and so not recognized by economists to generate further inequality and the misallocation of resources. Accounting doctrines exacerbate misallocation of resources and inequities by treating a proportion of investment returns as a cost to reduce reported profits by an imaginary expenditure described as depreciation. These processes contribute to the seven deadly sins of corporate capitalism discussed later.

Inequality is also generated from the private ownership of urban land that can capture windfall gains generated from the investment of others in providing site services, facilities, and amenities. These concerns are outlined in turn below.

The Problems of Modern Money and Credit

Markets allocate resources through prices, and prices are defined in terms of money. However, money is no longer defined in terms of any specific goods and/or services. As a result the price signals created by legal tender, that is now a national monopoly, can distort the allocation of resources to a greater degree than taxes and tariffs with "faulty feedback" signals (Jacobs 1985, 156).

A mind experiment can illustrate this point using the assumption that the demand for foreign exchange in any region is proportional to the population. This assumption illustrates the extent that governments establishing a monopoly currency over regions with diverse characteristics grossly distort prices, and so resource allocation. Take for example the situation of Western Australia where only 10 percent of population live but earn 60 percent of total Australian foreign exchange. This means that Western Australians are earning six times the foreign exchange they can consume. This means that the Eastern States with 90 percent of the population only earn 40 percent of the foreign exchange. Separate currencies would make Western Australian money worth much more internationally than the money circulating in the Eastern States. Manufacturing, tourism, and the export of education services in the Eastern States would boom with folk in the Eastern States migrating to the West to obtain a higher standard of living. This mind experiment illustrates a fundamental problem of the Euro and the concerns of Friedman and Schwartz (1996).

More importantly, it illustrates how monopoly money can seriously distort resource allocation. It supports the case presented by Hayek (1976a, 1976b) of denationalizing money to allow competing currencies. The price distortions and resulting inefficiency of modern money are exacerbated by it being allowed to earn interest that also introduces inequities.

Proudhon (1840) pointed out that all real assets depreciated and/or carried a storage cost while paper did not. Paper money that earned interest allows money holders to get richer without their money or themselves necessarily making a contribution to society. To create both an equity and a level investment playing field to create what Suhr (1990) described as "neutral money," Gesell (1919) proposed that money should only be issued if it carried a cost. The private issue of cost-carrying money was initiated in Germany in the 1920s and was so successful in stimulating depressed communities during the Great Depression that it soon spread in Europe and on to the United States (Fisher 1933). Keynes (1964, Chapter 23, part VI) supported cost-carrying money that was described as "Stamp Scrip." He described Gesell as "unduly neglected prophet" (Keynes 1964, Chapter 23, part VI).

So successful was the use of stamp scrip in Germany, Austria, and the United States that it threatened the monopoly of official money and so was banned. The carrying cost was created by the need to periodically affix a stamp on the back of the script. Revenues from the sale of stamps paid for the redemption of the money. It allowed communities to stimulate their economies with a self-financing, self-liquidating, locally issued currency.

The Economist (2009a) and Buiter (2009) suggested that "depreciating currencies" be reintroduced to stimulate economies after the Global Financial Crisis (GFC). Today, paper money and stamps would be replaced with cell phone money that is now spreading around the world. There are now four billion cell phones, mostly in developing nations (*The Economist* 2009c).

Cell phones have become electronic storehouses for money. In ancient Egypt, grain was used as money and deposited in storehouses. Deposit notes were issued in form of scratches on shards of pottery. Rather than earn interest, deposits incurred a storage fee and sometimes also a tax (Suhr 1989, 113). Cost-carrying money has been the rule throughout history until the duplicity of fractional banking was introduced.

With fractional banking, banks created more notes than it held to deliver hard currency, such as grain, gold, silver, and so on. As the bank only held a fraction of hard currency, this fraud meant that not all notes could be redeemed at once. Like a Ponzi scheme, only the first person to redeem their note would be able to obtain hard currency unless other investors deposited new hard currency.

The ability of private banks to create credit out of nothing in this way and then charge an interest rate exacerbates financialization, wealth concentration, inefficiencies, and instability in the financial system. Huber and Robertson (2000, 89) estimated that if instead the government carried out the credit creation then UK tax collections in 1999 could have been reduced by 15 percent. The governor of the Bank of England, Mervyn King, suggested that the practice of "fractional banking" be eliminated stating that "eliminating fractional reserve banking explicitly recognises that the pretence that risk-free deposits can be supported by risky assets is alchemy" (King 2010, 17).

King (2010, 18) went on to state: "Of all the many ways of organising banking, the worst is the one we have today." A number of the indefensible practices of the existing system are explained in my other writings.

The Problems of Perpetual Property Rights

Perpetual property rights allow investors to get overpaid. All intellectual property rights are time limited. Such investments are the norm as productive assets wear out or deplete. Perpetual property rights have only been created for owning land and corporations. To create a level investment playing field, time limits need to be applied to all investments. This can also ameliorate the overpayment of investors and the associated concentration of wealth. Overpayment of investors is also inconsistent with the objective and reason for having a market economy to efficiently allocate resources.

In making a decision to invest, a commercial investor will not rely on the unforeseeable future to recover their investment and obtain a competitive return. The foreseeable future is described as the investor's "time horizon." Any cash received afterward the time horizon is not required to provide the incentive for the investment to be made. It represents a surplus incentive that I describe as a "surplus profit." Unlike profits, or any excessive profits that are reported by accountants, surplus profits are not identified or reported because accountants do not identify investment time horizons. This makes surplus profits different from other types of economic rent that are reported by accountants.

Because surplus profits are not reported, economic analysts are denied the understanding of how wealth in the form of asset ownership becomes highly concentrated. Surplus profits can be very substantial to become many times greater than the original investment as I discovered when working as a financial analyst for one of the largest firms in the world. More critically, economic analysts do not have a basis for understanding the full cost to communities that host alien investment. As a result foreign investment is widely promoted even though it may introduce excessive cost over benefits from "the acceptance of an unlimited, unknown and uncontrollable foreign liability" (Penrose 1956, 235).

Another problem with the profits reported by accountants is that they under-report economic returns. This is created by accounting doctrines requiring accountants to describe part of the cash obtained from an investment as a return *of* the investment with the remaining cash being described as a profit *on* the investment.

The cash described as a return *of* the investment is called depreciation and is treated as a cost. This obscures the fact that investors can recover the cost of their investment from the artificial cost called depreciation. Governments typically allow this artificial cost as a tax deduction. The tax deduction provided to investors to recover the cost of their investment has to be made up by other taxpayers.

Consider an investment being depreciated over ten years producing a net cash return of 20 percent per year. By introducing an artificial cost of 10 percent per year for ten years, the before reported tax profit also becomes 10 percent per year. With a 30 percent tax rate, the reported return becomes a marginal 7 percent. The after-tax cash return to the investor becomes 17 percent that provides an acceptable 11 percent after taking into account the time value of money.

The policy lesson for governments from this insight is that ownership of any investment should be written off at the same rate that it is written off for tax purposes. This would not change the reported profits as the cost is already taken into account by the artificial cost of depreciation. For the various reasons set out in my other writings, it makes good sense for the ownership of the assets being written off to be vested in the individuals who are essential for a firm to exist such as its suppliers, employers, and customers. In this way, surplus profits become shared with stakeholders who participate in their creation. This provides one way to democratize the wealth of communities, and so nations.

The above discussion explains some of the seven sins of corporate capitalism. Corporations can be

1. inefficient by not distributing to shareholders all their surpluses, which allows their managers rather than shareholders and market forces to allocate their investment funds and also allows them to grow too big to be allowed to fail;
2. inequitable by over-paying investors with surplus profits not reported by accountants and not understood by economists;
3. exploitive by not sharing surplus profits with their stakeholders on whose contribution they depend for their existence as employees, suppliers, distributors, customers, and other members of their host community;
4. alienating by not sharing power with employees and other stakeholders;
5. not directly accountable to all the stakeholders on whom the firms depend upon for their existence and whose lives are affected by their operations;

6. nontransparent, hiding the identity of their ultimate ownership and control with owners voting on a plutocratic basis that provides the wealthy with the most votes; and
7. degrading for democracy by using corporate resources to influence politicians to protect and further the concentration of their economic, political, and social power.

The Problems of Private Windfall Gains from Public Investment

Another way in which the current rules of ownership create inefficiencies and inequities is from windfall gains obtained from the private ownership of urban land. The uplift in land values can occur from the site being approved for greater development and/or from surrounding improvements made in servicing the site with utilities, facilities, and amenities by various levels of government and/or by private investors.

It is both inefficient and inequitable for government expenditure spent on utilities, roads, transport, schools, hospitals, and other amenities to provide private profit to nearby landowners. The degree to which public investment creates private profit is not commonly revealed because economists or anybody else do not typically prepare balance sheets for communities. What is not measured is not managed. Windfall gains, like surplus profits, are not generally reported and so are not recognized by economists, policy makers, and governments.

An illustration of the extent of how government investment can generate private profits is provided by the construction in 1999 of the Jubilee underground tube line in London. The cost of the project was 3.5 billion pounds. The uplift in land values around each of its new stations totaled 13 billion pounds (Riley 2002, 46).

Public expenditure could have been avoided and greater equity and efficiency achieved by the landowners financing the construction from the uplift in values they obtained. Even if the landowners borrowed all the construction costs they would still have received a net benefit of 9.5 billion pounds. However, this would still be unequitable as it is not the owners who create the uplift in values but the users of the sites and facilities. Sites and services without users may be worth little.

As uplift in land/site values are created by the community, an equitable system of ownership would allow the community to share the values so created. If all the land, but not the buildings, within 1,000 yards of each of the 11 Jubilee station had been collectively owned by a cooperative of all residents, then each resident would receive a windfall gain of around 75,000 pounds. Each cooperative would have a net worth of 9.5/11=864 million pounds after paying for the project, with each resident owning cooperative shares worth around 75,000 pounds.

While mutual ownership of land would be created by the cooperative or Community Land Bank (CLB), the buildings would still be privately held by investors and/or residents. This is how the Garden City of Letchworth, 60 miles north of London, was financed at the turn of the last century (Howard 1946, 28). These examples demonstrate how urban development can be made self-financing by capturing the values created by the community and being owned and controlled by residents.

A condition precedent for any government to finance public works that generate windfall gains is that such gains be shared on a mutualized basis with only residence as described above. By eliminating alien and foreign ownership of land, this approach would reduce the leakage of values out of communities and their host nations. CLBs provide a way to make the financing of "transition towns"[2] self-financing to spread their emergence to create a green economy as envisaged in this chapter.

The cost of urban land typically represents around half the cost of a house in the United States, UK, and Australia (Davis and Palumbo 2006, 3; Moran 2006, 60). The ability of CLBs to make land self-financing as indicated above allows the cost of land to be removed in new towns or inner city redevelopment projects. In this way CLBs can provide half-cost housing and eliminate the cost of land for commercial investors in rental housing, retail outlets, office buildings, entertainment, and sporting facilities. However, the condition for providing land without cost to commercial developers could be tied to a requirement that as they wrote off their investment for tax purposes the ownership of their investment would be transferred to nominees of the CLB. In this way all tenants in rental housing would acquire ownership of their residence without cost and the CLB would become the owners of supermarkets, office buildings, and factories. The rent/rates from the commercial sector provide cross subsidies to sustain low cost housing over generations. In the event of depopulation, CLBs are well placed to restructure their community as they have integrated control over intergenerational facilities.

Making Capitalism Efficient, Equitable, and Sustainable

This section outlines how the adoption of ecological property rights for owning and controlling money, firms, and realty can make capitalism more efficient, equitable, and sustainable.

But more importantly, ownership of income producing assets becomes universal for all citizens to provide a "third way" to distribute national income without employment or welfare. It is by this means that prosperity can be achieved without growth. As the government is no longer required to raise taxes and distribute welfare, the size of government can be reduced. This in turn increases prosperity as the dead weight transfer costs of government are reduced.

Rules for owning money, firms, and realty created by society can be changed by society. The incentives to change the most fundamental defining feature of capitalism arise because the new rules provide the maximum benefits for the greatest number of people. Because of this there exists the opportunity of obtaining a political mandate to initiate the changes described. In this way the venal materialistic values of self-interest can assist change to overcome the concerns of Trainer (2010b). The new institutions created would then provide incentives for citizens to change their behavior from the collective interdependencies that would arise.

The introduction of ecological property rights would create three new types of market institutions: (1) cost-carrying money, (2) Ownership Transfer Corporations (OTCs), and (3) CLBs. However, while changing the nature of property rights is a necessary condition for building a sustainable society, it is not sufficient.

Also required is ecological control described as network governance that is ubiquitous in nature. Such is the efficacy of network governance that it spontaneously emerges when society become more complex and dynamic (Jones, Hesterly, and Borgatti 1997, 911). The reason for its success is because "nothing can be made simpler without becoming more complex," as noted by of the founding CEO of the Visa card organization, Dee Hock (1994, 8). In other words, as society gets more complex, it requires a requisite variety of complexity in its communication and control circuits (Ashby 1968, 243). In this way, tasks can be sufficiently simplified to match the limited ability of humans to multitask and/or process data (Turnbull 2000, 245).

Both evolution and the analysis by Simon (1962) provide evidence that the communication and control architecture of nature creates the most robust way to create or manage complexity. Innate physical structures of nature and biota always create or manage complexity by using simpler subcomponents. The universe is made up of components that Hock describes as "Chaords" (Hock 1995, 1) because they represent both chaos and order. The academic literature describes these components as "holons" (Mathews 1996, 33) as the whole creates more than the constituent parts.

A hierarchy of holons is described as a "Holarchy" (Koestler 1967, 104). Holarchies have properties diametrically opposed to hierarchies. Hock (1995, 4) highlighted the difference by writing:

> Industrial Age, hierarchical command and control pyramids of power, whether political, social, educational or commercial, were aberrations of the Industrial Age, antithetical to the human spirit, destructive of the biosphere and structurally contrary to the whole history and methods of physical and biological evolution. They were not only archaic and increasingly irrelevant, they were a public menace.

The ecological architecture developed by evolution provides a basis for designing the governance architecture of an advanced complex global society. A democratic society governed from the bottom up composed of self-financing, locally-owned and -controlled, self-governing communities are mostly self-reliant.

To allow communities to be self-governing, they must become self-financing to avoid economic and, so, political dependency. The same principle applies to all the higher levels in the political holarchy presented in Table 4.1. To allow communities to become self-financing, they need to stop economic value from leaking out. Many families spend over a third of their income on rents or mortgage payments. To stop rents and interest leaking out, it becomes essential for communities to establish their own local currency and minimize any external ownership of land, buildings, and enterprises. While CLBs provide a way to minimize external ownership of realty, OTCs as explained later provide a way to minimize external ownership of firms.

The establishment of local ecological currencies with ecological rules for owning firms through OTCs and realty through CLBs provides ways to plug the drains that invisibly suck out economic value from communities.

Table 4.1 Global governance and political economy

Level	Principle role[a]	Other roles[a]	Source of funding[b]
Family	Personal and social development	Community and cultural development	Work and/or dividends, rents, profits, etc.
Enterprises	Wealth generation	Fulfilling work	Self-financing
Neighborhoods	Social and cultural support	Substitution of paid services	Nonprofit and voluntary contributions
Land banks (CLBs)	Income distribution between entities	Health, education, welfare, and other infrastructure services	Enterprise rents and gains from site trades
Cities	Provide infrastructure	Balance income between CLBs	Taxes from CLBs
Bioregions	Federating economic and political systems	Coordinating infrastructure services	Green taxes from degrading enterprises
Regional biospheres	Federating bioregions	Coordinating economic structures in regional biospheres	Green taxes from bioregions
Global	Governance of global commons	Coordinating political structures in regional biospheres	Green taxes from regional biospheres

[a]Roles allocated on the basis that no level of government should carry out any function, which is better undertaken at a lower level as per the "Principle of Subsidiary Function" (Schumacher 1975, 203).

[b]Sources of funding based on the medieval cascade system of taxation where each level of government taxes the next lower level, which it represents. No taxes on individuals or the profits of enterprises. Redistribution of income is achieved through the private sector from the democratic distribution of income producing assets and cross-subsidization through land bank rentals, property trades and provision of welfare services.

Ecological Community Currencies

The reasons why the existing nature of money and the financial system should not be replicated have been indicated in the previous section. A community currency is required not only to plug economic leaks but also to establish a local unit of value that is defined by the natural endowment of the host bioregion. In this way the local environment can provide self-correcting price signals to maintain its sustainability that get lost with a national monopoly currency as discussed earlier and by Jacobs (1985, 156). Money redeemable into units of value defined by locally available renewable services of nature without necessarily being converted into the service will be described as "green dollars."

Table 4.2, outlines how green dollars contribute to building an ecological economy with quite different operating characteristics. Local Employment and Exchange Trading Systems (LETs) allows any person in a community to create and/or to obtain credit. There has never been a need since money was invented for either governments or banks to create credit as set out in Table 4.2, row 1. Anybody can create credit. Handwritten IOUs were used as hand-to-hand money in Sydney Town early in the nineteenth century before there was a printing press or the discovery of precious metals in the Colony (Butlin 1953, 26). Other parties also signing the notes would reinforce their creditability and acceptance. Creditability can also be provided with acceptable third party guarantors. The guarantee fee would create a carrying cost as noted in Table 4.2, rows 2 and 7.

Over the millenniums, money has always been a product of nature that incurred a storage and/or insurance cost (Table 4.2 rows 2 and 7). Cost-carrying money reduces the resources absorbed by the financial system because it removes the incentive to invest in synthetic paper assets (Table 4.2, row 8) rather than in the real economy (Table 4.2, rows 9 and 11). In this way cost-carrying money paradoxically reduced the cost of the financial system whose purpose is to service the real economy.

Cost-carrying money also improves equity as it removes the ability for money to make money from earning interest (Table 4.2, row 13). Instead of capturing "unearned income" (Gesell 1919, 36) an incentive is created to invest in "processes by which society expands its power to make nature yield its resource more abundantly" (Moulton 1935, 12–13). In this way productivity is increased to reverse inflation while limiting the ability of the finance sector to act like a leech on the real economy.

More importantly, procreative assets by their nature must become self-financing as they increase productivity, and crucially, they provide the ability for society to live more lightly on the planet by making "nature yield its resources more abundantly" (Moulton 1935, 13). Investments in procreative assets provide the key to increasing prosperity without consuming more. In addition, procreative assets can be owned by anyone or by more individuals who can obtain credit during their payback period. The provision of credit insurance to cover their payback period provides a way to encourage the formation and wide distribution of the ownership of procreative assets to reduce inequalities and increase prosperity without growth. Various ways of

Table 4.2 Existing and ecological money

	Difference between	Existing money	Ecological money
1	Money created by	Government and banks	Traders and investors
2	Interest rates fixed by	Central Bank	Cost of risk insurance
3	Expansion of money	Government ratios/ regulation	Value of transactions
4	Money defined by	Government fiat	Local resources of nature
5	Choice of currency	Government monopoly	Determined by community
6	Inflation control by	"Blunt" policy instruments	Value of renewable energy
7	Structure of money	Unlimited accrual of interest	Carrying cost limiting life
8	Economic flaw-1	Incentive to own money	Disincentive to hold money
9	Economic flaw-2	Allocates resources to finance	Real assets more attractive
10	Economic flaw-3	Distorts price relativities	Price related to sustainability
11	Environmental flaw-1	Incentive to burn carbon	Favors renewable energy
12	Environmental flaw-2	No feedback from nature	Nature controls price signals
13	Social flaw-1	Compounds unearned income	No unearned income
14	Social flaw -2	Concentrates influence	Localizes influence
15	Political flaw-1	Concentrates power	Enriches local democracy

providing selective credit insurance are described by Kelso and Hetter (1967, 102) and Turnbull (1975, 57).

No living thing can exist without processing energy, so electricity generated from renewable resources provides a universal inflation proof unit of value (Table 4.2, row 6). The relative value of the kilowatt-hour (kWh) generated in each community could vary according to its endowment of renewable resources. But some sort of renewable energy is available throughout the world. As there would be a cost incurred in not using green money, there would be an incentive to spend money as noted in Table 4.2, row 8. The role of money would be simplified to only being a unit of account and a medium of exchange and not also a store of value.

A reference value for green dollars can be established by anyone who invests in solar cells, wind farms, hydrogen producing bacteria, or other sources of renewable energy. To avoid manipulation of the reference value that establishes market prices, customers in the community should ideally mutually own the renewable energy generators. The generators would be financed by consumers buying their electricity in advance by accepting IOUs issued by the mutual association (that the note holders would then own) to deliver specified kWh at specified future times. The IOUs would be negotiable to become the reserve green currency of the community. Ideally also, the local government body or CLB would require its rates to be paid in green dollars issued to finance the conversion of renewable energy into electricity. The local government body could then redeem its notes to pay for its street lighting and other energy requirements.

The redemption of privately issued cost-carrying money into commodities was established in Germany in the 1920s. The idea was promoted by Gesell (1919, 191) so as to avoid the ability of money to make money and so make the rich richer.

Privately issued cost-carrying money described as stamp scrip rapidly spread through Europe and to the United States during the Great Depression because it was so successful in stimulating local communities (Fisher 1933, 66). The scrip was issued mainly by individual businesses in Europe, but in the United States, it was mainly issued by the local chambers of commerce. The merchants would agree to accept the scrip presented by their customers. Every seven days the notes became worthless unless the holder placed a stamp on the back equal to 2 percent of the notes nominated value. In this way the issuer sold stamps over a year valued at 52 by 2 percent being 104 percent to allow them to redeem the notes into official money and leave them with a 4 percent gross margin. While the merchants had to pay 2 percent of the value of the notes they held at the end of each week, it is but a fraction of the cost of paying over 2 percent on every credit card transaction.

How many "invisible hands" would support the introduction of cost-carrying money is discussed in my other writings. Another GFC could initiate the spontaneous introduction of cost-carrying money to complement, augment, and/or replace legal tender as it did during the Great Depression (Fisher 1933).

Today, stamp scrip could be created in electronic form that could be stored on the Subscriber Identity Modules (SIM) of cell phones. Cell phones that can transmit money electronically and/or be swiped at checkout counters have already been introduced in some countries.[3] Electronic green money, with its value determined by the value of locally generated kWh, would provide a way for communities to insulate themselves from another global financial crisis. Green dollars create the means to build economic lifeboats to float away from control and exploitation by big money center banks. To build the most efficient, equitable, and effective lifeboats, communities need to also establish OTCs and CLBs as described below.

Ecological Corporations

All the seven sins of corporations identified in the section "The Problems of Perpetual Property Rights" can be ameliorated and/or removed by providing a relatively modest tax incentive for investors to convert existing corporations to OTCs (Turnbull 1975, Appendix). OTCs convert investor-owned and -controlled firms to stakeholder-owned firms to provide a basis for introducing a comprehensive form of network governance (Turnbull 2000, 217).

The modest nature of the concession arises because investors discount twice the money that they may obtain in the future. First they discount the value of future money because of the lost opportunity to earn interest and profits today. They then discount future values again to recognize the uncertainty of any values being recovered.

Equity investors are much more concerned about not losing the money they put at risk than the prospects of obtaining a return on their money invested. No matter what accountants may report, equity investors cannot make a profit until they have recovered all their investment placed at risk. The time required to recover their funds is described as the payback period. As the payback period gets longer, the risk of loss gets bigger. The incentive for investors to vote at a shareholders meeting to convert existing corporations to OTCs in return for a tax concession is that they would obtain bigger, quicker profits with less risk. An analysis of the trade-off between perpetual ownership and a tax incentive at various rates is provided in Turnbull (1975, Appendix; 2000, 409).

No changes in the law need be required to create OTCs governed by their stakeholders. Corporations creating stakeholder shares that acquire all the property rights of the common shares over 20 years become an OTC. As patents commonly last for 20 years, this creates a more level investment playing field between innovations and corporations. Stakeholder shares would be issued without cost to residential individuals of the host community. In this way all OTCs would become locally owned and controlled to eliminate the draining out of the community profits that Penrose (1956, 235) described as "unknown, unlimited and uncontrollable." It makes operational sense to first include as new owners those citizens who can make a direct contribution to the success of the firm such as suppliers, employees, or customers or individuals employed by suppliers and customers. The identity of such operational stakeholders and the value of their contributions over time would be a matter of record in the various associated entities. This would allow stakeholder shares to be issued in proportion to the value each stakeholder contributed from being a customer and/or being an employee of the company or entity in the supply or distribution chains.

Besides being more economically efficient by limiting the export of surplus profits, OTCs distribute wealth according to the contributions of its stakeholders. Stakeholder shares would obtain votes on a democratic basis of one vote per person rather than the plutocratic one vote per share obtained by investors. Each class of stakeholder would elect a separate stakeholder council to protect and further their interests and that of the firm as described by Pirson and Turnbull (2011). Firms would become accountable to their host community. Firms would not become too big to fail because investors would require all profits to be distributed each year instead of any being reinvested as retained profits. This is because any retained profits would accrue to stakeholders rather than the common stock holders.

Table 4.3 Existing and ecological corporations

	Feature	Existing corporations	Ecological corporations
1	Rights to life	Perpetual	Limited to 20 years like patents
2	Ownership rights	Static and monopoly	Dynamic and co-ownership
3	Owners	Located anywhere	Mainly local
4	Creation of corporations	Entrepreneurs and investors	Entrepreneurs, investors, and mature fecund corporations
5	Size of corporations	No inherent limit by investors	Limited by investor's short-term return of and on investment.
6	Number	As at present	Many more smaller corporations
7	Governance by	Shareholders in theory but in practice by directors	Competitively and dynamically determined by stakeholders
8	Regulation by	Government	Stakeholders and so by local requirements

Firms would grow by establishing offspring corporations taking over part of the assets of the progenitor business. The offspring firms would be funded with dividends from their progenitor corporation and/or from other sources. This would also improve the efficiency of the capital markets, as shareholders, not managers, would undertake reinvestment decisions. Unlike managers, shareholders are not conflicted by being involved in the use of the funds and have many more investment options than managers. The result would be the creation of many smaller firms to improve competition and social and political accountability with the features indicated in Table 4.3.

Self-Financing Urban Communities

This section describes how communities can efficiently restrict the leakage out of value from their community to alien parties through rents, interest, profits, and/or capital gains. To achieve this objective, the title deed to land needs to be separated from the title deed to structures over the land (Turnbull 1975, 65) to create a CLB.

Combing the ownership values created in land with the ownership values of buildings creates both inefficiency and inequities because parties providing essential services enhance the value of the land/sites they service but do not share in the uplift in values they create. As a result, landowners capture unearned windfall gains generated by the investment by others, such as governments who finance the roads, water, sewerage, schools, and hospitals and the private sector providing shopping facilities, places of work, and amusement and recreation.

Efficiency and equity can be achieved by all buildings being privately owned with the sites on which they are built being owned mutually by all citizens residing in the community with a sufficiently large population to support a number of secondary schools and places of significant employment. In this way sufficient windfall gains created by urban development can be captured by the mutually owned CLB with sufficient rental income for it to become self-financing. As the cost of land is typically half the cost of a dwelling, this arrangement eliminates the cost of land for pioneer homeowners to half the cost of acquiring a house. It also makes more attractive commercial investment in rental housing, office buildings, and shopping facilities as the land cost is also eliminated for them.

All individual homeowners and individual residential tenants obtain one share in the CLB for each square meter of the site they occupy. As only residents who are voters can own shares, no nonresidents or commercial investors can capture any uplift in land values created by the community to extract value from the community. As residents typically only occupy around 20 percent of the land area in an urban precinct, the area of land in which residents obtain an ownership interest through the CLB becomes five times greater than a homeowner with a conventional unitary title.

Homeowners can finance and sell their dwellings in the usual way. However, for the buyer to obtain title to the house, she/he must buy at market value the CLB shares held by the vendors that are redeemed by the CLB and resold to the buyer. The CLB share redemption price discount reduces from 100 percent to zero over the time required to write off the dwelling for accounting purposes. The profit obtained by the CLB in redeeming its shares and reselling them provides another source of income to allow the CLB to become self-financing.

Because the CLB becomes self-financing, its shares can be gifted to pioneer homebuyers. As investors cannot acquire CLB shares, tenants in rental properties can likewise be gifted shares over the period the rental properties are written off by their owners for accounting purposes. Tenants acquire co-ownership rights to rental properties without cost at the same rate that the property is written off. This does not reduce the reported rate of return for investors. As co-owners, tenants have an incentive to undertake repair and maintenance to increase the return of investors who already obtain higher returns by not needing to buy land.

CLBs capture the surplus profits by becoming owners of all commercial developments except rental housing. As CLB offers a way to provide a minimum social dividend to all residents, every resident must become a shareholder. Residents involved as stakeholders from being suppliers, workers, and/or consumers of local enterprises would also obtain additional income from acquiring without cost stakeholder shares as described in the section "Ecological Corporations". It is by this means that national income can be equitably distributed to all citizens without work or welfare.

The provision of a minimum income to all residents of all generations resident in a CLB means that provision for pensions are no longer required. This would improve the level of prosperity without growth, as individuals would no longer need to forgo consumption to finance a private pension or to contribute to a public pension and medical insurance. As CLBs have a comprehensive integrated involvement in all aspect of community life at the neighborhood level, they

Table 4.4 History and vision of a transforming society

	Features	Past society	Present society	Future society
1	People treated as	Property	Resource	Potential
2	Role of women	Breeding	Cheap labor	Full partners
3	Purpose of work	Sustenance	Income distribution	Fulfillment
4	Sources of income	Work	Work or welfare	Work, welfare, dividends
5	Environment	Subservient	Dominant	Stewardship
6	Natural resources	Use	Exploit	Sustain
7	Source of land acquisition	Conquest or inheritance	Purchase or inheritance	Use
8	Land ownership	Through occupancy	Perpetual	Time of use and so limited
9	Firm ownership	Start up or inheritance	Purchase/start up and inheritance	Start up, investment, and stakeholder rights
10	Business owners	Proprietors	Shareholders	Stakeholders
11	Ownership period	Life of owner	Perpetual	Limited
12	Property rights	Discretion of Sovereign	Static, monopoly, and perpetual	Dynamic co-ownership and time limited
13	Structure of business	Paternal and centralized	Hierarchic and centralized	Nested networks of component holons
14	Monopolies	Granted to private interests by rulers	Banned or government control	Removed by time limited dynamic property rights
15	Institutions	Perpetual	Evolving	Dynamic
16	Basis of money	Commodities	Artificial	Services of nature
17	Creation of money	Decentralized in private sector	Government controlled	Decentralized competitive private sector nonbanks
18	Cost of money	Storage and testing	Interest	Cost of risk insurance
19	Allocation of resources	Command and control	Markets	Family, benevolence, semiotics, and markets
20	Value system	Absolute	Materialistic	Humanistic
21	Wealth distribution	Autarchic	Market forces	As to contribution and need
22	Accumulation of economic value	Limited by political power	Not limited	Limited by time and dynamic rights
23	Political power	Centralized in ruler	Government and big business	Spread to communities
24	Source of power	Inherited, physical	Democracy	Holonic by lot (demarchy)

are well placed to initiate preventive medical care and mobilize the unemployed in self-help and community care activities—refer to Table 4.1, row 4.

The type of society that could result from introducing ecology ownership and control of money, firms, and realty are considered in the next concluding Section.

Building Sustainable Communities

The type of society that would emerge by introducing ecological property rights to money, firms, and realty is outlined in Table 4.4. The changes required to create a stable state that is more efficient and an equitable resilient society with built-in feedback messages from its host environment are less than the changes achieved from the past. However, the time for achieving the changes needs to be very much shorter.

One of the results of introducing network governance within and between organizations is the decomposition of decision-making labor to allow people with little specialized knowledge or experience to make decisions. Life and death decisions in a number of societies have been made by a jury formed by randomly selected people to sit in judgment of people charged with murder. Random selection of qualified decision makers was an important element of Athenian democracy and in the governance of medieval cities of Italy (Burnheim 1985, 9). Electing decision makers raises the problem of rich vested interests using their resources to support and/or buy votes of candidates who undertake to make decisions to further the enrichment of those already rich. Political democracies that elect representatives create an inbuilt bias for the rich to get richer.

Network governance makes is practical to introduce an alternative to electoral politics (Martin 2001). The selection of decision makers by lot instead of votes is described as "demarchy" (Burnheim 1985, 9)—refer to the last row in Table 4.4. Some elements of demarchy are practiced in a number of employee-owned enterprises such as the MCC. The key to the constructive implementation of demarchy is only for appropriately qualified individuals to be available for selection. The process of filtering individuals according to their abilities is, in any event, typical of many preselection process in democracies based on political parties.

Another way of distributing political power, influence, and wealth is through the rotation of office bearers. The city leader of ancient Athens was rotated each month with a representative from the various suburbs. A practice adopted today by the European Union is to rotate the presidency every six months with leaders from their member states. To provide continuity, each presidency is shared among three member states over one and half years.

In considering how to design the governance architecture of society, scholars have identified six coordinating mechanisms. Economists focus on markets and private hierarchies. However, social relationships are also governed by families, networks, associations, and government (Hollingsworth 2002, Figure 2). Each of these six coordinating mechanisms has strengths and weaknesses but each can be used in various combinations as found in various societies over history as indicated by Turnbull (2000, 276–277).

In addition, governance architects need to consider the criteria and design concepts embedded in nature. How and why the architecture of nature provides a compelling model for designing an equitable, efficient, and sustainable society is illustrated in Turnbull (2000, 130). A contribution of this paper is to identify how this can be achieved by introducing ecological property rights and ecological governance.

The consumption of nonrenewable resources is likely to seriously exacerbate the problems of achieving sustainable society. Reduced consumption may well be forced upon society. Trainer (1985, 2010a, 2010b, 2010c) anticipates this possibility with his compelling arguments for adopting a much more frugal lifestyle.

Conclusion

The Trainer analysis leads to the conclusion that a good society that protects and nurtures the environment for future generations may only become possible with a much smaller global population. The contribution of this chapter is that it has identified a new type of capitalism that can simultaneously promote a good society today while also showing how to achieve environmentally sustainable prosperity. In this way ecological capitalism provides a politically attractive way to encourage both depopulation and de-growth to create a virtuous reenforcing process, which can transform society today and can establish a good society for future generations.

Notes

1. http://www.spiked-online.com/index.php?/site/article/3337/ (accessed November 10, 2012).
2. http://www.transitionnetwork.org/ (accessed November 10, 2012).
3. As described at http://www.nextbillion.net/remittances-mobile-globe-cash and at http://wirelessfederation.com/news/zain-bahrain-launches-zain-wallet-bahrain/ (accessed November 10, 2012.

References

Ashby, W. R. 1968. *An Introduction to Cybernetics*, University Paperback, London [1959]. http://pespmc1.vub.ac.be/ASHBBOOK.html. Accessed March 7, 2010.

Berger, C. 2010. *Better than Growth: The new economics of genuine progress and quality of life, a primer for policy innovation*, Australian Conservation Foundation, Melbourne. Available at http://www.acfonline.org.au/uploads/res/ACF_BetterThanGrowth.pdf

Berliner, J. S. 1999. *The Economics of a Good Society: The Variety of Economic Arrangements*. Malden, MA: Blackwell.

Burnheim, J. 1985. *Is Democracy Possible? The Alternative to Electoral Politics*. Berkeley, CA: University of California Press.

Buiter, W. (2009), *Negative nominal interest rates: Three ways to overcome the zero bound*, NBER Working Paper Number 15118 June, available at: http://www.nber.org/papers/w15118.pdf?new_window=1.

Butlin, S. J. 1953. *Foundations of the Australian Monetary System 1788–1851*. Sydney, Australia: Sydney University Press.

Daly, H. E. 1991. *Steady State Economics*. 2nd ed. Washington, DC: Island.

———. 1996. *Beyond Growth: Economics of Sustainable Development*. Boston: Beacon.

Davis A. M., and M. G. Palumbo. 2006. *The Price of Residential Land in Large US Cities*. Finance and Economics Discussion Series Divisions of Research & Statistics and Monetary Affairs. Washington, DC: Federal Reserve Board. http://www.federalreserve.gov/Pubs/feds/2006/200625/200625pap.pdf.

The Economist. 2009a. "Depreciating Currencies." January 24–30, 74. http://www.economist.com/finance/displaystory.cfm?story_id=12998254. Accessed March 17, 2012.

———. 2009b. "Fertility and Living Standards: Go Forth and Multiply a Lot Less." October 29. http://www.economist.com/node/14743589. Accessed November 10, 2012.

———. 2009c. "Mobile Marvels: A Special Report on Telecoms in Emerging Markets." September 24. http://www.economist.com/node/14483896. Accessed March 17, 2012.

Fisher, I. 1933. *Stamp Scrip*. New York: Adelphi. http://userpage.fu-berlin.de/roehrigw/fisher/. Accessed March 17, 2012.

Friedman, M., and A. J. Schwartz. 1986. "Has Government Any Role in Money?" *Journal of Military Economics* 17: 37, 60.

Gesell, S. 1919. *The Natural Economic Order*. Translated by Philip Pye, 2002. http://www.silvio-gesell.de/en/neo/index.htm. Accessed March 17, 2012.

Gummer, J., and Z. Goldsmith. 2007. *Blueprint for a Green Economy: The Low Carbon Economy, Security, Stability and Green Growth*. Policy Green Paper No. 8, London: Conservative Party. http://www.conservatives.com/~/media/files/downloadable%20files/lce.ashx?dl=true. Accessed January 27, 2011.

Hayek, F. A. 1976a. *Choice in Currency: A Way to Stop Inflation.* Occasional Paper 48, The Institute of Economic Affairs, London.

———. 1976b. *Denationalization of Money: An Analysis of the Theory and Practice of Concurrent Currencies.* Hobart Paper Special 70, The Institute of Economic Affairs, London.

Hock, D. W. 1994. "Institutions in the Age of Mindcrafting." Presented at the Bionomics Annual Conference, San Francisco, California, October 22. http://ntl.bts.gov/lib/jpodocs/repts_te/259.pdf. Accessed March 17, 2012.

———. 1995. "The Chaordic Organization: Out of Control and into Order." *World Business Academy Perspectives* 9 (1):5–18. http://www.ki-net.co.uk/graphics/Dee%20Hock%20-%20The%20Chaordic%20Organization.pdf. Accessed March 17, 2012.

Hollingsworth, J. R. 2002. "Some Reflections on How Institutions Influence Styles of Innovation." Paper presented to the Swedish Collegium for Advanced Study in the Social Sciences (SCASSS) September 26. http://history.wisc.edu/Hollingsworth/documents/Some_Reflections_on_How_Institutions_Influence_Styles_of_Innovation.htm. Accessed March 17, 2012.

Howard, E. 1946 [1902]. *Garden Cities of To-Morrow.* London: Faber and Faber. http://www.archive.org/stream/gardencitiestom00howagoog#page/n41/mode/2up. Accessed March 17, 2012.

Huber, J., and J. Robertson, J. 2000. *Creating New Money: a Monetary Reform for the Information Age.* London: New Economics Foundation. http://www.neweconomics.org/gen/uploads/CreatingNewMoney.pdf. Accessed January 26, 2011.

Jackson, T. 2010. *Prosperity without Growth?—The Transition to a Sustainable Economy.* London: Sustainable Development Commission. http://www.sd-commission.org.uk/publications/downloads/prosperity_without_growth_report.pdf. Accessed January 26, 2011.

Jacobs, J. 1985. *Cities and Wealth of Nations: Principles of Economic Life.* New York: Vintage Books.

Jones, C., W. S. Hesterly, and S. P. Borgatti. 1997. "A General Theory of Network Governance: Exchange Conditions and Social Mechanisms." *Academy of Management Review* 22 (4): 911–945.

Kelso, L. O., and P. Hetter. 1967. *Two-Factor Theory: The Economics of Reality.* New York: Vintage Books.

Keynes, J. M. 1964 [1936]. *The General Theory of Employment, Interest, and Money.* New York: Harcourt Brace Jovanovich. http://www.marxists.org/reference/subject/economics/keynes/general-theory/index.htm. Accessed January 26, 2011.

King, M. 2010. "Banking: From Bagehot to Basel, and Back Again." The Second Bagehot Lecture, Buttonwood Gathering, New York City, October 25. http://www.bankofengland.co.uk/publications/speeches/2010/speech455.pdf. Accessed March 17, 2012.

Koestler, C. O. 1967. *The Ghost in the Machine.* London: Hutchinson.

Martin, J. 2001. "Demarchy: a Democratic to Alternative to Electoral Politics." Posted at http://www.uow.edu.au/~bmartin/pubs/89demarchy.html. Accessed November 10, 2012.

Mathews, J. 1996. "Holonic Organizational Architecture." *Human Systems Management* 15: 27–54.

Milne, E. G. 2010. "Dynamics of Human Mortality." *Experimental Gerontology* 45 (3): 180–187. http://peer.ccsd.cnrs.fr/docs/00/56/72/29/PDF/PEER_stage2_10.1016%252Fj.exger.2009.11.008.pdf. Accessed March 17, 2012.

Moran, A. J. 2006. *The Tragedy of Planning: Losing the Great Australian Dream*. Melbourne: Institute of Public Affairs. http://www.ipa.org.au/library/MORANPlanning2006.pdf.

Moulton, H. G. 1935. *The Formation of Capital*. The Institute of Economics, The Brookings Institution, Publication No. 59, Washington, DC, 10–11.

Palley, T. I. 2007. "Financialization: What It Is and Why It Matters." Working Paper No 525, The Levy Economics Institute. http://ssrn.com/abstract=1077923. Accessed January 26. 2011.

Penrose, E. T. 1956. "Foreign Investment and the Growth of the Firm." *Economic Journal* 66 (262): 220–235.

Pirson, M., and S. Turnbull. 2011. "Corporate Governance, Risk Management, and the Financial Crisis—An Information Processing View." *Corporate Governance: An International Review* 19 (5): 459–470.

Proudhon, P. 2007 [1840]. *What Is Property? An Inquiry into the Principle of Right and of Government*, Reprint. Charleston, SC: BiblioBazaar LLC. http://www.historyofideas.org/toc/modeng/public/ProProp.html, (accessed 26 January, 2011).

Reddaway, W. B. 1939. *The Economics of a Declining Population*. London: Allen and Unwin.

Riley, D. 2002. *Taken for a Ride*. London: Centre for Land Policy Studies.

Schumacher, E. F. 1975. *Small Is Beautiful: a Study of Economics If People Mattered*. London: Abacus.

Simon, H. A. 1962. "The Architecture of Complexity." *Proceeding of the American Philosophical Society* 106 (December): 467–482.

Suhr, D. 1989. *The Capitalistic Cost-Benefit Structure of Money: An Analysis of Money's Structural Non-Neutrality and Its Effects on the Economy*. Berlin, Heidelberg, New York: Springer. http://www.sozialoekonomie.info/Info_Foreign_Languages/English_6/Suhr-Structure-of-Money.pdf. Accessed March 17, 2012.

———. 1990. "The Neutral Money Network: A Critical Analysis of Traditional Money and the Financial Innovation 'Neutral Money' (NewMoNe)." Paper presented at the University of Augsburg, Brussels, April 30.

Trainer, F. E. 1985. *Abandon Affluence and Growth*, London: Zed Books.

———. 2010a "De-Growth Is Not Enough." *International Journal of Inclusive Democracy* 6 : 4. http://www.inclusivedemocracy.org/journal/

vol6/vol6_no4_trainer_degrowth_not_enough.htm. Accessed January 27, 2011.

———. 2010b. "The New Economy: For the Simpler Way." http://ssis.arts.unsw.edu.au/tsw/TheNewEc.html. Accessed November 10, 2012.

———. 2010c. *The Transition to a Sustainable and Just World*, Sydney: Envirobook.

Tricker, R. I. ed. 2000. *Corporate Governance: The History of Management Thought*. Dartmouth: Ashgate.

Turnbull, S. 1975. *Democratising the Wealth of Nations*. Sydney: Company Directors' Association of Australia. http://ssrn.com/abstract_id=1146062. Accessed January 26, 2011.

———. 2000. "The Governance of Firms Controlled by More Than One Board: Theory Development and Examples." PhD Thesis, Macquarie University, Sydney. http://ssrn.com/abstract=858244. Accessed January 26, 2011.

United Nations. 2001. "Replacement Migration: Is It a Solution to Declining and Aging Populations?" Population Division, Department of Economic and Social Affairs, ST/ESA/SER.A/206. http://www.un.org/esa/population/publications/ReplMigED/Cover.pdf. Accessed November 10, 2012.

———. 2003. *World Population in 2300: Highlights*. New York: United Nations. http://www.un.org/esa/population/publications/longrange2/Long_range_report.pdf. Accessed November 10, 2012.

Weiner, J. 2010. *Long for This World—The Strange Science of Immortality*. New York: HarperCollins.

———. 2011. "Our Ageing Future." Discussion broadcast in Future Tense program on Radio National, Australian Broadcasting Commission, January 24. http://www.abc.net.au/rn/futuretense/stories/2011/3068037.htm#transcript. Accessed November 10, 2012.

Chapter 5

Green Consumerism: A Path to Sustainability?

Valerie K. Kepner and Paula M. Cole

Introduction

Green (or environmentally conscious) consumers are making consumption choices among an ever-growing selection of green products. Producers, seeing a new market, are meeting the demand for green products by devoting resources to the development of greener technologies and green product lines. This green evolution is happening all in the spirit of capitalism. However, a truly green consumer would necessarily consume less, which is a direct contradiction to the role of consumers established by the previously mentioned capitalist spirit. We will, ultimately, propose to reconsider the green consumer as a social provisioner and reframe the economic system to be an inclusive and sustainable institution (Power 2004, 6–8).

While it is appropriate to acknowledge the trend toward green consumerism as a first step in creating institutional change, we have significant work remaining before us if we desire to function as social provisioners within a truly sustainable economy. A starting place to support social provisioners would be to improve the effectiveness of green regulations and the truthfulness in green advertising. Additionally, careful consideration is necessary if we are to develop and support an effective green evolution of institutions. Importantly, we must acknowledge and use our social natures to change not only the way we consume but also how much we consume and the place of consumption within our economic system. A truly green revolution requires institutional change that reconstructs our economy and the provisioning of life by changing customs, social norms, and policies.

In summary, our research will explore how environmentally conscious consumers operating within a capitalist economy are limited in their ability to produce a sustainable economy. We will then consider how advertising impacts the green movement and how government regulations produce (or do not produce) a sustainable economy. We will also examine what a true green revolution would look like. Toward the end, we will propose recommendations for encouraging the development of social provisioners through ethical guidance, government regulation, and reforms to institutions and social norms.

Buy, Buy, Buy

The capitalist economic system's promotion of the division of labor and the institution of private property makes the individual's participation in exchange essential in the acquisition of the means of subsistence. In mainstream economics, this individual, *homoeconomicus*, is assumed to be rational, autonomous, self-interested, and well-informed (Nelson 1996, 22). These characteristics of economic man allow him to carefully construct his preferences for goods and services, maximizing his utility function given a budget constraint. This mainstream analysis leads to economic man's conclusion that "more is better" and that interpersonal utility comparisons between individuals will not (and cannot) be made (England 2003, 40–42). The result is an individual who is an economic individual focused on consumption with mainstream economists prohibited from utilizing positive economic analysis to critique his consumption choices.

However, the assumptions and theoretical implications of economic man described above have been well critiqued. Examples of critiques include those enumerated by institutional, feminist, ecological, and post-Keynesian economists. Institutional economists highlight the importance of culture, customs, and norms in our decision-making processes. For example, Veblen's perspective of consumer behavior enables us to see the social nature of consumption decisions. His theory of the leisure class provides analysis of conspicuous consumption and emulation as defining characteristics of consumer behavior (2007, 20–27, 49–69). Feminist economists raise awareness of the importance of socially constructed identities, such as gender and race, creating differences in the way individuals experience economic systems (Power 2004, 5). This perspective of the economic individual calls for discussion of privilege and asks the mainstream economic models and theories to be more inclusive; an instance of one such opportunity would be the inclusion of nonmarket work as an economic activity. Ecological economists remind us that our economic system is only one component of our life systems and is situated within an ecological system (Harris 2003, 6–8).

All of these critiques suggest the need for redefining the economic individual as a social provisioner and reinventing economic theories to be more reflective of the reality of our economic and social lives. For example, Julie Nelson (2003, 84–85) argues for a socially and materially situated individual. This alternative construction of an economic individual is more reflective of a social provisioner's life as it is inclusive of one's different lived experiences, the social and environmental nature of one's life, and one's need to live a full, complete life. Changing the social construction of the economic individual would, naturally, change the story of our economy and the models and theories we use to tell this narrative (Nelson 2003; England 2003; Eisler 2007). This new story would begin with a discussion of the provisioning of life by examining how we meet our needs to support the subsistence of all life; this is a very different narrative than the mainstream one of an economy's sole function being the allocation of scarce resources among unlimited wants utilizing a system of exchange. These competing views on the appropriate identity of the economic (and social) individual inform our understanding and analysis of green consumers.

The Green Consumer: An Oxymoron?

Individuals identifying as "green" are conscious of their environment and concerned for how their actions impact the well-being of the planet. As green consumers, they strive to bring this environmental awareness to their consumption decisions. Green consumption is defined as sustainable consumption, where sustainability addresses the economic, environmental, and social needs of our communities in a reproducible and equitable way (Harris 2003, 6–8). An important component, but maybe less obvious, is that sustainability also demands environmental justice. An economy is not considered sustainable unless all members of society are treated justly and have the same opportunity to meet their needs (Johnson 2009, 20; Agyeman 2005, 5). Here we see acknowledgment of the individual as not only focusing on the economic sphere but also on the environmental and social spheres.

Although many individuals may desire to sustainably consume, today's environmentally conscious consumers may have difficulty reaching this goal because they are (1) unwilling to change their lifestyles and are uncertain about the difference a change will make and

(2) motivated by social status, not sustainability. Peattie (2001, 192) provides a framework for understanding the green consumer's degree of confidence (the likelihood of achieving a green outcome) and degree of compromise (the likelihood her lifestyle will be impacted) in making a green purchase. The green consumer's willingness to change her lifestyle is connected to her belief that her efforts actually improve the health of the environment. For example, purchasing compact fluorescent light bulbs is a relatively easy and inexpensive way to be green as the green consumer can physically see the monetary reward of this decision in lower electric bills, yet she does not have to substantially alter her daily routine. Cloth diapers, on the other hand, require significantly more effort from the consumer and there is greater uncertainty in the green outcome cloth diapers might generate.

There is also the serious problem of a lack of transparency in the production and consumption of goods and services. While it is relatively easy to determine the monetary cost and visual quality of products or services purchased, it is much more difficult to ascertain the information needed to make a fully green purchasing decision. Goleman (2009, 6) proposes a "radical transparency"; a radical transparency attaches to a product its numerous impacts including, say, its carbon footprint and chemical impact. The idea is that if we, acting as social provisioners, have all the relevant information before making our purchasing decisions, then we will make purchasing decisions that better align with our values (Power 2004, 5; Schwartz 2010, 87). The power of information is significant. As capitalism currently functions, producers largely determine the range of products and services available for purchase; however, with full information, consumers can utilize their power as consumers to "become the shapers of our destiny rather than passive victims" (Goleman 2009, 10). The time has come when it should no longer be acceptable to ignore our duty to act as social provisioners; our purchasing decisions are more than small drops in a big pond. The development of a consumer ethic will be addressed in a later section.

When making consumption decisions, social relations will also play a key role. Written by Rogers and Kostigen (2007), *The Green Book* is meant to be a guide for consumers on how to be green, yet this book illustrates the social aspect of green consumption well. This book acts as a simple guide allowing celebrities to be conspicuous green consumers by providing a forum for them to show off how they are green. Additionally, the book supports less well-off consumers in their green emulation efforts by teaching them how they can be green just like celebrities. It is conceivable that for many green consumers, sustainable consumption is driven by their desire to maintain or improve their social standing, rather than to assuage their environmental concerns. Referring back to the earlier discussion of Veblen and his theory of conspicuous consumption, the social nature of green consumption provides a contemporary example. However, the powerful force of social relations may well play a positive role in the formation of responsible social provisioners. For example, Czech (2000, 110) cites the possibility of the dismantling of lasting and ingrained institutions by a majority that recognizes and rejects the reprehensible nature of earth-damaging institutions. Our current long-term and revered institution of consumption can be changed.

So, what is so wrong with the act of consuming? If one desires to be a green consumer, this is a contradiction in words because consumerism, by its very definition in mainstream economics, is not a green practice. Being green necessarily requires that an individual think more like a social provisioner and adopt a "less is more" attitude, which is in direct contrast to the "more is better" mantra of homoeconomicus. For example, within the preface of *The Green Book* (mind you, a book with the express purpose of guiding individuals to be green) the authors state the following: "This book is derived from our desire to be environmentally friendly while remaining selfish consumers" (Rogers and Kostigen 2007, x). The challenge then, as Wilk (2004, 27) discusses, is that simplifying being green to consuming less does not account for our need to be consumers. As Schwartz (2010, 112) highlights, the capitalist economic system is fueled by consumption, and marketers are well aware of this dependence on consumption. In consequence, marketers do well to foster an individual's primary responsibility to consume from a very early age. This apparent paradox of sustainable consumption may, ultimately, be extended to questioning whether capitalism can be a sustainable economic system (Eisler 2007; McKibben 2007).

Going Green: Just a Marketing Ploy?

It is expected that producers will respond to green consumers' signals for more environmentally friendly products by making the necessary product changes, and the producers might even expect stronger profits. Yet, it may be very tempting for directors of operation to skimp on adopting the more expensive green technologies but market the production process as accommodating the concerns of the green consumer. If we assume a consumer with full information, such a scenario would not be possible as truly green consumers will choose to purchase from genuinely green producers. However, with the absence of a regulatory agency or trusted green label to which a consumer might turn for full information on products marketed as green, the possibility of making false claims is plausible.

Upon review of regulations regarding the branding of products as green, there appears to be no public or private regulating body in the United States overseeing generally acceptable marketing and labeling standards, that is, there is no one agency to which a green consumer can turn to vet producers' claims. However, it is not difficult to find studies describing for producers the typical green consumer. Green consumers are portrayed as wanting the benefits of buying green but without paying a premium for those benefits. For example, one green marketing guide asserts that few consumers will pay more than a premium of two percent for green benefits and then only so long as those benefits are perceived to add value to the product. The guide further emphasizes that green consumers are unwilling to be inconvenienced in the finding or use of a green product; the quality of the product must also be well-established (International Institute for Sustainable Development 2007).

The 2009 National Green Buying Study, commissioned by Green Seal and EnviroMedia Social Marketing (2009), sheds some light (and sometimes contrary light) on the data behind marketers' perceptions of green consumers. Fifty percent of the study's 1,000 survey respondents reported they had not reduced their spending on green products even though economic conditions had deteriorated. Another 19 percent said they had purchased more green products while 14 percent reported buying fewer such products. The survey also revealed green consumers' preference for recycling over moving to cleaner energy, reducing packaging, or buying environmentally friendly personal care products. Thirty-nine percent of respondents said they believed recycling to be the best way for them to benefit the environment.

Given the previous discussion of marketers' perceptions of green consumers, the survey results are surprising as buying green might be considered a luxury item and therefore easily dispensable during times of economic distress. The statistics are also interesting in that environmentally aware consumers are not indicating a strong interest in reducing consumption as a way to reduce waste, pollution, and other harmful environmental consequences of a consumptive society. However, there has not been a strong push to reduce overall consumption while campaigns to recycle, to lessen the country's dependence on foreign oil, and to buy more green, yet new, products have been emphasized.

The survey also indicated consumers desiring to be environmentally responsible when making their purchases faced difficulties in validating environmental claims. Some consumers just assumed that the products' claims were true. For example, approximately one-third of those surveyed replied they did not know if environmental claims were true. Ten percent of respondents put their trust in product claims, 17 percent researched claims, and 24 percent of people surveyed said they used the package to educate themselves about a product. Reputation, word of mouth, brand loyalty, certifications, and manufacturers' labels were the highest ranked reasons given for consumers purchasing specific green products; product advertisements actually influenced consumers the least (Green Seal and EnviroMedia Social Marketing 2009).

The US Federal Trade Commission (FTC) (2011) has published guidelines in an effort to assist producers in making consistent and accurate environmental claims. These guidelines should be beneficial to consumers as at least one benefit is the reduction in time and effort that would normally be needed to validate green claims. However, note the Commission labels the following as guidelines, that is, "they provide the basis for voluntary compliance with such laws by members of industry" (2011). Environmental marketing claims should be clear and prominent, with the ability to substantiate all claims. Producers should refrain from making misleading statements when marketing their products' green characteristics. The FTC's guide includes recommendations regarding the use of the terms degradable, biodegradable, photodegradable, compostable, recyclable, recycled content, source reduction, refillable, ozone safe, and ozone friendly (2011). With consumers and producers concentrating on their own well-being in capitalism, how can we achieve a green outcome, especially when the green vocabulary is ever-expanding and marketers have incentives to manipulate the vocabulary to best position their products?

The Role of Product Regulation

Our review of the marketing literature revealed marketer savvy in utilizing the decentralized green labeling standards to better position their products in the market. The US government does, however, utilize its power to influence the production process by rewarding those companies that produce green products with substantial government contracts. This is done through the use of government purchasing guidelines and recommendations. A significant government green purchasing guideline includes the US Environmental Protection Agency's (EPA) (2002) Comprehensive Procurement Guideline (CPG), and a government purchasing recommendation program is the Environmentally Preferable Purchasing (EPP) program.

To begin with purchasing guidelines, the CPG and the EPP, both sponsored by the EPA, are guidelines used when purchasing decisions are being made by procuring agencies, in the case of the CPG, and federal agencies, for the EPP. Procuring agencies include local and state agencies as well as any government contractor spending at least $10,000 a year on a CPG item; all federal agencies are subject to CPG's standards. The CPG has been promoting the use of products made with recovered materials since 1995 designating 61 products in eight categories, including paper, construction, and nonpaper office products, as preferable. CPG is the direct result of Congressional action instructing procuring agencies to favor the purchasing of recycled items. Further, agencies are required to advertise their interest in purchasing recycled-content products (EPA 2007). In this way, it is not the producer attempting to generate demand for goods already produced but a buyer demanding particular features or a particular production process from producers. Additionally, in 1993, the EPA launched the EPP to help agencies meet the environmental demands placed on their purchasing activities. Environmentally preferable purchases will favor goods or services demonstrating less potential damage to the environment and human health in comparison to competing goods or services. The EPA (2011) emphasizes the buying power exercised by federal agencies as generating greater demand for environmentally friendly products and services thereby impacting the availability of green products for the average green consumer. One could cite the inclusion of such governmental purchasing programs in "greening your business" recommendations and green marketing strategies as further evidence that the government's demand is positively influencing the major producers to be more mindful of their environmental impacts (EPA 2002; International Institute for Sustainable Development 2007).

A document prepared for the EPA's Office of Pollution Prevention and Toxics discusses tactics to green products including becoming familiar with the major federal purchasing programs (EPA 2002). The International Institute for Sustainable Development (2007) put together a global guide to business and sustainable development where it provides information on a number of resources including Green Seal. The Institute notes that in order for a business to be successful in marketing and selling its products to consumers concerned about the environment, the green claims must be considered credible. From the consumer's point of view, determining credibility can be difficult. In the review of green marketing strategies, such strategies emphasize the winning of the green consumer's business, and the drive to maximize profits may conceivably lead business leaders to make debatable green claims in the hopes of acquiring a new consumer base without all the necessary costs of going green. However, the move away from a consumption focused homoeconomicus to a social provisioner, who is engaged in the revolution of institutions and the creation of a consumer ethic, will actively limit the possibility of exploitation by business.

Green Recommendations

Right Relationship

Brown and Garver (2009, xi, xvi), in their book *Right Relationship: Building a Whole Earth Economy*, propose the creation of a whole earth economy based on an ethic of right relationship; this ethic joins concern for the environment with individuals' access to the means of life. Providing a guiding ethic for social provisioners, right relationship "offers a guidance system for functioning in harmony with scientific reality and enduring ethical traditions" (Brown and Garver 2009, 4). Major questions posed in the formation of an ethic of right relationship include (1) what is the economy for? (2) how does the economy work? (3) how big should the economy be? (4) what is a fair distribution of the economy's benefits and burdens? and (5) how should the economy be governed? A right relationship ethic answers these questions in such a way that the purpose of an economy encompasses more than maximizing profits and individuals' utility functions. With the economy maintaining "the integrity, resilience, and beauty of life's commonwealth," both individuals and communities will be acknowledged (Brown and Garver 2009, 10).

Right relationship emphasizes the importance of situating the economy as not only serving humans but also as functioning within and supporting the health of the earth's ecosphere. Importantly, the current anthropocentric economy emphasizes the importance of consumption activities; yet, humans typically do not acknowledge the damage consumption causes to the ecosystem. Even if production processes were made to be environmentally neutral, there remains the problem of disposing of "used up" products (Brown and Garver

2009, 11). Yet, at the same time, Brown and Garver (2009, 60) acknowledge that individuals should not be denied the conditions under which they can meet their needs even while society does not (or should not) have the right to permanently deplete the earth's natural resources. This is tricky. How does one structure a society that supports consumption in the meeting of one's needs without going so far as to condone the permanent depletion of resources? David Schwartz (2010, 88) suggests the development of a consumer ethic that would guide individuals in making their own consumption decisions. This consumer ethic, in tandem with a right relationship ethic, may be just the approach needed to evince a revolution calling for humans to live an ecologically sustainable lifestyle while navigating within a capitalist economic system.

Brown and Garver's ethic of right relationship modifies Ehrlich and Holdren's framework, I = f(PAT), to include an element of ethics, that is, the relationship now becomes I = f(PATE) (2009, 76). Hypothesizing that the human impact on the ecosystem (I) is a function of the population (P), affluence (A), technology (T), and ethics (E), the ethics variable provides an avenue for compelling individuals to live a life compatible with right relationship. While many economists cite the efficacy of the "invisible hand" and consumer sovereignty in directing consumption, the ethics of consumption in right relationship would set a new standard of lower per capita consumption (Brown and Garver 2009, 76–81). The role of consumption (and advertising for the purpose of generating consumption) carries too much significance in the lives of humans, and with right relationship, the ever-present desire to generate economic growth as a solution to many of the human population's problems would be rejected. Instead, a steady state economy, as proposed by Herman Daly in 1973, would replace the goal of ever increasing economic growth. In a steady state, population, technology, and per capita consumption stabilizes (Czech 2000, 94). With the introduction of an ethics variable, a steady state would be embraced while ever increasing rates of consumption would be viewed negatively. The core question then is whether it is possible to alter social norms such that only necessary consumption is revered while conspicuous or wasteful consumption is derided. The formation of a consumer ethic will be a critical step in the process.

An effective consumer ethic will challenge consumers to always and everywhere think of themselves as social provisioners. An appropriate consumer ethic will, according to Schwartz (2010, 88), take into account all potential negative outcomes associated with consumption of a particular good or service. More specifically, Schwartz highlights three categories into which such negative outcomes may be placed including (1) harm to others, (2) bad consequences, and (3) moral offense. These broad categories form a useful framework for social provisioners to use when making consumption decisions. In this way, the entire ecosystem will be respected during the consumption process as negative environmental consequences may easily enough be tied to harm to others. Now, it may be argued that this anthropocentric approach is too narrow to be an acceptable green consumer ethic, but Schwartz points out that this approach is all that is necessary to compel an individual, living by this consumer ethic, to act as a green consumer (2010, 94). Ultimately, damage to the ecosystem threatens the viable existence of future generations of humans. Is this not enough to place nongreen consumption within Schwartz's first two categories: harm to others and bad consequences? The discussion then becomes whether social provisioners are morally *obligated* to boycott a particular nongreen product or service, not should they *choose* to boycott (2010, 92).

Even after a successful evolution from homoeconomicus to social provisioner, it is going to be nearly impossible to separate oneself from consumption associated with negative outcomes. Schwartz (2010, 88–92) suggests four practical rules to be applied in daily consumption. Rules applicable to this discussion include the following: (1) if at all possible, avoid those products and services that harm others; (2) choose the lesser of the evils if a bad outcome cannot be avoided; and (3) determine whether the good or service one is purchasing is a necessity or a luxury, and if it is a luxury that causes harm, then refrain from purchasing that good or service. However, to follow these rules, one needs to know the relevant information. The viable provision of such information will be crucial in the formation of a society made up of social provisioners (in contrast to robotic unthinking consumers).

The question, then, is whether we can expect a social provisioner to expend the energy necessary to gather basic information about potential purchases. As articulated by Schwartz (2010, 107), much of the information is either not available or imposes additional costs (time and energy) on the ethical consumer. Environmentally conscious consumers in the United States lack a distinct trustworthy green label approving organization, but, according to the consumer ethic proposed by Schwartz, an ethical consumer cannot willfully remain ignorant (2010, 111). Yet, what ethical consumers need is help in the gathering of accurate product information. Thus, a call for government-mandated labeling and advertising standards will aid in the efficient functioning of markets—full information is an underlying assumption of homoeconomicus and deserves more attention than it currently receives.

Government Regulations

The government, because of its major purchasing guidelines and recommendations, is already encouraging the development of producers who are mindful (or maybe not so mindful but at least recognizing the profitability of environmental practices) of the desires of social provisioners. We recommend the government go further and create a centralized environmental labeling initiative in the spirit of labeling standards in countries such as Norway, Sweden, Denmark, Finland, and Iceland. Following a model that has already been successful in the United States, a standardized government-mandated green label could follow the model of nutritional labels found on all packaged food for sale. We are now also seeing caloric and other nutritional information on restaurants' menus. While it may be said that the government does not always have the wherewithal to command the results desired and it not be the only institution instituting change, Goleman (2009, 72) points out that "when it comes to the environmental or health impacts of a product, manufacturers and suppliers may know the answers, but they rarely go out of their way to offer up such data unless compelled to by government fiat."

Aside from government-mandated labeling initiatives, private organizations are another avenue to providing greater product transparency. An example of such a transparency-generating organization already in existence is Green Seal. Green Seal operates as a nonprofit entity setting environmental criteria and certifying those products that meet the criteria (EPA 2002). Using the International Organization for Standardization's environmental labeling standards, Green Seal (2011) develops its standards utilizing the life-cycle approach. This approach takes into consideration all phases of a product's development "from raw materials extraction through manufacturing to use and disposal." Green Seal has secured the accreditations and positive reviews from its peers including GENICES (GEN Internationally Coordinated Ecolabelling System), ANSI (American National Standards Institute), and Green America (Green Seal 2011).

Another example of a private organization meeting the information demands of consumers is GoodGuide, Inc. Environmentally conscious consumers may soon be able to tap into GoodGuide's pool of information gathered from hundreds of databases using just their cell phones. GoodGuide is on the cutting edge of communication technology providing the consumer standing in the grocery store aisle a product's life-cycle impacts as measured according to social, health, and environmental impacts. A beta version of GoodGuide allows consumers to take a picture of a product's bar code and upload the image to GoodGuide's server to then receive information on the product's life-cycle impact (Goleman 2009, 83–93). As O'Rourke, the visionary behind GoodGuide, is quoted as saying: "We want to give consumers the information they need to apply their values" (Goleman 2009, 92).

Given the spontaneous development of private organizations rising to meet the needs of consumers desiring to make more environmentally friendly purchases, the public sphere is going to be an important, but not the only, institution enabling society to move closer to the idea of living in harmony with the ecosystem. The evolution of our institutions, including our schools, will be instrumental in the changing of customs, social norms, and policies. The following section addresses the potential pitfalls of leaving institutions to evolve on their own.

A Green Evolution of Institutions—Yes and No

A truly green revolution requires institutional change that reconstructs our economy and the provisioning of life by changing customs, social norms, and policies. A starting point for this green revolution is by encouraging the evolution of our institutions. The following examples examine how, if we are not careful, efforts to be green run up against institutional barriers illustrating the necessity of evolutionary change. All of the following examples are set in the context of green campaigns of a collection of colleges and universities. As educators of future generations of social provisioners and leaders of change in society, higher education institutions provide an interesting setting for studying the complex reality of being green.

The first example of an institutional barrier to being green focuses on a university's recycling policy. The university provides all offices and buildings on campus with recycling containers to promote recycling, but it does not regularly collect the materials from all bins, and many recycle bins are regularly overflowing. Notably, many classrooms are without recycling bins. However, the university does empty all trash bins on a nightly basis. This recycling program allows the university to present the image of being green without really having concern for their environmental impact. This example also highlights the potential for an ineffective policy to act as an impediment to being green because even when an economic individual chooses to recycle university policy falsely supports them in this effort.

Another example critiques a college green campaign in the context of environmental justice. This aspect of being green is particularly challenging for private colleges and universities because of the innate privilege of their student bodies. At the end of every academic year when students are packing up their dorm rooms, one institution collects unwanted and unneeded furniture, home decorations, kitchen items, and other home furnishings from its students and general campus community and then holds a sale open to all members of the local community with proceeds going to a local charity. The sale was initially billed as "Trash to Treasure" reflecting that many of the items collected would previously have ended up in trash bins, a particular reality considering the many privileged members of the campus community. Although this event is commendable so far as it is reducing campus waste and generating a positive outcome for the local community (one that is not as privileged as the campus community), it does not address the flippant campus attitude toward consumption.

A final example of the institutional barriers to a true green revolution on university campuses compares how two universities approached bicycle sharing programs on their campuses. One university purchased brand new bicycles and new bicycle racks, while another asked for donations of used bicycles that were then refurbished. Both of these bicycle programs can be promoted as environmentally friendly programs. We can see the limitation of one university's environmental impact in their inability to see beyond consumer norms by purchasing new products to support their program. However, the other university did not have the foresight to consider the need for additional bike racks. This green activity attempted to create a bike culture on campus as a way to reduce environmental impacts without addressing all of the institutional barriers impeding the success of a bike culture. For example, both universities have yet to address the need for bike lanes on campus or taken measures to reduce their car cultures. This example shows that even in our efforts to change our lifestyles we have difficulty in constructing the institutions necessary to support this change (i.e., bike lanes) and in seeing beyond the current institutional structures (i.e., acting as consumers).

All of these campus efforts to be green are attempts to reduce environmental impacts. Although these small steps may support us in our move toward a sustainable economy, they are all limited at producing positive change because of larger institutional constraints (technology, policy, addressing privilege, resistance to institutional change) impeding the evolution to a green outcome. To be successful, social provisioners need an institutional structure that promotes a sustainable economy; the road to living as social provisioners will not be without its bumps.

Conclusion: Creating a Green Economy

According to mainstream economic theory, the meeting of consumers and producers in a market where price is used as a signaling device thereby dictating the efficient level of production (and subsequent consumption) is a thing of beauty. If consumers cease signaling their desire for unbridled production and consumption, theory predicts producers are to respond by scaling back production (or changing the production process to address consumers' concerns). This is as it should be. The question then is why consumers tend to assume that what they desire in the way of production matters only so far as producers are willing to bow to their demands. As Hawken (1993, 14) states: "It is important to understand that we consumers are accessories before and after the fact." It is not right to place full blame for our environmental problems on producers' shoulders, although producers are significant players in the solution.

We propose that moving toward a whole earth economy will be one right step in the green direction. Four steps in this process of creating a whole earth economy will include: (1) establishing a sense of awe for the cosmos and adopting an ethic that correctly places the human species within the cosmos and the earth; (2) developing the institutions, models, programs, and techniques necessary to develop a whole earth economy while retaining an emphasis on localized decision-making; (3) bearing witness to a guidance system based on right relationship; and (4) initiating a social movement of action that is nonviolent yet changes hearts and minds toward right relationship (Brown and Garver 2009, 20–21).

A truly green revolution requires institutional change that reconstructs our economy and the provisioning of life by changing customs, norms, and policies. It may be that our current approach of green consumerism within a capitalist economic system is the first step in creating institutional change of the consumer. However, we have significant work to do before we can be a sustainable economy. A beginning place to support green consumers in their efforts to be more environmentally aware would be to strengthen and centralize the regulations on green products and green advertising. To go further, a change in society's acceptance and encouragement of ever more consumption might be curtailed with the honest discussion and presentation of right relationship coupled with a reasonable, yet responsible, consumer ethic. Additionally, careful consideration and thought is required to support an evolution of our institutions to align with this new right relationship. We need to acknowledge and use our social natures to change the way we consume, how much we consume, and the place of consumption in our economic system. While there are several points from which to start this discussion, human consumption needs to be a part of the discussion.

Bibliography

Agyeman, Julian. 2005. *Sustainable Communities and the Challenge of Environmental Justice*. New York: New York University Press.

Brown, Peter G., and Geoffrey Garver. 2009. *Right Relationship: Building a Whole Earth Economy*. San Francisco: Berrett-Koehler.

Czech, Brian. 2000. *Shoveling Fuel for a Runaway Train: Errant Economists, Shameful Spenders, and a Plan to Stop Them All*. Berkeley: University of California Press.

Eisler, Riane. 2007. *The Real Wealth of Nations: Creating a Caring Economics*. San Francisco: Berrett-Koehler.

England, Paula. 2003. "Separative and Soluble Selves: Dichotomous Thinking in Economics." In *Feminist Economics Today: Beyond Economic Man*, edited by Marianne A. Ferber and Julie A. Nelson, 33–60. Chicago: University of Chicago Press.

EPA (Environmental Protection Agency). 2002. "Greening Your Products: Good for the Environment, Good for Your Bottom Line." February. http://www.epa.gov/epp/pubs/jwod_product.pdf.

———. 2007. "EPA Comprehensive Procurement Guideline Program." October. http://www.epa.gov/osw/conserve/tools/cpg/pdf/cpg-fs.pdf.

———. 2011. "Basic Information." *Environmentally Preferable Purchasing*. http://www.epa.gov/oppt/epp/pubs/about/about.htm.

Federal Trade Commission. 2011. "Part 260—Guides for the Use of Environmental Marketing Claims." http://www.ftc.gov/bcp/grnrule/guides 980427.htm.

Goleman, Daniel. 2009. *Ecological Intelligence: How Knowing the Hidden Impacts of What We Buy Can Change Everything*. New York: Broadway Books.

Green Seal. 2011. "How Green Seal Develops Standards." http://www.greenseal.org/GreenBusiness/Standards/HowGreenSealDevelopsStandards.aspx.

Green Seal and EnviroMedia Social Marketing. 2009. "Top Line of Findings from 2009 National Green Buying Study." http://www.enviromedia.com/news-item.php?id=688.

Harris, Jonathan M. 2003. "Sustainability and Sustainable Development." *International Society for Ecological Economics Internet Encyclopedia of Ecological Economics*. February. http://www.ecoeco.org/education_encyclopedia.php.

Hawken, Paul. 1993. *The Ecology of Commerce: A Declaration of Sustainability*. New York: HarperBusiness.

International Institute for Sustainable Development. 2007. "Business and Sustainable Development: A Global Guide." http://www.bsdglobal.com.

Johnson, Glenn S. 2009. "Environmental Justice: A Brief History and Overview." In *Environmental Justice in the New Millennium: Global Perspectives on Race, Ethnicity, and Human Rights*, edited by Filomina Chioma Steady, 17–46. New York: Palgrave Macmillan.

Lavoie, Marc. 2009. "Post Keynesian Consumer Choice Theory and Ecological Economics." In *Post Keynesian and Ecological Economics: Confronting Environmental Issues*, edited by Richard P. F. Holt, Steven Pressman, and Clive L. Spash, 141–157. Cheltenham: Edward Elgar.

McKibben, Bill. 2007. *Deep Economy: The Wealth of Communities and the Durable Future*. New York: Holt Paperback.

Nelson, Julie A. 1996. *Feminism, Objectivity, and Economics*. London: Routledge.

———. 2003. "Separative and Soluble Firms: Androcentric Bias and Business Ethics." In *Feminist Economics Today: Beyond Economic Man*, edited by Marianne A. Ferber and Julie A. Nelson, 81–100. Chicago: University of Chicago Press.

Peattie, Ken. 2001. "Golden Goose or Wild Goose? The Hunt for the Green Consumer." *Business Strategy and the Environment* 10 (July–August): 187–199.

Power, Marilyn. 2004. "Social Provisioning as a Starting Point for Feminist Economics." *Feminist Economics* 10 (3) (November): 3–19.

Rogers, Elizabeth, and Thomas M. Kostigen. 2007. *The Green Book: The Everyday Guide to Saving the Planet One Simple Step at a Time*. New York: Three Rivers.

Schwartz, David T. 2010. *Consuming Choices: Ethics in a Global Consumer Age*. Lanham, MD: Rowman & Littlefield.

Veblen, Thorstein. 2007. *Theory of the Leisure Class*. Oxford: Oxford University Press.

Wilk, Richard. 2004. "Questionable Assumptions about Sustainable Consumption." In *The Ecological Economics of Consumption*, edited by Lucia A. Reisch and Inge Ropke, 17–31. Cheltenham, UK: Edward Elgar.

Chapter 6

Sustainability in a Good Society: Alternate Visions from Australia and the United States

*Janet Spitz**

Introduction

Widely held values and attitudes toward sustainability increasingly differ from practices of globalized business as conducted under free trade, where emphasis is placed on short-run profit. Prevalent views among the US citizens, for example, support sustainability both in the generalized concept and in specific manifestations of sustainable economic and political development. These include minimizing pollution (Pew Research Center 2010, Carlson 2005), paying a reasonable wage (Pew Research Center for the People and Press 2010), and promoting democracy (Pew Research Center for the People and Press 2009).

This chapter finds significant differences along national identity, workplace identity, and gender identity lines on these sustainability-related views. Using an original data set collected from US and Australian academics in 2008 and 2009, the main finding is that academics in the field of Business, and Americans, tend to value these aspects of sustainability and democratic development significantly less than comparable academics in Australia and in other fields of study. Women academics value all aspects of sustainability more highly than do comparable men.

These results suggest that a more cosmopolitan approach than "Free Trade" is needed if global business activity is to lead to a good society for more than business owners and managers themselves. In particular, to the extent that workplace and national identity ideological norms are carried forward into business decisions which reflect those values and beliefs, a case may be made for greater regulation governing global business development, regulation specifically focused on economic and political development, as well as on resource use. Given business views, rules such as these will be needed to mediate tendencies to restrict good society outcomes to an increasingly select few.

Values and Workplace Identity—The Importance of Occupational Social Norms

Social norms have been found to be tightly coupled with meaningful and positive workplace identity across types of jobs and in varied locales (Dutton, Roberts, and Bednar 2010; Ashforth and Mael 1989). Our connections to our jobs in general comprise an essential element of who we are and how we think of ourselves (Pratt 2000; Butler 1998). Because we wish to hold a positive self-view, at least two mechanisms operate to render workplace norms congruent with those held more personally.

First, many people self-select into college majors, workplaces, jobs, and careers for which at least part of the attraction is the "fit" between values and expectations held by the prospective employee, and the occupational social codes (Judge and Bretz 1992; Arlow 1991; Lindholm 2003; Kezar 2001). Second, once employed, social codes at work "tell people how they are supposed to think of themselves and how they are supposed to interact with each other" (Akerlof and Kranton 2010, 1).

Some workplace norms and ideological beliefs function as legitimating tools for control and maintenance of hierarchical status across a variety of organization types and locations (Salaman and Thompson 1980; Lincoln and Kalleberg 1990; Jost and Major 2001; Barley and Kunda 1992 provide a review). As newcomers join an established order, they may experience a felt pressure to adopt majority views. Ridgeway (1997) argues that the process of workplace interaction itself promotes and conserves a preference for already high-status dominant type workers (i.e., males) for "good" jobs, particularly under conditions of economic change.

In the case of business school and management education, social codes and self-selection mechanisms occurring across workplaces, in general, operate to help shape who business students are (Petriglieri and Petriglieri 2010) and establish guidelines for junior faculty as well as students. Spitz (2011) found, for example, that business school junior faculty views, across cultures, increasingly became "more like" the views of senior faculty, as faculty ascended through the academic ranks. Much of this social coding may be subtle: both women and men in MBA programs have been observed to deny the relevance of gender even as their language endorses the systemic nature of gender-based business inequality (Kelan and Jones 2010).

The social codes within management education constitute a kind of moral philosophy. These have recently been well-studied, not only as a result of recent corporate scandals occurring in Italy, the United States, and several other locations but also as a consequence of mandated inclusion of ethics into business school accreditation agencies including the ACBSP (Accreditation Council for Business Schools and Programs) and the AACSB (The Association to Advance Collegiate Schools of Business) as noted by Bell and others (Bell 2009; Adler and Jermier 2005; Ghoshal 2005; Mitroff 2004; Neubaum et al. 2009). The question that ethics-based research explores is whether specific training in ethics per se impacts management students' values, beliefs, and subsequent decision-making choices. Most such research found that requiring coursework in business or accounting ethics does impact student decision-making choices and ideological views (Luthar and Karri 2005; Bloodgood, Turnley, and Mudrack 2010; Uysal 2010), much of that focused on the trade-off between the maximization of short-run profit traditionally emphasized in business education and long-run sustainability concerns.

The emphasis of MBA and undergraduate Business education on short-term profit measured quarterly (Callahan 2004) has been found to impact students' personally held values and beliefs, altering these toward greater material gain (Mitchell and Scott 1990; Giacalone 2004; Kasser 2002). For example, in a matched entry and exit assessment, Krishnan (2007) found graduates from a two-year MBA program to become significantly more interested in a personally comfortable, pleasurable, and exciting life, and significantly less interested in world peace, natural beauty, national security, or in being helpful and polite.

The business community influences student beliefs as well through business school practices (Rynes and Trank 1999), which include business leaders as guest speakers in class, business leaders as actual course instructors, and business leaders as speakers at special events. One example of how this might influence student values and carry over into workplace decisions once graduates gain employment in corporations is that business leaders who drastically downsized their organization's workforce—particularly during times of positive earnings—earned 42 percent more on average than chief executive officers in the Standard and Poor's largest 500 corporation list (Anderson et al. 2010). This cannot fail to be noticed by students whose career paths steer them toward business firms. Business students tend to be most interested in higher-paying financial, consulting, or marketing careers (Branch 1997) and thus self-identify with business leaders' successes (Mael 1991).

Research in academic fields other than business, and at levels other than University, has similarly found students' personal views to shift over time into greater congruence with the views of their teachers. Literature at the elementary-, middle-, and high-school levels confirms that students adopt views of teachers (Wittrock 1992), especially those whom they like or regard as role models (see Maylor [2009] for a review). College students were found to absorb personal views of professors whom they admire and respect (Light 2001; Hong and Shull, 2010), particularly when student-faculty interaction extends beyond the classroom itself (Kuh and Hu 2001). Graduate students in teacher education are likewise recognized to shift beliefs and expectations into greater congruence with faculty dispositions, causing them to act in accord with those beliefs (Villegas 2007).

Beyond the general case of workplace norms, then, the social norms, values, and beliefs *in academia* have thus been found to matter a great deal to the resulting values, beliefs, and actions of students, and within the field of management education, this result has been shown to hold as well. The research in this chapter, by its ability to glean patterns of values and beliefs directly from academic faculty across various disciplinary fields, enables us to create a window into the social codes operating in colleges and universities today carried forward by graduating students and presumably utilized in decision choices once former students are employed, including those employed in business management. One question we ask is whether those academic social codes vary by nationality across otherwise similarly structured, and in many ways similarly operational, locales.

Values emphasizing short-term profit and material gain characterizing business education are particularly troubling in a sustainability sense. Should these values be found to be pronounced among business academics, prognosis will not be good for sustainable development if it is guided by these business precepts.

National Differences in Values and Beliefs

Values and Beliefs about sustainability are likely to vary by more than area of specialization or field. Much work has concerned itself with cultural differences across nations (Hofstede 2001) or other identity groups (Bisin and Verdier 2010). Cultural difference associated with national identity has been used to explain patterns of tourism (Reisinger and Crotts 2010), corruption (Pillay and Dorasamy 2010), knowledge sharing in virtual communities (Siau, Erickson, and Nah 2010), and of course management (Chevrier 2009; Inkpen and Ramaswamy 2006). National differences in structures of values and beliefs impact group cohesiveness (Lauring and Selmer 2010), gender interaction and tension (Gentry et al. 2010), organizational willingness to engage in modernization (Kragh and Djursaa 2006), and humor (Kalliny, Cruthirds, and Minor 2006).

More to the point of sustainability, this tendency for values of business school students to become more individualistically competitive, and attaching more importance to careers and money rather than social goals such as helping others and the physical environment, is a set of characteristics that also has been found to vary by national culture (Hofstede 2001). The extent to which national culture dilutes or strengthens convergence of management practices across nations (Carr and Pudelko 2006) can be informed by this chapter's research on academics' values and beliefs. That is, are cultural values exhibited in business decisions by dominant management and business players adopted cross-nationally, or is there nation-based resistance to that? In particular, this research tests whether there are differences in values and beliefs about sustainable business development between academics in Australia and the United States, national differences strong enough to emerge even among otherwise similar academics. Or, would field of specialization override otherwise culturally distinct inclinations toward greater equality, less pollution, more democracy, and other characteristics of a good society? In American terms, legitimate globalization in economic development involves adding to the wealth of those already at the global top (Stiglitz 2006; Caldentey 2006; Milanovic 2002). This research tests whether that value set is shared by Australian academics in business whose larger society is structured in a more egalitarian way.

Both Australia and the United States are similar in many ways as modern industrialized English language nations with quite similar standards of living (World Bank 2009);[1] both are members of the Organisation for Economic Co-operation and Development. The nations differ substantially, however, on social provisioning, specifically social welfare, where certain differences are quite stark. Australia's minimum wage was roughly 1.86 times that of the United States at the time of this 2008–2009 data collection (Saunders, Hill, and Bradbury [2008], adjusted for exchange rate) indicating a more generous social provisioning standard. Australia provides extensive support to families in terms of birth payments, compensated parental time off, and day care support, none of which occurs in the United States where parents cope individually with these challenges.

A third notable difference in is health care: basic health care is nationally provided in Australia without requiring patient responsibility for excessive costs and bills. By contrast, health care in the United States is a mixture of government-funded "last resort" Medicaid available only to those with demonstrably little to no income; privately insured health care with—generally speaking—strict coverage limits; and those earning too much for Medicaid but with no health insurance at all, roughly 16 percent of citizens who pay directly out of pocket (Gallup Wellbeing 2009). Limits on health coverage in the United States is the single largest contributor to household bankruptcy filings, medical bills causing about 60 percent of these (Tamkins 2009). That same year, 2009, saw private US health insurance companies post profit increases of 56 percent to $12.2 billion while 2.7 million US citizens lost private health insurance coverage (HCAN 2011). In these and other ways, social provisioning differs significantly between Australia and the United States.

The Australian social context, because of its emphasis on a more inclusive society (Carney and Ramia 2011), may thus create an expectation that these types of good society elements are normal, just, and right (Eisler 1987). If so, residents of Australia are likely to understand higher levels of social provisioning from a taken-for-granted point of view, rather than something that needs to be attained, in a society that is otherwise in many ways quite similar to that experienced in the United States (Hofstede 2001).

The Australian provision of social welfare follows patterns established in Britain and the European Union, which has defined sustainable development as a combination of protecting the natural resource base, poverty eradication, making globalization sustainable, and enhancing good governance and participation (Caratti and Lo Cascio 2006). Others echo the inclusion of well-being as a measure of economic success, as well as the inclusion of power relations (Power 2004). Grote (2009) and others also understand the link between sustainable economics and shared power, discussing the Living Wage movement in the United States and globally, not simply as a higher minimum wage but as a redefinition of power relations toward positive employment, which, in the long run, enables sustainably higher participation of wage earners in their local and regional economies.

In sum, each nation's social context, as well as the particular workplace social identity associated with each job, is influential, if not determinative, in its creation of a common interpretation of social reality and of our place within it: each person's interaction with those around us creates and substantiates a social reality of such strength that not only does its maintenance become taken for granted, but also its violation becomes almost unthinkable (Berger and Luckmann 1966). Similarly, Lukes wrote of influence at its most powerful when it forms the assumed context within which we even think about what possibilities might be considered (2005). C. Wright Mills defined this more institutionally, viewing the social context as the historical institutions and structures in which are organized the milieu of our everyday lives; of these structures, the nation-state is the unit, which he called both the history-making unit and the unit within which types of people are formed (Mills 1958). Mills thus viewed political and economic struggles as contests for which type of humanity might prevail.

As the topic of "sustainability" moves from being considered one of many unattainable ideals coveted by environmental utopianists onto a far more robust center stage, pushed in part by increased visibility of business globalization, the concept of what sustainability exactly is has widened. Beyond pollution or climate change, is economic exploitation sustainable in a good society? How about political orders governed by corruption? Questions such as these are increasingly discussed at all levels of society in nations whose citizens seek a reliable and steady standard of living enduring beyond the short-term flash of windfall profits followed by recession's unemployment and social service cuts, a cyclical pattern increasingly characteristic of nations heavily engaged in the largely unregulated investment and withdrawal of capital under agreements of free trade.

The conversation about what type of humanity will prevail, then, speaks directly to the issue of sustainability. And for sustainability to be practically actualized, in any sense beyond corporate public relations imagery, one of two conditions must be met: either personally held value commitments congruent with broadly defined sustainability are required among those whose decision-making choices consequentially impact the environment, the economy, and the political governance of societies in which we live, or, absent that personally held commitment, significant regulatory constraint must emerge as a needed mediating element to otherwise largely unregulated business globalization activity.

Support for Sustainability and a Good Society: Hypotheses, Model, Sample, and Data

Hypotheses

The hypotheses follow the sustainability categories outlined above: a sustainable environment reasonably unpolluted by hazardous materials, a sustainable economy sufficient to provide a reasonably good standard of living for employed citizens, and a sustainable political governance election mechanism needed for an overall good society. Together, these compose a larger level of concern with sustainability as global business development. In each particular aspect, we hypothesize both a field of specialization effect (Business/Management vs. other field of specialization) and a national culture effect (Australia vs. the United States). Academics working in the field of business are expected to show levels of support for sustainability that are lower than academics working in other fields, and residents of Australia are expected to show levels of support for sustainability that are greater than the levels of support shown by residents of the United States.

Three control variables are included in the model: gender, age, and years of international experience. The views of women academics may be impacted by ongoing differences in hiring and promotion (Fraumeni 2011).[2] Age and years of international experience are included as controls on the theory that greater exposure to the complexities of different aspects of life, and different national cultures, may impact values and beliefs about dimensions of sustainability.

H1(a): Business academics will show lesser support for sustainability than comparable academics in other fields in terms of (1) environmental sustainability, (2) economic sustainability, and (3) democratic election sustainability.

H1(b): Business academics will show less concern about the sustainability of business globalization than similar academics in other fields.

H2(a): Australia academics will show more support for sustainability than academics residing in the United States in terms of (1) environmental sustainability, (2) economic sustainability, and (3) democratic election sustainability.

H2(b): Australian academics will show more concern about the sustainability of business globalization than similar academics in the United States.

The Model

To test these hypotheses we use the model,

Y = f(X1, X2, Z1, Z2, Z3)

where Y = specific sustainability dimensions including

1) support for environmental sustainability in the traditional climate-related definition, focusing on business production of hazardous waste;
2) support for economic sustainability as workplace compensation adequate to provide a reasonably good standard of living, with medical care available to all;
3) support for a sustainably democratic society, absent of coercive domination through business' private use of military forces or suppression of dissent through business' influence of public elections; and
4) support for sustainability of business globalization in general.

X1 represents respondent field of academic specialization (coded: Business or Management=1, Other field of specialization=0);
X2 represents national identity (coded: Australia=1, United States=0);
Z1 is a control variable for gender, where the respondent is female (coded: female=1, male=0);
Z2 is a control variable for age in years; and
Z3 is a control variable for the number of years the person has lived internationally (no international living experience=0).

The Sample

During the 2008–2009 academic year, hardcopies of anonymous surveys with introductory cover letters and return envelopes were distributed in three waves.[3] In all, there was a total response rate of 12.55 percent;[4] emailed surveys to academics yielded 220 additional responses from Australia and the United States. Because this chapter focuses on differences between academics in Australia and the United States, this analysis included only responses from academics residing in Australia and the United States, and responses which identified academic field; this resulted in a final sample size of 1,580 cases. This included 1,195 respondents who identified their residence as the United States, and 385 who identified their residence as Australia.

The Data

Data were structured in the form of value-laden statements with which the respondent was invited to strongly agree, agree, disagree, or strongly disagree. Information was also requested about field of specialization, gender, and other demographic characteristics.

For purposes of this analysis, four value-laden statement groups were used. First, "Hazardous waste is an unavoidable result of business production" indicated (when reverse-coded) belief that a sustainable environmental approach is reasonably possible absent the production of hazardous waste. Second, economic sustainability for citizens was composed by adding responses from the two statements, "Businesses should pay all employees enough to live well" and "Everyone world-wide should have medical care" (note that this wording did not place the cost of providing that medical care on business). Economic sustainability was further explored with the more detailed statement, "It is OK that some enjoy Luxuries while others do without." Third, a sustainably democratic society absent of coercive domination was composed by adding (reverse-coded) responses from the two statements, "Businesses should be able to influence election outcomes" and "It is reasonable for business to hire private military forces." Last, concerns about the sustainability of business globalization overall were explored with the statements, "Globalization spreads inequality" and "Nations should be able to deny Business Opportunities."

Results

Table 6.1 shows the mean values for each of the variables used.

Column 1 shows that Australian respondents make up about 1/4 of the sample; due to intentional oversampling, 43 percent work in Business. About 32 percent of the respondents are women.

On average, respondents agree that hazardous materials are avoidable in business production. Contrary to the effect hypothesized, this does not appear to vary much by either national identity or academic field. The rest of the sustainability measures do differ, both by national identity and by academic field.

Australian academics show stronger support for a sustainable economy than academics living in the United States (columns 2 and 3). Australians are also less likely than US respondents to agree with the idea that it is okay for some to have luxuries while others do without, an attitude consistent with the higher level of equality and basic structure of social provisioning in Australian society.

Table 6.1 Overall means, values, and beliefs of academics in Australia and the United States.

	Means of Full Sample	Means of Divided Samples			
		AU	US	Business	Other Fields
	(1)	(2)	(3)	(4)	(5)
Australia	0.245				
Business	0.43	0.21	0.5		
Academic Field					
Female	0.32	0.38	0.31	0.29	0.35
Hazardous Materials are Avoidable in Business Production	0.903	0.919	0.897	0.86	0.934
Wages Sufficient to a Reasonable Life with Medical Care	2.142	2.614**	1.987	1.653**	2.508
OK for Some to have Luxuries, while Others do Not	0.362	0.006**	0.478	0.697**	0.111
Citizens Should Control Democracy	2.088	2.504**	1.952	1.802**	2.3
Nations Should have the Right to Deny Business Opportunities	0.409	0.599**	0.346	0.354**	0.45
Globalization Spreads Inequality	−0.502	−0.060**	−0.647	−0.796**	−0.274

** $p<0.01$, indicating that the values of the two divided samples are statistically significantly different from each other, where marked.

Attitudes toward political sustainability similarly vary by nation, with Australians significantly more supportive of citizen-controlled elections. Finally, in terms of global sustainability, Australian academics show significantly more concern with potentially negative consequences of business globalization: compared with academics in the United States, they believe to a greater extent that nations should have the right to deny business opportunities, largely because of the inequality they believe that globalization spreads.

Similar divisions in values may be seen in the last two columns of Table 6.1, which compares academic respondents working in the field of business (column 4) to academic respondents working in other fields (column 5). This chapter argues that this business-nonbusiness division in values, attitudes, and beliefs about sustainability is consequential, especially in terms of business global development because of the influence that business academics exert over national, international, and global trade policy, in addition to the direct decision-making in which business school students, soon after graduation, engage. The values and beliefs held in business schools as social codes matter, and it is in columns 4 and 5 of Table 6.1 that these differences in values are shown.

Beliefs about the inevitability of hazardous materials in business production are consistent across fields: both business and nonbusiness academics believe on average that such non-sustainable pollutants can be successfully avoided.

Differences emerge in other sustainability dimensions. Business academics agree less than academics in other fields that wages should enable employees to live at a reasonable standard of economic health, and they do not support the concept of universal medical care. Moreover, in terms of the question "a sustainable society for whom?," business academics agree that it is acceptable for some to have luxuries while others do without, more so than comparable academics in other fields.

Business academics support citizen democratic control but to a significantly lesser extent than academics in other fields, and they agree less as well that nations should be able to deny businesses opportunities, perhaps because they disagree that globalization spreads inequality, more so than do academics in other fields. This overall pattern of values and beliefs is confirmed in Table 6.2, which shows results of Ordinary Least Squares Regression Analyses on the four sustainability dimensions of pollution, economic sustainability, sustainable democracy, and sustainable global development.

Again, while views on pollution generated no business or national identity effects, working in the field of business did consistently and negatively predict sustainability views for economic sustainability, democratic sustainability, and sustainability of business globalization. Australian national identity positively predicted views about these same issues.

In terms of the control variables, gender and life experience also mattered. Women academics, across fields and regardless of national location, more strongly supported sustainability than did comparable academic men. Women opposed hazardous materials generation, believing this was not an inevitable part of business production; women academics endorsed a sustainable standard of economic citizen well-being; and they supported a sustainable citizen controlled democracy.

Table 6.2 Ordinary least squares regression results, full sample, values, and beliefs of academics in Australia and the United States

	Dependent variables:			
	Hazardous Materials are Avoidable in Business Production (1)	Economic Sustainability (2)	Sustainable Democracy (3)	Sustainable Business Globalization (4)
predictors:				
Constant	0.317	1.917	1.266	0.271
Business	−0.032	−0.662**	−0.343**	−0.375**
Australian	0.033	0.409**	0.511**	0.724**
Female	0.516**	0.478**	0.427**	0.056
Age	0.008**	0.005	0.013**	−0.008*
Yrs Int'l	0	−0.000*	−0.000*	0
F	12.83**	25.82**	14.59**	16.942**
R-sq	0.043	0.083	0.049	0.054

**p<0.01, two tail
*p<0.05, two tail

Life experience, both in terms of age and years spent living internationally, mattered as well. Older academics were more concerned with democratic sustainability and sustainability of business globalization, while international living experience led to less concern with economic sustainability and sustainable democracy.

Concluding Remarks

As the global population moves toward a broader recognition of, and a deeper concern about, factors of sustainability, the disconnect swells between widespread citizens concerned with creating a good society broadly sustainable in the long run, and the non-sustainable business approach characterized by a focus on short-term profit whose benefit goes to a select few.

The United States is by far the largest and strongest economic global power at this time: by wealth it is the dominant global player. In its globalizing business activities, it exhibits a set of national cultural values, and business values, that endorse a system which benefits a small number who enjoy a great deal while the rest of the populace receives far less. Specific values consistent with this outcome are documented in self-reports of academics reviewed in this chapter's research. Yet this work also shows that the national cultural values and workplace social codes, exhibited by this globally dominant player, are not (or at least not yet) adopted cross nationally, but that there exists nation-based—as well as gender-based and field-based—resistance to those views.

This research therefore contributes a piece of the much larger story of why it may be that business globalization activities seem not to advance the less wealthy nations in the manner that David Ricardo's (1821) theory of comparative advantage predicts and which the World Bank uses as its primary rationale to justify promotion of free trade (World Bank 2002). The role that identities, including national identity and identity of academic field, play in this business globalization pattern of investment, outcomes, and trade emerges as salient.

The field of business is one whose social codes contain significantly lower levels of support for important specific aspects of sustainable economic, democratic, and global development. This view of sustainable vs. unsustainable activity may help explain strong institutional support for international trade policies that have general goals that sound as if they promote economic betterment but have the actual effect of maintaining and exacerbating current wealth disparities (Kacowicz 2007; Rapley 2004; Bourdieu 2003; Milanovic 2007).

All decision makers select choices consistent with personally held culture, values, and social systems of beliefs. When business decision-makers choose actions consistent with economically, politically, and globally unsustainable outcomes that advantage some while not others, laissez-faire policies which permit enactment of those decisions, while hoping for general betterment, are unrealistic at best. One element of awareness that sustainable thinking has taught us already is that realism is an important requisite of measureable progress.

Given that, these results suggest that business decisions will not on average, result in economically, democratically, or globally sustainable global progress leading to good society outcomes on their own. To generate that widespread, more-sustainable result, some type of regulated guidance will be needed, perhaps not unlike those explicitly spelled-out codes that govern aspects of economic, political, and cross-national development within the European Union. Regulations such as these will be required globally, rather than nationally or within a limited trading bloc, to guide business development toward a more economically and politically sustainable, citizen-oriented future where the populace, rather than only business managers, benefit in an ongoing way.

Notes

*The Author would like to thank The College of Saint Rose and the University of Queensland for their research support.

1. Current World Bank data shows 2008 Gross Domestic Product per capita at 46,700 US and 47,400 AU in US Dollars, and Gross National Income per capita at 40,350 US and 47,580 AU, all in U.S. dollars (World Bank 2009).
2. Gender is a critically important consideration in its own right, and a full paper is elsewhere devoted to the intricacies of gender identity, with values relating to these sustainability dimensions, as well as the intersections of these values and identities with income and academic rank. In this paper, where gender is limited to merely a place-holder as a control, these considerations are beyond the scope of this chapter's focus on national identity and academic field.
3. The first wave in November of 2008 was a US postal service mailing, with stamped return envelopes, to a sample of faculty across every department at seven major US universities. 8,795 solicitations were sent in this wave, with faculty names taken from posted University Departmental Website faculty listings; of these, 255 were returned to sender with addressee unknown and 498 were returned fully or partially completed. After cleaning, 444 useable surveys remained. The response rate (498 of the 8540 nonrejected addresses) was 5.83 percent, although it is likely that many of those not returned were also not undeliverable but simply discarded by university departments, rather than returned.The second wave in February of 2009 consisted of 4,908 anonymous surveys with cover letters saluting recipients as AOM colleagues, and business reply envelopes, sent to members of the Academy of Management who were identified as members of either the Business Policy and Strategy or the International Management cluster groups; this mailing list was purchased to over-sample business academics, as some 65 percent of AOM members are academics in business or related fields. Of the surveys sent, 11 were returned to sender as undeliverable and 625 were completed and returned; 547 were useable, for an effective response rate of 12.76 percent.The third wave in April and May of 2009 consisted of 1,442 anonymous surveys distributed either directly into academics' mailboxes, or via campus mail, at two major universities in Australia; these contained cover letters noting local university approval and included campus mail return envelopes. None were returned as undeliverable (presumably these were simply discarded), 419 were returned partially or fully completed of which 349 were entirely useable. This yielded a response rate of 18.67 percent.
4. This rate does raise the concern of nonresponse bias. Unfortunately, no resources were available for follow-up contact; worse, errors in envelope printing omitted a return address on more than half of the

sent envelopes, an error which both decreased the response rate and prevented return-to-sender activity.

References

Adler, N. J., and J. Jermier. 2005. "Developing a Field with More Soul: Standpoint Theory and Public Policy Research for Management Scholars." *Academy of Management Journal* 8: 941–944.

Akerlof, G., and R. Kranton. 2010. "Identity Economics." *The Economists' Voice* 7 (2): 1–3.

Anderson, S., C. Collins, S. Pizzigati, and K. Shih. 2010. *CEO Pay and the Great Recession: 17th Annual Executive Compensation Survey.* Washington, DC: Institute for Policy Studies.

Arlow, P. 1991. "Characteristics in College Students' Evaluations of Business Ethics and Corporate Responsibility." *Journal of Business Ethics* 10: 63–69.

Ashforth, B. E., and F. Mael. 1989. "Social Identity Theory and the Organization." *Academy of Management Review* 14: 20–39.

Barley, S. R., and G. Kunda. 1992. "Design and Devotion: Surges of Rational and Normative Ideologies of Control in Managerial Discourse." *Administrative Science Quarterly* 37: 363–399.

Bell, M. P. 2009. "Introduction: On Evidence, Ethics, Values and Corruption." *Academy of Management Learning and Education* 8 (2): 252–254.

Berger, P. L., and T. Luckmann. 1966. *The Social Construction of Reality.* New York: Doubleday.

Bisin, A., and T. Verdier. 2011. "The Economics of Cultural Transmission and Socialization." In *The Handbook of Social Economics*, edited by J. Benhabib, A. Bisin, and M. Jackson. Elsevier Science.

Bloodgood, J. M., W. H. Turnley, and P. E. Mudrack. 2010. "Ethics Instruction and the Perceived Acceptability of Cheating." *Journal of Business Ethics* 95 (1): 23–37.

Bourdieu, P. 2003. Firing Back: Again the Tyranny of the Market 2. Translated by L. Wacquant. London: Verso.

Branch, S. 1997. "MBAs Are Hot Again." *Fortune* 135 (7): 155–157.

Butler, S. 1998. *The Way of All Flesh.* New York: Random House.

Caldentey, E. Perez. 2006. "The Recent Rise of Bilateral Free Trade Agreements: Issues, Implications and Lessons for the Smaller Economies of Latin America and the Caribbean." Paper presented at the Eastern Economics Association, Boston, March; working paper, Economic Commission for Latin America and the Caribbean (ECLAC).

Callahan, D. 2004. *The Cheating Culture: Why More Americans Are Doing Wrong to Get Ahead.* Orlando: Harcourt.

Caratti, P., and G. Lo Cascio. 2006. "Sustainable Development Policies in Europe." Fondazione Eni Enrico Mattei. FEEM Working Paper No. 152.06.

Carlson, D. K. 2005. "Public Priorities: Environment vs Economic Growth." Gallup Poll. http://www.gallup.com/poll/15820/Public-Priorities-Environment-vs-Economic-Growth.aspx.

Carney, T., and G. Ramia. 2011. "Welfare Support and Sanctions for Non-Compliance in a Recessionary World Labour Market." Sydney Law School Legal Studies Research Paper no. 11/11. http://papers.ssrn.com/sol3/papers.cfm?abstract_id=1753362.

Carr, C., and M. Pudelko. 2006. "Convergence of Management Practices in Strategy, Finance and HRM between the USA, Japan and Germany." *International Journal of Cross Cultural Management* 6 (1): 75–100.

Chevrier, S. 2009. "Is National Culture Still Relevant to Management in a Global Context?" *International Journal of Cross Cultural Management* 9 (2): 169–183.

Derrida, J. 1996. *Monolingualism of the Other or the Prothesis of Origin.* Translated by P. Mensah. Stanford: Stanford University Press.

Dutton, J. E., L. M. Roberts, and J. Bednar. 2010. "Pathways for Positive Identity Construction at Work: Four Types of Positive Identity and the Building of Social Resources." *Academy of Management Review* 35 (2): 265–293.

Eisler, R. 1987. *The Chalice and the Blade.* San Francisco: Harper.

Fraumeni, B. 2011. "Report of the Committee on the Status of Women in the Economics Profession 2010." CSWEP website. http://www.aeaweb.org/committees/cswep/annual_reports.php.

Gallup Wellbeing. 2009. "About One in Six U.S. Adults are Without Health Insurance." http://www.gallup.com/poll/121820/One-Six-Adults-Without-Health-Insurance.aspx.

Gentry, W. A., L. Booysen, K. M. Hannum, and T. J. Weber. 2010. "Leadership Responses to a Conflict of Gender-Based Tension: a Comparison of Responses between Men and Women in the u.s. and South Africa." *International Journal of Cross Cultural Management* 10 (3): 285–301.

Ghoshal, S. 2005. "Bad Management Theories Are Destroying Good Management Practices." *Academy of Management Learning and Education* 4 (1): 75–91.

Giacalone, R. A. 2004. "A Transcendent Business Education for the 21st Century." *Academy of Management Learning and Education* 3 (4): 415–420.

Grote, D. 2009. "Recombinant Slave Equilibria and Their Cure: Living Wage Full Employment." *Review of Social Economy* 67 (2): 175–200.

HCAN. 2011. "Flagging Economy Doesn't Dampen Health Insurers' Excessive Profits." http://healthcareforamericanow.org/site/content/reports/.

Hofstede, G. 2011. *Culture's Consequences: Comparing Values, Behaviors, Institutions and Organizations across Nations.* Thousand Oaks, CA: Sage.

Hong, B. S., and J. P. Shull. 2010. "a Retrospective Study of the Impact Faculty Dispositions Have on Undergraduate Engineering Students." *College Student Journal* 44 (2): 266–278.

Inkpen, A., and K. Ramaswamy. 2006. *Global Strategy: Creating and Sustaining Advantage Across Borders*. New York: Oxford University Press.

Jost, J. T., and B. Major. 2001. *The Psychology of Legitimacy: Emerging Perspectives on Ideology, Justice, and Intergroup Relations*. Cambridge: Cambridge University Press.

Judge, T. A., and R. D. Bretz. 1992. "Effects of Work Values on Job Choice and Decisions." *Journal of Applied Psychology* 77: 261–271.

Kacowicz, A. M. 2007. "Globalization, Poverty, and the North-South Divide." *International Studies Review* 9: 565–580.

Kalliny, M., K. W. Cruthirds, and M. S. Minor. 2006. "Differences between American, Egyptian and Lebanese Humor Styles: Implications for International Management." *International Journal of Cross Cultural Management* 6 (1): 121–134.

Kasser, T. 2002. *The High Price of Materialism*. Cambridge, MA: MIT Press.

Kelan, E. K., and R. D. Jones. 2010. "Gender and the MBA." *Academy of Management Teaching and Learning* 9 (1): 26–43.

Kezar, A. 2001. "Investigating Organizational Fit in a Participatory Leadership Environment." *Journal of Higher Education Policy and Management* 23 (1): 85–101.

Kragh, S. U., and M. Djursaa. 2006. "Modernization and Management." *International Journal of Cross Cultural Management* 6 (1): 19–36.

Krishnan, V. R. 2007. "Impact of MBA Education on Students' Values: Two Longitudinal Studies." *Journal of Business Ethics* 83: 233–246.

Kuh, G. D., and S. Hu. 2001. "The Effects of Student-Faculty Interaction in the 1990s." *Review of Higher Education* 24 (3): 309–332.

Lauring, J., and J. Selmer. 2010. "Multicultural Organizations: Common Language and Group Cohesiveness." *International Journal of Cross Cultural Management* 10 (3): 267–284.

Light, R. J. 2001. *Making the Most of College*. Cambridge, MA: Harvard University Press.

Lincoln, J. R., and A. L. Kalleberg. 1990. *Culture, Control and Commitment*. Cambridge: Cambridge University Press.

Lindholm, J. A. 2003. "Perceived Organizational Fit: Nurturing the Minds, Hearts, and Personal Ambitions of University Faculty." *Review of Higher Education* 27 (1): 125–150.

Lukes, S. Power. 2005. *Power, Second Edition–A Radical View*. 2nd ed. New York: Palgrave Macmillan.

Luthar, H. K., and R. Karri. 2005. "Exposure to Ethics Education and the Perception of Linkage between Organizational Ethical Behavior and Business Outcomes." *Journal of Business Ethics* 61: 353–368.

Mael, F. 1991. "A Conceptual Rationale for Domains and Attributes of Biodata Items." *Personnel Psychology* 44: 763–792.

Maylor, U. 2009. "They Do Not Relate to Black People Like Us: Black Teachers as Role Models for Black Pupils." *Journal of Education Policy* 24 (1): 1–21.

Milanovic, B. 2002. "The Two Faces of Globalization: Against Globalization as We Know It." World Bank Working Paper, Development Research Group. http://papers.ssrn.com/sol3/papers.cfm?abstract_id=320287.

———. 2007. "An Even Higher Global Inequality than Previously Thought: A Note on Global Inequality Calculations Using the 2005 ICP Results." (December 28). World Bank Policy Research Working Paper Series. http://ssrn.com/abstract=1081970.

Mills, C. Wright. 1958. "Psychology and Social Science." *Monthly Review* (October). Reprint December 2009, 61(7): 47–52.

Mitchell, T. R., and W. G. Scott. 1990. "America's Problems and Needed Reforms: Confronting the Ethic of Personal Advantage." *Academy of Management Executive* 4 (3): 23–35.

Mitroff, I. I. 2004. "An Open Letter to the Deans and Faculties of American Business Schools." *Journal of Business Ethics* 54: 185–189.

Nelson, J. A. Feminism. 1996. *Objectivity and Economics*. London: Routledge.

Neubaum, D. O., M. Pagell, J. A. Drexler, Jr., F. M. McKee-Ryan, and E. Larson. 2009. "Business Education and Its Relationship to Student Personal Moral Philosopies and Attitudes toward Profits: An Empirical Response to Critics." *Academy of Management Learning and Education* 8 (1): 9–24.

Petriglieri, G., and J. L. Petriglieri. 2010. "Identity Workspaces: The Case of Business Schools." *Academy of Management Learning and Education* 9 (1): 44–60.

Pew Research Center for the People and Press. 2009. "America's Place in the World Survey." http://people-press.org/questions/?qid=1751787&pid=51&ccid=51#top.

———. 2010. "For Public, Tough Year Ends on a Down Note: Little Progress Seen on Major Domestic Issues." http://people-press.org/report/686/.

Pew Research Center. 2010. "Wide Partisan Divide over Global Warming." http://pewresearch.org/pubs/1780/poll-global-warming-scientists-energy-policies-offshore-drilling-tea-party.

Pillay, S., and N. Dorasamy. 2010. "Linking Cultural Dimensions with the Nature of Corruption: An Institutional Theory Perspective." *International Journal of Cross Cultural Management* 10 (3): 363–378.

Power, M. 2004. "Social Provisioning as a Starting Point for Feminist Economics." *Feminist Economics* 10 (3): 3–19.

Pratt, M. G. 2000. "The Good, the Bad, and the Ambivalent: Managing Identification among Amway Distributors." *Administrative Science Quarterly* 45: 456–493.

Rapley, J. 2004. *Globalization and Inequality: Neoliberalism's Downward Spiral*. London: Lynne Rienner.

Reisinger, Y., and J. C. Crotts. 2010. "Applying Hofstede's National Culture Measures in Tourism Research." *Journal of Travel Research* 49 (2): 153–164.

Ricardo, D. 1821. *On the Principles of Political Economy and Taxation.* London: John Murray.

Ridgeway, C. L. 1997. "Interaction and the Conservation of Gender Inequality: Considering Employment." *American Sociological Review* 62 (April): 218–235.

Rynes, S. L., and C. Q. Trank. 1999. "Behavioral Science in the Business School Curriculum: Teaching in a Changing Institutional Environment." *Academy of Management Review* 24 (4): 808–824.

Salaman, G., and K. Thompson. 1980. *Control and Ideology in Organizations.* Cambridge, MA: MIT Press.

Saunders, P., T. Hill, and B. Bradbury. 2008. "Poverty in Australia." Social Policy Research Centre Report 4/08, Australian Council of Social Services.

Siau, K., J. Erickson, and F. F. Nah. 2010. "Effects of National Culture on Types of Knowledge Sharing in Virtual Communities." *IEEE Transactions on Professional Communication* 53 (3): 278–292.

Spitz, J. 2011. "Academy of Management Then and Now: Values and Beliefs among Business Academics." Working paper.

Stiglitz, J. 2006. *Making Globalization Work.* New York: W. W. Norton.

Tamkins, T. 2009. "Medical Bills Prompt More Than 60% of u.s. Bankruptcies." CNNHealth. http://articles.cnn.com/2009-06-05/health/bankruptcy.medical.bills_1_medical-bills-bankruptcies-health-insurance?_s=PM:HEALTH.

Uysal, O. 2010. "Business Ethics Research with an Accounting Focus." *Journal of Business Ethics* 93 (1): 137–160.

Villegas, A. M. 2007. "Dispositions in Teacher Education." *Journal of Teacher Education* 58 (5): 370–380.

Wittrock, M. C. 1992. "Generative Learning Processes of the Brain." *Educational Psychologist* 27 (4): 531–542.

World Bank. 2002. *Development, Trade and the WTO: A Handbook.* Washington, DC: World Bank.

———. 2009. "Key Development Data and Statistics." http://web.worldbank.org/WBSITE/EXTERNAL/DATASTATISTICS/0,,contentMDK:20535285~menuPK:1390200~pagePK:64133150~piPK:64133175~theSitePK:239419,00.html.

Part III

Economic Development, Employment, and Good Society

Chapter 7

Not Just Fun and Games: Reconceptualizing the Role of Young People in Economic Development

K. Maeve Powlick

> *[N]o matter how consistent and effective a parent you think you are,* your child is separate from you. *In the end, he will make his own decisions. Your job is to use every opportunity you have during his youth to teach him how to make good choices—and why... You are teaching your child to "be in charge of me" in a way that is thoughtful and wise. This is the essence of being a mature adult... [C]hildren determine their own futures and affect others' as well.*
>
> *The Successful Child* by
> Dr. William Sears, Martha Sears, and
> E. Pantley (2002, 148, emphasis in original).

Introduction

A good society is one where people, including young people, are able to participate in decisions that affect them. This is especially important regarding economic development policy, which directly impacts the ability of people to make a living, support a family, and make choices about employment and career. The understanding of children as people, who make choices affecting themselves, others, and the future, is limited in economic analysis.

> Children tumble out of every category economists try to put them in. They have been described as consumer durables providing a flow of utility to their parents, investment goods providing income, and public goods with both positive and negative externalities. Children are also people, with certain rights to life, liberty, and the pursuit of happiness (Folbre 1994, 86).

Folbre makes a strong case for treating children as public goods, producing benefits that accrue to those other than providers of caring labor. Raising the next generation also produces the important public good of the perpetuation of the species. Children act both as capital (the produced means of production) and as assets used to generate income. However, as Folbre asserts, children are also people. They are active participants in the public goods generation process of which they themselves are a public good. Children make economic choices, they build capabilities, and they enact agency in ways that affect institutions relevant to the economy. Raising children is intimately connected to development in the long-term—a "long-term" time frame is intergenerational.

Below I discuss the active involvement of young people in economic development as an important component of a good society. I approach development from a human development perspective, building on Sen's (1983, 1985) concept of capabilities. First, I discuss the mixed-method study from which data is drawn to support my arguments in this chapter, involving youth programs in New York State. Then, I address the issue of why it is important to consider young people when addressing economic development at the community level. I address the role of young people as economic actors in the community, and the ways youth settings and informal institutions contribute to development through a coevolution of individuals and institutions discussed.[1] I use after-school programs, also called Out-of-School Time or OST programs, as an example. The third section addresses how to proceed in order to involve young people in economic development, first discussing the degree to which meaningful participation is ignored in decision-making in local economic development policy and standards for creating participatory structures. I then discuss two examples of how young people are included in development through their participation in community change projects and the fostering of agency. Again, both of these are examples of the coevolution between individuals and institutions.

In a good society, people are able to make choices for themselves and are able to successfully enact those choices. The ability to do so is cultivated in youth and involves not only individual beliefs, values, and assets but also institutional constraints. By promoting the agency of youth, informal institutions promote long-term development through both individual and institutional channels, providing young people with skills to consciously challenge institutions that influence and potentially limit their lives.

Data on Youth Programs in Communities of Concentrated Poverty

Throughout the chapter I support my arguments with qualitative data generated through a multi-year, mixed-methods research project with OST programs for youth living in communities of concentrated poverty in New York State, funded through 21st Century Community Learning Centers (21st CCLC) grants.[2] This research included qualitative research with five 21st CCLC programs—the Harvey Milk High School (HMHS) academic enrichment program in lower Manhattan, the Youth for Real programs at an elementary and middle school in the South Bronx, the school-run program at Yonkers Middle School, the BOCES program at an elementary school in rural Otsego County, and the YMCA program at an elementary school in Albany. I conducted a minimum of three site visits at each program, working with research assistants at Skidmore College. These visits included observation, interviews, and focus groups with youth and staff. In addition, I maintained a more intensive relationship with HMHS and Youth for Real. Over the course of one academic year, I taught a weekly Participatory Action Research class at HMHS, including in-class discussion, the creation of a survey conducted by students in Union Square and Washington Square Park, and the collaborative creation of a half-hour long documentary that was screened at the school. I worked with Youth for Real for more than two years, conducting many hours of observation, interviews, and focus groups with staff, participants, and parents.

Young People and Economic Development

Raising children is an integral part of community development, including economic development. As discussed in the introduction, however, children are often not treated as economic actors if at all in economic literature. In this section, I explore the relationship between community, economic development, and children. I then discuss the importance of assets to low-income communities, including human and social capital, and the ways young people participate in building these assets. Explored in detail are informal institutions, especially OST programs, which are a site of adult-youth partnership and a vehicle for building assets in low-income communities.

Children and Community

Community can be defined as "a group of people who interact directly, frequently, and in multi-faceted ways" (Bowles and Gintis 2002). Youth participating in focus groups in the Bronx defined community as "all around" and "surrounding" them. One child offered the definition "people gathering and telling each other about projects," identifying community as a place of action. The market, the state, and the community are institutions that each perform different economic functions well. Markets are good at producing easily tradable, tangible goods when there is a minimum of externalities, and the state is the only institution capable of providing large-scale public goods, such as transportation networks (Bowles 2004). The community, however, is often the best institution to govern common pool resources (Ostrom 1991, 1999; Ostrom et al. 1999). Another function best accomplished by the community—the site of long-lasting relationships, multifaceted interaction, small geography, and real and fictive kinship relations—is caring for and supporting the development of children. Young people play an important role in the economy at the community level, through their participation in nonmarket productive activities (such as caring for siblings, helping neighbors, etc.) and their participation in collective action. Additionally, many children's activities are capability building, developing both human and social capital. During focus groups at two statewide trainings of 21st CCLC staff, I asked participants to define development. Over and over these youth workers defined development as working with youth and providing them with increased opportunities.

Building Assets for Community Development

Communities of concentrated poverty are limited in the assets they may use to accomplish economic development. Natural, human, and social capital provide the foundation for community-based development, although they are not typically thought of as assets in poor communities. Poor communities are especially limited in natural capital, such as safe public space (Boyce and Pastor 2001; Sampson 1999; Sampson, Sharkey, and Raudenbush 2007). School buildings are often a key natural asset, although they are also likely to have problems such as lead paint, unsanitary bathrooms, and a lack of appropriate technology (Noguera 2003). Extending the use of school buildings by keeping them open for OST programs democratizes access to this aspect of the commons, increasing the ability for individuals to use the asset productively.[3]

Human and social capital, likewise, are often treated as a problem rather than an asset for poor communities, but these assets are built intergenerationaly through raising children. Social capital is important for building human capital (Coleman 1988). This is especially true for children, who need support in every area of their development, including social relationships, in order to successfully develop their human capital (Tsoi-a-Fatt 2008). Young people rely on relationships with others to meet their basic needs, and youth in poor communities may have few if any other assets of their own. Social capital refers to social connections that facilitate economic behavior—most simply it has been labeled trust (Dasgupta 2005). Because one person cannot own social capital, it may more appropriately be termed "community governance" (Bowles and Gintis 2002) or "social cohesion" (as used by Sampson [1999]). Good community governance means that a community is able to maintain its norms and values, and is able to engage in collective action when necessary.

Human and social capital can both take many forms, some of which are scarce in poor communities. Youth in communities of concentrated poverty may have excellent street smarts, but are simultaneously lacking in the formal education that would allow them to obtain highly paid work. Investing in formal education may be subject to a disincentive if the only work opportunities they see available are in the black market. While poor urban and rural youth possess social capital imbedded in a network of friends and caregivers, their social capital is less likely to provide them with access to resources that can help them escape poverty, such as finding a job (Payne 2001; Durlaf 2002; Dasgupta 2005). Community-specific social capital is also likely to be bonding social capital, and is less useful for economic development than bridging social capital, which facilitates building new relationships across difference.

Informal Institutions and Development

Informal institutions[4] such as youth programs are necessary to capitalize on assets available in poor communities, leveraging them to generate, maintain, and utilize social capital, and to provide public goods underprovided by the state, including education in communities with failing schools. They also facilitate the utilization of social capital to engage in collective action and can strengthen formal institutions as well. For example, many after-school programs include partnership between community based organizations (CBOs) and public schools, including a liaison who works at the school during the day. Program directors spoke in interviews about using these relationships to advocate for struggling children and to suggest curricular changes in Schools in Need of Improvement (SINI).

In other cases, informal institutions can mitigate ongoing problems, such as a lack of parental involvement, with the school. Parents may face barriers to participation in their children's education due to immigration status, language barriers, fear, and negative attitudes held by teachers and school administrators (McDermott and Rothenberg 2004). Several parents at a focus group at Youth for Real lamented that, while they feel they have good relationships with the Youth for Real program, they cannot say the same of the school. They were able to explain in detail what their child does in the after-school program but could not offer the same information for day school activities. By developing parent relationships in the CBOs, children can reap the benefits of increased parental involvement in their education even as the institutional barriers with schools remain.

OST Programs and the Work of Community Development

Because of their difference from schools, after-school programs or OST programs can act in the role of "community as family," which has been important in African American communities since Emancipation (Barkely Brown 2000, 124). After-school programs do not assign grades, allowing children to work together in peer groups without evaluation or competition, and OST practitioners tend to follow different pedagogies than in schools, deemphasizing the role of teacher as source of knowledge (Rahm and Grimes 2005). A teacher participating in a focus group at the Yonkers Middle School program stated: "The fact that there is less stress after school allows them the freedom to express themselves more openly and maybe even take some chances that they don't take during the regular school." Parents and youth in my research identified opportunities for *expression* as important components of their after-school program—music, dance, and art programs that have been cut from schools in low-income communities.

OST programs also provide other benefits related to building human and social capital. For example, many Spanish-monolingual parents at Youth for Real stated that homework help was one of the most important benefits of the program because they were unable to help their children themselves. High quality after-school programs have also been found to strengthen social skills (Durlak and Weissberg 2007), which was echoed in my research—when asked what their children learned at Youth for Real, one parent offered "*a compartir*," and another proudly stated: "Well, basically she was very timid, very shy. Now I can't control her. I cannot say this is this, because she sort of knows it is this way. Now she is very opinionated."

Human and social capital are built, not depleted, through use. By providing help for homework, academic enrichment, and support for the many interlocking aspects of youth development, after-school programs foster the acquisition of human capital. They also support social capital, bringing youth together to engage in "transformative work" in a nonschool environment (Townsend 2003, 3) and developing constructive relationships between youth and adults (Butcher 2004). Moreover, some programs engage in conscious efforts to develop social capital, providing youth with opportunities for service learning, volunteering, lobbying, and other forms of activism. Informal institutions such as these OST programs provide one of the key pathways through which young people may participate in economic development. Participatory decision-making, however, is neither common nor easy. The next section addresses the absence of participation in local development policy, as well as two examples of participatory development being accomplished through OST programs with low-income youth in New York State.

Participation in Economic Development

The Lack of Participation in Economic Development Policy-Making

The economic development policy practiced in communities throughout the United States is rarely participatory in nature, sometimes going to the opposite extreme. Eve Weinbaum (2004) did extensive interviews with local economic development officials in the Appalachian region of the United States from 1992 to 1995, titling her chapter on economic development policy "Selling Poverty." Unfortunately, the type of policy she describes is not limited to this region. She describes how economic development policy-makers formed private entities with questionable legality in order to avoid any public input (44) because "privatization of economic development puts industry at ease" (52). As one interviewee stated, describing such a private entity, "decision-making processes tend to be closed until the project is about to be consummated" (20). When asked to define democracy, one city manager said, "I don't know what to say. It didn't cross my mind. Lord, I guess I've really never thought about it. I haven't heard that word in so long, I thought you was cussing or something! Thought it was a cuss word!" (59). Another defined democracy as anarchy (61). Attitudes Weinbaum identified among the policy-makers involved in her study include: a belief that any job is worthwhile, no matter what the ratio of benefit-to-cost is or the length of time a business stays in the area (55); the legitimacy of luring jobs away from other communities, even as close as the next county over (46); business, rather than tax payers, as the constituents of development policy-makers (53); and a firm belief in the "magic" of the market, even though policy-makers themselves have a hard time fully explaining such magic (59). The policy goals among Weinbaum's interviewees were to make their communities look attractive to businesses, portraying workers as compliant, willing to accept any jobs at any pay, uninterested in unions, and racially homogenous—that is, white (see pp. 29, 31, 32, and 49). Weinbaum concludes that the economic development policy, at least in this portion of the American south, relies on people remaining poor and desperate (56).

This type of nonparticipatory, business-focused development policy is supported by much research in the field of local development policy. For example, Feiock and Cable (1992), building on the empirical work by Sharp (1991), found that the relationship between need and economic development policy "is stronger when the process is closed rather than open" (397). They defined economic development policy as the number of incentives offered to businesses, implicitly treated as the only type of policy available. Thus, their results mean that poorer communities were likely to offer more incentives to businesses when there is a lack of participation in the development process. Likewise, Sharp (1991) offers a list of economic development policies under study—"ranging from loans, tax abatements, and other financial incentives to infrastructure improvements, zoning reform, and promotional activity" (129), otherwise known as "corporate welfare" (Weinbaum 2004, 34)—and investigates differences in the application of these policies, not questioning whether the policies are the best ones to address community problems. Feiock and Kim (2000) addresses the role of democracy, arguing that reformed governments (more insulated from political elections) issue development policy more responsive to economic interests while unreformed governments (less insulated from political elections) are more likely to be influenced by political incentives—but this chapter also fails to question the nature of economic development policy in the first place.

When economic development policy is focused on attracting jobs at any cost, even if those jobs are miserable and low paying, it would seem obvious that a good society requires a different type of policy. The capabilities approach to development offers another perspective, where development is a continual process involving both adults and young people. By definition, building capabilities is a participatory process—one cannot build a capability to be or do something for someone else without their cooperation and participation. Sen (2000a) argues that participation is one of the most important freedoms to be maintained in the development process: "Among the opportunities that we have reason to value is the freedom to participate. If participatory deliberations were to be hindered or weakened, something of value would be lost" (5).

Fostering Effective Participation of Children

When community members do participate in economic development, there are many important questions that need to be addressed. "Have all the social actors the same importance (i.e. weight)? Should some veto power be conceded to minorities? Are income distribution effects important?" (Munda 2004, 667). Moreover, effective participation goes beyond "verification processes" to "creation processes" where stakeholders have power over the decisions at hand (ibid.). Creation implies that stakeholders can come up with new alternatives and are involved in changing the nature of evaluation and decision-making through an iterative, "learning," or adductive process. Policy evaluation and decision-making is not a one-shot interaction. Iterative processes are also advocated by Sen (2000b). Using participation in a creative rather than verification function requires transparency in the decision making process. When participation is at a surface level only, it can be disempowering to participants, further alienating them (Munda 2004; Weinbaum 2004).

It is especially challenging to encourage effective participation of young people. Even in programs that value youth empowerment, there is a tendency to limit the power young people have over the program due to a belief that the adults know what is best—interviewees cited fears of "chaos," especially if children are allowed to choose what they do on a daily basis. Respecting adult wisdom and acknowledging adult responsibility for youth does not require limiting youth participation to verification processes. Munda (2004) offers five key lessons regarding participation that can be gleaned from experiences in Multi-Criteria Evaluation, each of which has relevance for the participation of youth: (1) the relationship between decision maker and analyst is always embedded in a social framework, (2) a variety of participatory methods, such as those used in qualitative research, should be combined, (3) a cyclic or iterative evaluation process is necessary to incorporate learning by the scientific team undertaking the study, which allows for "continuous testing of assumptions and unavoidable biases of the study team," (4) the first step in the process should be an analysis of the relevant institutions in order to identify stakeholders, and (5) the decision analysts/study team should not accept participatory inputs uncritically, as such a process may leave out some important social actors and/or privilege the voices of certain actors (670–671).

Young people are part of the social framework within which decision makers and decision analysts are involved. The role of children in relevant institutions and the impact of institutions on youth behavior are both relevant. A variety of participatory methods can help elicit the most useful participation of young people, as some children may be best able to offer their insights in one-on-one interviews, some in group discussions/focus groups or a formal Youth Advisory Board, some in brainstorming where individual participation is subject to less attention, and some in informal settings such as participant-observation. Using these various methods, decision analysts can process the inputs that come from young people to understand their deeper significance. For example, children might say they think the program should serve ice cream for snacks, and the underlying factor behind this statement may be that they do not like the food being served. After processing this information, the decision makers can go back to young people in a cyclic manner, with a partial list of snacks more acceptable than ice cream and ask children for their input. With young children especially, priming the pump can greatly increase the number of ideas generated in brainstorms and discussions, and starting with a partial list may jumpstart a productive conversation to learn what type of healthy snacks would be appealing to the children involved. Working with children takes creativity, patience, and a willingness to communicate at their level, but doing so can reap great rewards when young people are given the chance to experience ownership over decisions and rules that affect them—including greater engagement, cooperation, and enthusiasm (Sears, Sears, and Pantley 2002).

What follows is two examples of development activity involving children, both of which utilize participatory processes. These examples highlight the complex, coevolutionary relationship between change in individuals and change in institutions. First, many youth workers incorporate goals of "community change" into their programming, which impacts both children and the community directly. Second, the development of the important "capability" of agency impacts children directly and impacts the community when children enact their agency.

Community Change and Free Choice

Increasing the capabilities of young people increases the range of choices available to them, which in effect increases their freedom. As Sen (1985) argues, it is important not only to consider the choices that individuals make but also the range of choices that are available to them, and this is nowhere more apparent than with life choices made by young people living in poor communities. The range of choices available to youth is a characteristic of the institutions that influence and potentially limit their lives. A choice to stay in a decaying neighborhood is very different when it is an active choice based on evaluation of multiple alternatives than when it is a passive choice due to a lack of other options. This is something well-known to community workers and is highlighted in Sara Hill's (2004) article on Sweet Cove and Waterside Homes, when she quotes the executive director of Harmony Center:

> A role for Harmony Center is transition. Not so much to get kids out, as to mentally get out. If they decide that [this village] is their home and they want to live here for the rest of their lives, and they've made good choices where they want to go in life, I'm happy. So they don't necessarily have to leave the area...or leave Waterside or Sweet Cove Homes, but they should know that there's another world, and go out and explore it, and then when they say, "This is my home," I'm happy with that (7).

Another way to view this individual/institution duality is the importance of not only making good choices but also having the ability and resources to successfully enact those choices. Young people living in communities of concentrated poverty face many constraints on their choices, including a lack of knowledge about the true extent of choices available to them and a lack of resources to enact adaptive choices, such as the choice to seek higher education. The isolation of living in housing projects, for example, has well-documented effects on young people (Pratt Center for Community Development 2009, Furman Center for Real Estate and Urban Policy at NYU 2010, Schwartz et al. 2010). If the most successful members of their community leave, the field of view is further limited—if the only people a young person knows who went to college are in no better shape financially than those who did not go to college, or possibly even those who did not graduate from high school, college will not seem like a viable choice for improving their economic wellbeing.

Young people living in concentrated poverty may also believe it is impossible for them to attend college at all. This issue emerged among students in my Participator Action Research (PAR) class at HMHS, several of whom discussed their perceptions of insurmountable financial constraints to seeking higher education. The principal of the school agreed that one of the biggest challenges in encouraging attendance and graduation is the lack of hope for a college education. The returns to a high school diploma are much less than the returns to a college degree, especially for youth of color (Gamoran 2001), and so students who do not believe they will be able to earn a college degree may see little value in graduating from high school at all. Thus, the real or perceived inability to successfully enact adaptive choices can lead young people to dismiss life choices that have the most potential to build capabilities. Programs and policies directed at youth opportunity must focus both on the individual capacity for adaptive choice and on institutional constraints that limit feasible choices for young people.

OST programs such as 21st CCLC include objectives with both an individual focus on facilitating and teaching good decision-making and objectives with an institutional focus of increasing the feasible range of choices available to youth, many of which overlap. Examples include internships, creative work, part-time jobs, and college application support, all of which are demanded by adolescents participating in youth programs (Wahl Moellman and Rosenbaum Tillinger 2004). There are also programs specifically targeted at activism or advocacy, founded on the belief that these types of experiences are valuable for both youth and their community. One example is the Juvenile Justice organizations highlighted in Austria (2006), where young people who have been involved in the juvenile justice system are engaged in lobbying trips and other advocacy programs directly related to their own problems and challenges.

The Community Change Project at Youth for Real is another example of a program with an explicit community focus, where elementary and middle school youth spend an entire academic year analyzing and engaging in community action on an issue chosen by each group at the start of the project. As a culmination, the program hosts a rally involving parents, other family members, and friends. In interviews, most parents stated they participated in this rally annually, even if they did not participate in the program in any other way. As one staff member describes the project, "I think one of the strengths of this program is that it really is trying to instill in young people a set of core sort of character development principles that we hope will lead them and stay with them throughout their lives—and time will tell there." The activism is directed at the community, including a target population identified by youth in the program, but the goals of the project are to positively impact the young activists as well.

Additionally, program staff from multiple sites repeatedly stated an objective of giving youth who are failing in school a place to excel, thereby earning deserved praise from adults. Receiving deserved praise is an important developmental asset for young people (Scales and Leffert 1999). When young people are failing in school, they continually receive negative messages from teachers and other authority figures, which limit their beliefs about their own abilities and the range of choices open to them. OST programs provide a community setting where young people can form meaningful relationships with adults, providing them with a new opportunity to be valued for who they are.

This expansion of choices leads to increased freedom when young people not only get to make choices for themselves but also are able to influence the institutions that limit the range of choices available to them. Agency, defined by one after school practitioner as working past structures (Lyons 2000), is a skill required to effect such institutional change.

Agency and Voice as a Means and an End

Agency is both a method for producing institutional change and an important capability itself. When young people are in situations that limit their choices, agency can be used to work past these limiting structures, thereby expanding their capabilities. While agency is more than simply using voice, the use of voice is important in achieving the goals of agency-led action. In *Exit, Voice, and Loyalty:*

Responses to Decline in Firms, Organizations, and States, Albert Hirschman (1970) started with the analogy of the firm: when customers are dissatisfied with a decline in quality of products, they may either leave the firm and do business with another (exit), or they may let the managers know they are upset (voice). Both mechanisms, according to Hirschman, may induce a firm or other organization to improve quality if they are applied in the right amounts at the right time, but this balance is difficult to achieve. The situation Hirschman described as having inspired the book was one in which there was just enough exit so that the national railway in Nigeria could remain inefficient. The customers who might have been the most vocal and persuasive were leaving to use other means of transportation, and so the rail management was not pressured to fix its problems. At the same time, Hirschman argued that voice is most effective when it is not overly harassing and most potent when combined with a threat of exit. While exit may induce change, it does not provide a mechanism for directing that change, and the agent who exited the organization does not get to enjoy any changes that are made.

The Housing and Urban Development program Moving to Opportunity is an example of a policy that utilizes exit in response to concentrated poverty, requiring families in the program to move to communities with poverty rates under 10 percent. However, participants leave behind communities no less concentrated in poverty. Young people rarely have the option of exercising exit on their own, whether in response to their community as a whole or in response to specific institutions like their schools. Additionally, poor communities are not actors the same way firms are. They are an amorphous collection of individuals and institutions and, while individuals engage in conscious action, the aggregate results of evolutionary changes are most likely not the direct result of individual choices (Bowles 2004). Unlike a firm, a poor community cannot "respond" to the exit of some of its residents because there is no one to enact the response. Participation in changes and development requires the effective use of voice.

Youth have voices, but for these voices to translate into agency and to motivate development, they must develop the character of their voices (Ellsworth 1994) as well as receive an adequate response to their voices (Dowdy and Golden 2004). These are interrelated goals (Weinbaum 2004). Both aspects of the use of voice—character (individual) and response (institutional)—impact the way speakers will be changed by it. Youth develop the character of their voices and learn what types of responses to expect not only in settings such as families, schools, and after-school programs but also in gangs and juvenile detention facilities. Low-income youth often experience harsher reactions from police than those from more affluent communities (Sampson and Bartusch 1999). Their attitudes about law enforcement will be different if they are discussing the problem in a youth gang or in a 21st CCLC program. If impassioned voices are ignored, the experience can be disempowering and discouraging, and for the opposite to be true, voices must be heard by those with the power to act on the demands of the dissatisfied (Weinbaum 2004). Additionally, it is important for the critical use of voice to move beyond the rhetoric of personal betrayal to address the deeper causes of a problem (ibid.). When the use of voice is empowering and effective, voice is a tool for exercising agency.

Defined above as working past structures (Lyons 2000), agency is also conceptualized as "deliberate public participation in decision-making and collective action," but this definition should be expanded to include "more complex ways of understanding agency in collective action as deeply relational, and constituted by routine practice as well as purposive action" (Cleaver 2007, 223). Changes in routine practice include habits, norms, and culture.

While everyone has the capacity for agency, not everyone will be able to act upon their agency and watch those actions become fruitful. Power relationships limit the ability to engage in effective agency both because of the self-disciplining that goes along with following norms, the "acceptance of relations of inequality . . . [that] may ensure the reproduction of power through everyday acts and relationships," (230) and because of roadblocks such as a lack of access to resources, stereotyping, and discrimination. The development of effective agency requires a coevolutionary relationship between individual agency and institutions that support its effectiveness.

Youth are in an unusual position vis-à-vis power, because their position is shifting—they are a people-in-process. The self-discipline of norms and structure is about "knowing ones place" (235), and this is something that children are still in the process of learning, while also simultaneously determining what that place will be. Moreover, they have not yet experienced the disillusionment and frustration of failed attempts to exercise agency. If they are provided with opportunities for successful agency, such as in youth program with an "agency culture," they have the opportunity to build a foundation of experience to apply agency in more challenging situations later on (Lyons 2000).

While many who work with youth have objectives of increasing the agency of youth or of empowering them, the definitions they use of these terms differ. Empowerment and agency are often treated as synonymous. Rahm and Grimes (2005) identify providing youth with opportunities to earn a wage and/or operate within a business structure as empowerment. Wilcox, Lazarre-White, and Warwin (2004) identify positive individual experiences, such as celebrating rites of passage, as empowering. Others identify the importance of providing youth with the opportunity to use their critical voices and produce transformative work as empowerment (Soep 2006; Townsend 2003). There are many other examples of programs with objectives to empower youth, such as debate leagues (Hall 2006), political lobbying activities (Austria 2006; Blank, Friedman, and Carlson 2006), and media literacy and filmmaking skills (Fanscali and Nevarez 2005).

Program staff in my study defined empowerment in many different ways, mostly centering around the idea of choice—a common thread in interviews is that youth empowerment involves allowing youth to choose what they want to do, such as choosing their activities from a list on a given afternoon. Some interviewees, such as at the YMCA program in Albany, NY, included allowing youth input into choosing what activities could go on the list itself as an element of empowerment and agency. Many programs and researchers highlight the importance of including youth in program development and governance (Lyons 2000; Butcher 2004; Hill 2004). Involving youth in the creation of knowledge has also been recognized as both important and empowering (Fanscali and Nevarez 2005; Wahl Moellman and Rosenbaum Tillinger 2004).

At HMHS, the agency of youth is supported by providing an environment where youth are free to express themselves outside the boundaries of heteronormativity, challenging a culture that constrains their expression of identity and enacting agency through changes in every day practice. Students in my PAR class had different reasons for choosing HMHS, but all of them were at risk of dropping out before applying to transfer. One student faced violent threats and discrimination because of his transgendered identity, while another explained that he faced the same because of his homosexuality. Other students choose not to identify with older LGBT (lesbian, gay, bisexual, and transgender) labels, but dress and date how they please, fluidly crossing and recrossing boundaries of gender expression and sexual orientation. HMHS provides students with a school setting where they can be themselves without conflicts and danger over their expression of identity dominating their educational experience. In the survey we conducted in Washington Square Park and Union Square, several respondents said they believed HMHS would help to create LGBT leaders—in later discussions, students identified these responses as a source of pride for themselves.

Agency is also supported through involving youth in activism, outside of daily practice. The agency of youth is supported at Inwood House's Youth for Real programs in the Bronx by engaging young people in the Community Change Project. Youth from kindergarten through middle school work in age-segregated groups to conduct a deep analysis of a problem in their community, eventually choosing a specific action they believe will help alleviate the problem. They are encouraged to distinguish between the symptoms and causes of the problem, and to distinguish between actions that address the symptoms and those that address deeper causes. Youth for Real exposes youth and their guardians to activism, often for the first time.

These types of experiences, I would argue, differ from an empowerment project, like the gardening business discussed in Rahm and Grimes (2005), because rather than seeking to fit youth into adult roles in an existing structure—in this case, giving them their first job—youth are being taught to assume more adult roles while simultaneously challenging the structure itself in a conscious, self-critical way.

While fostering agency is clearly important to many youth workers, there are obstacles to its achievement. Participants may have basic needs that must be addressed, and there may be a real or perceived trade-off between meeting these needs and meeting higher-order needs such as developing agency. One day when I was observing the kindergarten group at Youth for Real, there were several children in tears at the beginning of the afternoon, prior to receiving the hot snack they are served every day. Two children said they had toothaches. One boy said he had not eaten anything all day, although he had access to free lunch—he said the food tasted bad. Two children complained of other health problems, a stomachache and a headache. One girl was tired and wanted to go home so she could take a nap, which she is not allowed to do during the school day. Regardless of other programming possibilities, these children required that their needs be met before they were able to listen, participate, and think about the activities they were doing.

Another barrier to developing agency is its widespread absence in the daily experiences of youth (Lyons 2000). Settings of agency culture are difficult to find for low-income youth faced with punitive social policy and schools that increasingly resemble prisons (Noguera 1995). Along with giving youth a place to excel, changing the "culture," "mindset," and "values" of youth is a common goal articulated by after-school program staff, including line staff, site coordinators, and program directors. When youth programs providing agency culture operate in a climate with few other sources of such culture, they may be unable to achieve their stated objectives, no matter how high the quality of their program and staff. Behaviors and norms related to youth are density dependent and thereby subject to unpredictable positive feedback effects (Himmelweit 2000). By increasing the density of norms they wish to produce, after-school programs can promote change as "successful failures" even if they do not achieve their stated objectives, laying groundwork for future activism, as Eve Weinbaum argues occurred around plant closures in rural Appalachia in the 1990s.

> Organizing campaigns that scholars and journalists alike would have labeled as failures, in fact led to institution-building, activist networks, and long-term coalitions to protest economic injustice and develop public policies. These failures were the early battle-grounds in which men and women developed the strategies, arguments, and methods for the larger struggles to come. Failures, in retrospect, were actually critical turning points that created the conditions for later success. By closely studying these nascent grassroots social movements, this research points toward new avenues for labor and community activism around the global economy. (Weinbaum 2004, 8)

The success in successful failures with youth occurs when young people build capabilities, learn to exercise their voices and have early experiences of success doing so, and go on to the next stages in their lives with a strong sense of agency.

Conclusion

Youth are important to community economic development, which must leverage the assets available to low-income communities, including public space like public school buildings, human and social capital, and informal institutions including CBOs. Involving youth in development requires substantive participation in decision-making, which is both new and difficult. Examples of participatory development with young people, enacted by OST programs, include programs focused on creating community change and activities to develop agency among youth. Both of these approaches lead to changes in individuals, especially the children and families involved, as well as institutions, including local culture and norms.

Youth programs that build capabilities, expand the range of choices available to youth, develop effective youth voice, and promote youth agency are an important component of participatory community-based development. Programs already performing these functions should be valued for such, but those activities are rarely included in evaluations. In the case of 21st CCLC, evaluations tend to be limited to changes in grades, test scores, and teacher reports. Improving the evaluation of youth programs with the potential not only to impact individuals but also to promote community-based development requires a paradigm shift in evaluation research—more than just a new "formula" for incorporating benefits not easily quantified (Ackerman and Heinzerling 2004). Methods such as Multi-Criteria Evaluation and Benefits Analysis, which include qualitative data, offer a starting point for such methodological change (Burgha 2004; Mathieson 2004; Munda 2004).

Additionally, the role of young people should be included in economic development theory. A better understanding of the behavior, choices, and rationality of youth would greatly improve models and theories of long-term development. Improved theory is important for including young people in local economic development policy, because policy-makers often take their cues from theorists. Local economic development policy requires a drastic overhaul in order to meet the ideals of a good society. As policy hopefully becomes more participatory, young people should not be left out. When the participation of youth is part of the policy debate, it facilitates moving the discussion beyond a narrow range of policies limited to subsidies, tax breaks, and other business incentives—such a change is good not only for young people but also for whole communities.

The world being created by today's business-focused development policies will not be enjoyed by the current development officials or their critics—instead it will be enjoyed, for better or worse, by our children. Children also participate in creating that future world, whether their choices are understood and encouraged by economists or not. The capabilities built by young people today will determine how they will utilize and interact with the institutional environment of their adulthood. Moreover, young people can have an impact on that institutional environment itself. Young people are especially important in communities of concentrated poverty, which are lacking in assets. Young people energized with a sense of agency are themselves assets for community development. The promotion of youth agency addresses both individual and institutional aspects of community development and, cumulatively in the long-term, is an important part of creating a good society.

Notes

1. The importance of coevolutionary processes in social change is discussed at length by Bowles (2004).
2. In addition to the qualitative data used in this paper, the research project included quantitative analysis of data on 735 programs in New York State. See Powlick (2011).
3. See the Natural Assets Project—Boyce and Pastor 2001.
4. In my usage of the term "informal institution," I am following Goeffrey Hodgson and Calatrava (2006) who define it as institutions with no direct relationship to the government, that is, those not codified in law.

Bibliography

Ackerman, F., and L. Heinzerling. 2004. Priceless: On Knowing the Price of Everything and the Value of Nothing. New York: New Press.

Austria, R. 2006. "Toward a Movement: Uniting Organizers and Direct Service Providers in a Movement for Juvenile Justice Reform." *Afterschool Matters* 5: 20–40.

Barkley Brown, E. 2000. "To Catch the Vision of Freedom: Reconstructing Southern Black Women's Political History, 1865–1880." In *Unequal Sisters: A Multicultural Reader in U.S. Women's History*, edited by Ellen DuBois and Vicki Ruiz. Amherst: University of Massachusetts Press, 124–146.

Blank, S., L. Friedman, and K. Carlson. 2006. "Democracy in Action: Experiential Civics Learning in after School Advocacy Days." *Afterschool Matters* 5: 5–29.

Bowles, S. 2004. *Microeconomics: Behavior, Institutions, and Evolution*. New York: Russell Sage Foundation.

Bowles, S., and H. Gintis. 2002. "Social Capital and Community Governance." *Economic Journal* 112 (483): 419–436.

Boyce, J., and. Pastor. 2001. "Building Natural Assets: New Strategies for Poverty Reduction and Environmental Protection." PERI Research Report 13.

Burgha, C. M. 2004. "Structure of Multi-Criteria Decision-Making." *Journal of the Operational Research Society* 55 (11): 1156–1168.

Butcher, S. 2004. "Youth-Adult Partnerships: A Powerful Force for Community Change." *Afterschool Matters* 3: 37–43.

Cleaver, F. 2007. "Understanding Agency in Collective Action." *Journal of Human Development* 8 (2): 223–244.

Coleman, J. S. 1988. "Social Capital in the Creation of Human Capital." *American Journal of Sociology* 94 (1): 95.

Dasgupta, P. 2005. "Economics of Social Capital." *Economic Record* 81 (1): S2–S21.

Dowdy, J., and S. Golden. 2004. "GED Scholars Initiative at Kent State University: Inspiring the Inspired." *New Horizons in Adult Education* 18 (3): 13–26.

Durlak, J. A., and R. P. Weissberg. 2007. *The Impact of After-School Programs that Promote Personal and Social Skills.* Chicago: Collaborative for Academic, Social and Emotional Learning.

Durlauf, S. 2002. "Groups, Social Influence, and Inequality: A Membership Theory Perspective on Poverty Traps." Working Paper 18, Madison, WI.

Ellsworth, E. 1994. "Why Doesn't This Feel Empowering? Working through the Repressive Myths of Critical Pedagogy." *Harvard Educational Review* 10 (2): 300–327.

Fanscali, C., and N. Nevarez. 2005. "The Connection between Afterschool Programs and In-School Success." *Afterschool Matters* 4: 19–35.

Feiock, R., and G. Cable. 1992. "Need, Institutional Arrangements, and Economic Development Policy." *J-PART* 2 (4): 387–398.

Feiock, R., and J. –H. Kim. 2000. "Form of Government, Administrative Organization, and Local Economic Development Policy." *J-PART* 11 (1): 29–34.

Folbre, N. 1994. "Children as Public Goods." *American Economic Review* 84 (2): 86–90.

Furman Center for Real Estate and Urban Policy at NYU. 2010. "Public Housing and Public Schools: How Do Students Living in nyc Public Housing Fare in School?" http://furmancenter.org. Accessed August 2010.

Gamoran, A. 2001. "American Schooling and Educational Inequality: a Forecast for the 21st Century." *Sociology of Education* 74: 135–153.

Hagedorn, J. M. 1998. "Gang Violence in the Postindustrial Era." *Crime and Justice* 30: 365–419.

Hall, G. 2006. "Civic Connections: Urban Debate and Democracy in Action during Out-of-School Time." *Afterschool Matters* 7: 21–37.

Hill, S. 2004. "Community-Based Youth Organizations Negotiating Educational and Social Equity." Robert Bowne Foundation Occasional Paper Series.

Himmelweit, S. 2000. "Alternative Rationalities, or Why Do Economists Become Parents." Open Discussion Papers in Economics, Open University. http://www.nuff.ox.ac.uk/.

Hirschman, A. O. 1970. Exit, Voice, and Loyalty: Responses to Decline in Firms, Organizations, and States. Cambridge: Harvard University Press.

Hodgson, G. M., and J. Calatrava. 2006. "What Are Institutions?" *Journal of Economic Issues* 40 (1): 1.

Lyons, E. C. 2000. "Creating an Agency Culture: a Model for Common Humanity." *Afterschool Matters* 1 (1): 18–29.

Mathieson, G. L. 2004. "Benefits Analysis: a Robust Assessment Approach." *Journal of the Operational Research Society* 55 (4): 390–402.

McDermott, P., and J. Rothenberg. 2004. "Why Urban Parents Resist Involvement in Their Children's Elementary Education." In *Approaches to Qualitative Research: A Reader on Theory and Practice,* edited by S. Hesse-Biber and P. Leavy, 286–302. New York: Oxford University Press.

Munda, G. 2004. "Social Multi-Criteria Evaluation: Methodological Foundations and Operational Consequences." *European Journal of Operational Research* 158 (3): 662–677.

Noguera, P. 1995. "Preventing and Producing Violence: a Critical Analysis of Responses to School Violence." *Harvard Educational Review* 65 (2): 189–212.

———. 2003. "Schools, Prisons, and Social Implications of Punishment: Rethinking Disciplinary Practices." *Theory into Practice* 42 (4): 341–350.

Ostrom, Elinor. 1991. Governing the Commons: The Evolution of Institutions for Collective Action. New York: Cambridge University Press.

———. 1999. "Coping with Tragedies of the Commons." *Annual Review of Political Science* 2 (1): 493–535.

Ostrom, E., J. Burger, C. Field, R. Norgaard, and D. Policansky. 1999. "Revisiting the Commons: Local Lessons, Global Challenges." *Science* 284 (5412): 278–282.

Payne, R. K. 2001. *a Framework for Understanding Poverty.* Highlands, TX: Aha! Process.

Pratt Center for Community Development. 2009. "Public Housing in New York City: Building Communities of Opportunity." Pratt Center for Community Development Research Report. http://prattcenter.net.

Powlick, K. M. 2011. "Youth and Economic Development: A Case Study of Out-of-School Time Programs for Low-Income Youth in New York State." PhD thesis, University of Massachusetts, Amherst. Open Access Dissertations. Paper 475. http://scholarworks.umass.edu/open_access_dissertations/475.

Rahm, J., and K. Grimes. 2005. "Embedding Seeds for Better Learning: Sneaking Up on Education in a Youth Gardening Program." *Afterschool Matters* 4: 33–41.

Sampson, R. J. 1999. "What 'Community' Supplies." In *Urban Problems and Community Development*, edited by R. Ferguson and W. Dickens, 241–292. Harrisonburg, VA: RR Donnelly.

Sampson, R. J., and D. Bartusch. 1999. "Attitudes toward Crime, Police, and the Law: Individual and Neighborhood Differences." US Department of Justice. http://www.ncjrs.gov.

Sampson, R. J., P. Sharkey., and S. Raudenbush. 2007. "Durable Effects of Concentrated Disadvantage on Verbal Ability among African-American Children." *Proceedings of the National Academy of Sciences* 105 (3): 845–852. http://www.pnas.org/.

Scales, P., and N. Leffert. 1999. *Developmental Assets: a Synthesis of the Scientific Research on Adolescent Development.* Minneapolis, MN: Search Institute.

Schwartz, A. E., Brian J. McCabe, I. G. Ellen, and C. C. Chellman. 2010. "Public Schools, Public Housing: The Education of Children Living in Public Housing." *Urban Affairs Review* 20 (10): 1–22.

Sears, W., M. Sears, and E. Pantley. 2002. *The Successful Child: What Parents Can Do to Help Kids Turn Out Well.* New York: Little, Brown.

Sen, A. 1983. "Development: Which Way Now?" *Economic Journal* 93 (372): 745–762.

———. 1985. *Commodities and Capabilities.* New Delhi: Oxford University Press.

———. 2000a. *Development as Freedom.* Norwell, MA: Anchor.

———. 2000b. "The Discipline of Cost-Benefit Analysis." *Journal of Legal Studies* 29 (S2): 931–952.

Sharp, E. B. 1991. "Institutional Manifestations of Accessibility and Urban Economic Development Polity." *Western Political Quarterly* 44 (1): 129–147.

Soep, E. 2006. "Youth Media Citizenship: Beyond 'Youth Voice.'" *Afterschool Matters* 5: 1–11.

Spergel, I. 1990. "Youth Gangs: Continuity and Change." *Crime and Justice* 12: 171–275.

Stoll, M. 2001. "Race, Neighborhood Poverty, and Participation in Voluntary Associations." *Sociological Forum* 16 (3): 529 – 557.

Townsend, L. O. 2003. "Transformative Work in Programs for Children and Youth." *Afterschool Matters* 2: 47.

Tsoi-A-Fatt, R. 2008. "a Collective Responsibility, a Collective Work: Supporting the Path to Positive Life Outcomes for Youth in Economically Distressed Communities." Center for Law and Social Policy. http://www.clasp.org. Accessed August 2010.

Wahl Moellman, L., and J. Rosenbaum Tillinger. 2004. "Civic Spaces: Retooling Public Libraries to Attract and Engage Teens after School." *Afterschool Matters* 3: 30.

Wilcox, S., K. Lazarre-White, and J. Warwin. 2004. "Rites of Passage: Preparing Youth for Social Change." *Afterschool Matters* 6: 47.

Weinbaum, E. 2004. *To Move a Mountain: Fighting the Global Economy in Appalachia.* New York: New Press.

Chapter 8

The Making of a Good Society: Lowe's Instrumental Method and the Pursuit of Full Employment

Michael J. Murray

Introduction: Economics and the Good Society

I have titled this chapter the "The Making of a Good Society." I have paraphrased it from Robert Heilbroner's now famous PhD dissertation; however the title suggests that a good society is something that is made. It is a process; in fact, it is a continual process—a process by which clearly defined (though modifiable) goals are forged and effort garnered toward their eventual achievement.

The policy goals for a good society should be toward enhancing society's general welfare. This presents economists and policymakers with three overarching concerns: (1) the problem of unemployment or the goal of full employment, (2) the problem of recessions or the goal of macroeconomic growth, and (3) the problem of inflation or the goal of price stability.

The objective of macroeconomics is toward the development of a theory that both aids in the analysis and provides solutions for policy makers toward the achievement and maintenance of the goals of a good society. There is little consensus among macroeconomists as to how to analyze such phenomena and as to what the viable solutions are. An ideological divide has been forged among economists. This divide has led to a methodological debate in both the analysis and the construction of viable solutions for macroeconomic problems.

The ideological debate to the present day centers on neoliberal policies backed up by the mainstream neoclassical economic approach versus active government involvement backed up by heterodox economic theory.[1] Neoliberalism is premised on the faulty assumption that the promotion of individual freedom leads to the promotion of societal welfare. In other words, the neoliberal view assumes no misalignment between the microeconomic goals of self-interested individuals and the macroeconomic goals of society; promoting the former promotes the latter. This connection leads policy makers to advocate for the protection of individual property rights, the protection of institutions that provide for freely functioning markets, and the promotion of free trade (Harvey 2005, 64). The neoliberal agenda has become dominant in both the economic dialog and the American political strata.

> Common interests and values among the great powers are also the basis for promoting peace and security around the globe.... As we preserve the peace, America also has an opportunity to extend the benefits of freedom and progress to nations that lack them. We seek a just peace where repression, resentment and poverty are replaced with the hope of democracy, development, free markets and free trade.... Free trade and free markets have proved their ability to lift whole societies out of poverty—so the United States is working with the entire global trading community to build a world that trades in freedom and therefore grows in prosperity. (Bush 2002)

The quotation from the former president of the United States embodies the neoliberal tradition of free markets and free trade. The agenda can be reduced to the promotion of individual freedom.

The neoliberal agenda is not new; it has its roots in England with Friedrich Hayek and is further rooted in the United States with Milton Friedman and the Chicago School of Economics. Hayek's (and the Chicago School's) view of the individual is centered on the "knowledge problem."

The knowledge problem deals with coordination and action of economic actors. For Hayek, individuals lack all the information that is necessary to coordinate economic activities. Hayek's viewpoint is that individuals are filled with limited and mostly erroneous knowledge. Because of this it then becomes impossible for centrally planned economies to collect, much less filter, all the knowledge that is required for answering questions related to production and distribution. Thus, Hayek defends free market capitalism and suggests that the market, not the government, is clearly the most efficient device to coordinate economic activity.

For Hayek, free markets coordinate economic activity through the formation of spontaneous order. "The formation of spontaneous orders is the result of their elements following certain rules in their responses to their immediate environment" (Hayek 1973, 43). As such, it is the result of "human action not of human design" (Forstater 2003, 189). In other words, macroeconomic order is assumed as the unintended consequence of individuals pursuing their own self-interest (Fehl 1994, 197). If such order is to be consistent with the goals of a good society, it must be shown that the promotion of individual freedom and free markets can always produce such macroeconomic results.

There are (at least) two problems to this conclusion for heterodox economists. The first problem can be immediately recognized from Hayek's definition of spontaneous order. According to Hayek, macroeconomic order is the unintended consequence of individualistic behavior *if and only if* "[the] elements follow certain rules in their responses to their immediate environment" (ibid., 43). The "rules" that must be followed are that businesses always engage in profit-maximizing behavior and consumers always pursue utility maximization. Profit and utility maximization guide economic behavior both in response from, and according to, the rules of supply and demand (Lowe 1987b, 143).[2]

Adolph Lowe (2003) suggests that "spontaneous order" (what Lowe terms "spontaneous conformity") presupposes a level of rational understanding of social processes. Lowe submits that such understanding of complex processes, such as industrial capitalism, exceeds the normal capacity of an individual (Lowe 1987a, 12). Henceforth, it is highly unlikely that the behavior of all individuals will conform to the strict rules of free market processes. Individual behavior can neither conform to the laws of supply and demand nor make rational, profit, and utility-maximizing decisions required for free market processes (Lee and Keen 2004, 188–192). The promotion of individual freedom cannot, at the same time, promote the larger goals of a good society. Lowe (1942, 1987b, 1951, 2003) was highly critical of such a deterministic relationship between supply and demand. Many contemporary heterodox theorists share Lowe's early objections.[3]

The neoliberal approach of the traditional economics confounds individualistic microeconomic goals with macroeconomic goals. Unlike the neoliberal approach, the methodological approach of Adolph Lowe (1965) termed the "instrumental method" requires the separation of microeconomic goals and macroeconomic goals of society.

By isolating the goal of full employment as our macroeconomic objective as a case study, here we address that the promotion of free markets in the United States over the past three decades has not achieved, and cannot achieve, this objective. Further, the "unintended consequences" of the promotion of free markets has not led to advancing societal welfare in the United States. Rather, it has led to the deterioration of the working class, an increase in crime, and a deterioration of the psyche of those affected by unemployment. It is conveyed below that contrary to neoliberal thought, there must be a clear separation between the macroeconomic goal of full employment and the microeconomic goal of profit generation. The latter does not promote the former. Private sector businesses are guided by the profit motive and will always and everywhere not only fail to achieve a fully employed society but also, rather by promoting pecuniary self-interest, create a society where unemployment is the norm. If full employment is to be maintained, it must be an actively pursued policy by the federal government. These issues will be discussed below, and the chapter will end with a brief discussion of the current Employer of Last Resort (ELR) proposal, which advocates direct government involvement toward the goal of full employment at the same time maintaining the pecuniary interests of capitalists.

Traditional Methodology versus Lowe's "Instrumental Methodology"

Traditional neoclassical analysis is ill-equipped to provide any meaningful policies toward the goal of full employment. We can go into a variety of reasons why but this is a distraction. Therefore, we will abandon the traditional neoclassical method in favor of the heterodox approach of Adolph Lowe. For Lowe, the postulates of traditional economic analysis are neither suitable nor even capable of deriving confirmable predictions of economic activity (Lowe 2003, 1942, 1965. However, Lowe's instrumental method assumes that the "actual forces that rule economic movements and in particular bring about a change in their direction cannot be known a-priori, but themselves fall in a category of unknowns" (Lowe 1965, 15). The instrumental method inverts the technique of traditional economic theory and departs from neoclassical theory.[4]

The first point of departure is that the macroeconomic goals are an a priori judgment made by governing officials who represent the general interests of society. The second point of departure is that the instrumental method assumes that the initial state of the economy is directly observable and complex. The microeconomic elements that make up the macro-economy represent the data that need to be studied. Lowe asserts that behaviors of consumers and producers cannot be generalized as in neoclassical analysis. Economic analysis needs to be grounded in the "sociological raw material" (2003, 148) that makes up everyday life that guide decision making regarding what to produce, how to produce, and how to distribute the output. The bulk of the work of the instrumental method is studying the sociological influences guiding production and distribution and gaining an understanding of its effect on the macro-economy. This framework is in stark contrast to neoclassical analysis that assumes a priori that consumption is based upon constrained optimization and producers maximize profits. For Lowe's instrumental method, consumer and producer behavior needs direct observation.

Following an investigation of the sociological and economic factors that guide production and distribution, the task of the instrumental method turns to discovering the conditions suitable, including necessary governmental regulations, for the attainment of the pre-declared macroeconomic goals. The instrumental method is a normative approach; it is "the logic of economic goal seeking" (ibid., 17).

To demonstrate Lowe's instrumental method, let us isolate and examine one macroeconomic goal of US policy makers, the goal of full employment as outlined in the Full Employment and Balanced Growth Act:

> An Act to translate into practical reality the right of all Americans who are able, willing, and seeking to work to full opportunity for useful paid employment at fair rates of compensation; to assert the responsibility of the Federal Government to use all practicable programs and policies to promote full employment, production, and real income, balanced growth, adequate productivity growth, proper attention to national priorities, and reasonable price stability.

The Full Employment and Balanced Growth Act was passed by the ninety-fifth US Congress as a macroeconomic goal irrespective of the current economic, political, or social makeup of the system. Given the lofty goal of full employment, the next challenge of the instrumental method becomes defining the current state of the U.S. economy, and studying both the economic and sociological impediments to maintaining our goal of full employment.

The Problem of Unemployment in Capitalist Economies

The Full Employment and Balanced Growth Act calls for "government to use all practicable programs and policies to promote full employment, production, and real income." Traditional Keynesian type of government intervention, such as priming-the-pump, has been one popular approach to promote full employment, but it is limited in its effectiveness (Tcherneva 2008). This limitation is partly because pump-priming policies are designed to work countercyclically with only the attempt to pull economy out of a downturn but not to maintain full employment; thus no attempt is made to address the long-term social and economic consequences of unemployment (Wray and Forstater 2004. In reality, the unemployment problem is multifaceted; therefore it requires intervention in many areas.

True to Lowe's instrumental method, to understand how and where government should intervene requires an understanding of what the economic and sociological factors are that deter the unemployed from gaining and holding on to private sector employment. Further, what other social consequences are coupled with unemployment that may need to be contemporaneously addressed? These questions must first be investigated before devising policies for government intervention.

Sociological Affects and Consequences of Unemployment

Government legislation to promote full employment cannot be articulated without first analyzing the sociological factors or the "sociological raw material," (Lowe 2003, 148) which impedes workers' ability to regain private sector employment. Mark Granovetter (2005) proposes that the ability to attain (and maintain) employment will vary depending on the size and strength of a worker's social network. Social networks are the ties that individuals have with one another. There are strong ties and weak ties, strong ties being ties with family members and close friends. Similarly, weak ties are more impersonal, such as ties with acquaintances and colleagues. Weak ties further connect individuals who are more distant and are likely gained through employment. A weak social tie expands a worker's social network. The greater an individual's social network the greater an individual's prospects of maintaining employment throughout their lives. Likewise, Granovetter's (1983) analysis on "the strength of weak ties" argues that individuals with fewer "weak ties" are less likely to be exposed to employment opportunities than those with many. Frequent contact between network members is connected with the persistence of social relationships (Feld 1997). The persistence of relationships among the unemployed can diminish over time due to feelings of social isolation and depression.

The social and psychological effects of unemployment add a further barrier to regaining employment as evidenced from Browman,

Hamilton, and Hoffman's (2001) study of the unemployed in Michigan following the General Motors plant closings in the late 1980s. The study is important as it links social and personal effects, such as, increase in crime, increase in divorce rates, deterioration of mental and physical health, and so on, as all consequences of stress (Brenner 1973). Browman, Hamilton, and Hoffman find that high stress leads to social, physical, and psychological consequences. The initial response to unemployment becomes imperative to the overall level of stress that the unemployed are subjected to. It is not surprising that the response to unemployment is different for different individuals. One's support network at the time of unemployment plays an important role, as does the current financial situation and the original reason for unemployment. Browman, Hamilton, and Hoffman (2001) find evidence that unemployment due to mass layoffs (such as plant closings) is not an initial stressor in workers' lives. These groups of the unemployed tend not to fault themselves for circumstances that, in their minds, are beyond their control.

Nevertheless, stress and distress is of a circular, cumulative, and causative nature. Exposure to stress causes additional stressful situations, such as unemployment as an initial stressor that in turn causes financial hardship. Financial hardship in turn leads to anxiety, hostility, and depression. Anxiety, hostility, and depression will open the door for further exposure and vulnerability to additional stressors (Browman, Hamilton, and Hoffman 2001, 11). As the authors conclude:

> Simply put, to have become unemployed and hence distressed—depressed, anxious, whatever—is to less likely gain reemployment or more likely to lose a subsequent job. Unemployment deals a double whammy because its consequence, distress, has further consequences—reduced employability—which make it harder to get back to square [one], unemployment leads to family stress and disruption, this too can have consequences for future employment, if only because it feeds the spiral of distress. (10–12)

Even when the initial cause of unemployment is of no fault of the worker, as time passes, workers' inability to become reemployed becomes a major cause of stress in their own lives. Workers may now see themselves as being at fault for their inability to acquire employment, and stress mounts especially in the midst of continuing financial hardship. Stress then leads to lower self-worth, anxiety, depression, family disruption, increase in drinking and drug use to cope with the stress, poor physical health of the unemployed and their families, and increased thoughts of suicide (Brenner 1973). Stressful situations simply do not pass; these are life-altering situations. The prolonging of unemployment further impedes the possibility of reemployment. Soon the unemployed could become unemployable.

Regular employment provides not only a basic income for individuals but also sets up a much needed social environment that is important and necessary for individuals. Losing one's regular job decreases their level of social activity that they were previously engaged in (Kelvin and Jarrett 1985). Workers become friends, and they engage in social activities inside and outside the workplace. Unemployment causes dependency issues within families. Inside and outside the family structure, the unemployed, especially the long-term unemployed, are seen as second-class citizens (Kelvin and Jarrett 1985, 6). The marginialization of the unemployed disrupt their day-to-day functioning within society and the normal functioning of the family. In these situations, both strong ties and weak ties dissipate further inhibiting the unemployed's possibility of regaining employment.

The relationship between unemployment, racial inequality, and crime could also be considered. As of the 2010 US census, 35 percent of Americans claim minority status. Of these Hispanics make up the largest share with 48.4 million Hispanics residents, accounting for over 15 percent of the US population, and African Americans comprising the second largest minority group with 37.7 million, accounting for over 13 percent of the US population. The distribution of unemployment in the United States is disproportionately skewed toward that of minorities. The two largest minority populations (Hispanics and African Americans) consistently have higher unemployment rates as compared to whites.

From 2000 to 2008 Hispanics narrowed the unemployment gap between themselves and whites to a difference of about 2.5 percent. Following the "Great Recession" of 2008–2009, this margin has increased to roughly 4 percent. The unemployment data for African Americans is not as promising. The unemployment rate for African Americans has consistently been about twice that of their white counterparts since 1980. During the Clinton expansion of the 1990s, the African American unemployment rate averaged just a little short of 8 percent. During this same period, the unemployment rate for white Americans was about 4.5 percent, 1 percentage point below the Federal Reserve Bank of Philadelphia's definition of "full employment."

One measure of economic inequality between minorities and whites can be illustrated by examining the black-white and Hispanic-white unemployment ratios. The ratio is calculated by dividing the minority

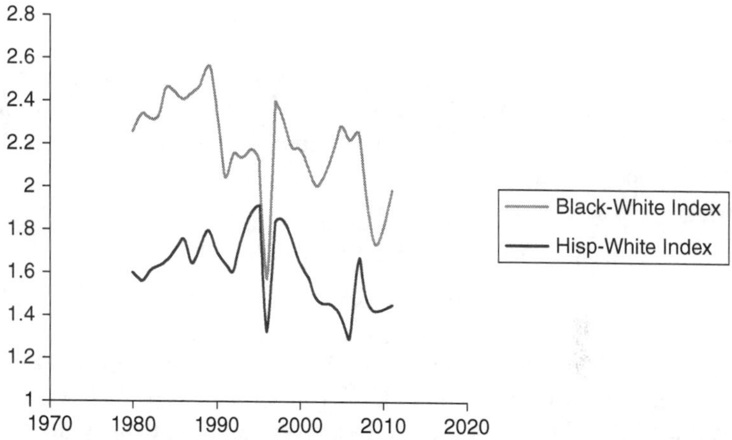

Figure 8.1 Black-white, Hispanic-white unemployment ratio.
Source: US Bureau of Labor Statistics and author's calculations.

unemployment rate by that of the white unemployment rate. A ratio of 1.00 is defined as economic equality between minorities and whites; the higher the ratio, the greater the degree of economic inequality. The unemployment ratios between these groups are graphed in Figure 8.1 for the period 1980–2011. It is seen from Figure 8.1 that African Americans are disproportionately affected by unemployment. With the exception of 1996, African American unemployment has continuously been 2.0–2.5 times that of whites for the past three decades.

Hispanics have fared better than African American. From 1999 to 2008, the economic outlook for Hispanics was improving as evidenced in Figure 8.1 by the steadily decreasing Hispanic-white unemployment ratio during this time. Since the Great Recession of 2008, any improvement in economic equality over the previous five years was lost; current economic policies have been unable to neither solve the problem of aggregate unemployment nor tackle the disproportional distribution of unemployment.

Addressing unemployment can also reduce criminal activity. Empirical studies illustrate a positive correlation between crime and unemployment (Raphael and Winter-Ebmer 2001). So government's active pursuit of the problem of unemployment also assists in the "war on crime" as evidenced by the 1990s, which witnessed a decade long expansion and a concurrent drop in overall crime (Wallman and Blumstein 2005, 319–348). During the Clinton expansion, the official unemployment rate fell to a 30-year low of 4.5 percent between

1992 and 1997, while the crime rate dropped 30 percent (Raphael and Winter-Ebmer 2001, 259).

Unemployment contributes to poverty, psychological and mental anguish, criminal activity, and racism. So public policy put toward alleviating unemployment is a large stepping stone to solving many other social problems.

The Macroeconomic Goal of Full Employment

A fully employed economy includes the whole of the labor force that is willing and able to work. It has become clear that current free market policies do not result in a good society (Murray 2010a). The neoliberal agenda of Hayek and the Chicago School, embedded in policy making of the United States, created a society where unemployment is persistent and is the norm rather than promoting full employment.

The promotion of free markets saw a brief period of high employment in the 1990s, but the Clinton free-market agenda also created a culture of private sector corruption and fraud that led to the collapse of giant companies such as Enron, WorldCom, and Tyco. High levels of output could not be maintained through the Bush presidency, and the Obama presidency has seen the highest official unemployment rates in decades; a corrupt corporate culture; the deterioration of the entire US financial system; and the rise of grassroots movements protesting the lack of job opportunities, corporate greed, and rising inequality. If the past two decades can serve as a yardstick, the macroeconomics outcomes of a laissez-faire policy are far from promoting public welfare as hypothesized by the neoliberal agenda of free markets.

The government must be an active player in the pursuit of full employment. The type of policies enacted by legislators must also be considerate of, and work with, interdependent firms operating in a capitalist society. One policy approach is for the creation of a direct-government-jobs program through an ELR program. The nature of the ELR program is to guarantee public employment for those who are willing to work, which is historically consistent with a number of legislative measures to remedy the problem of unemployment.

The federal government has historically subscribed (at least on paper) to actively pursue full employment as a policy agenda. Franklin D. Roosevelt proposed an "Economic Bill of Rights," which would have given Americans "[t]he right to a useful and remunerative job in the industries or shops or farms or mines of the nation"; however Roosevelt died in office before he could see the plan through.

Shortly after Roosevelt's death the Employment Act of 1946 was enacted, which called for the federal government to ensure "maximum employment." This legislation was followed in 1973 by the Comprehensive Employment and Training Act (CETA). Its purpose was to train workers and provide them temporary federal jobs. The Humphrey-Hawkins Full Employment Act of 1978 mandates that one of the four goals of the federal government is for full employment. The Humphrey-Hawkins Act replaced the earlier Employment Act of 1946 and has a more stringent goal of full employment rather than maximum employment.

Humphrey-Hawkins Act has been upheld, but the Reagan years saw the repeal of CETA, which was replaced by the Job Training Act of 1982, which provided job training for economically disadvantaged groups. The Job Training Act of 1982 was later repealed in 1998 under the Clinton administration and was not replaced with a federal jobs program. Rather it was replaced with watered down legislation that attempts to encourage private industries to assist in workforce and career development. The repeal of the Job Training Act and of similar legislation is despite the mandate under the Humphrey-Hawkins Act that one of the responsibilities of the federal government is to promote full employment.

The ELR approach is a solution to the full employment mandate required under Humphrey-Hawkins. Stemming from the earlier work of Hyman P. Minsky (1986), the government-job-guarantee approach to full employment is to hire off the bottom, hiring the workers who are unable to find private sector employment. As Minsky argued:

> The policy program is to develop a strategy for full employment that does not lead to instability, inflation, and unemployment. The main instrument of such a policy is *the creation of an infinitely elastic demand for labor* at a floor or minimum wage that does not depend upon long- and short run profit expectations of business. Since only government can divorce the offerings of employment from the profitability of hiring workers, in infinitely elastic demand for labor must be created by government. (1986, 307)

Much focus in discussions of the ELR approach involves affordability and feasibility. Concerning affordability, the main proponents of the ELR approach take a functional finance perspective, positing "that any nation that operates its own currency, and which adopts a floating exchange rate, can implement an ELR program, each nation might formulate the specifics of its program in accordance with its own political and economic situation" (Wray 2000, 1).

The functional finance approach to the ELR program is built upon Abba Lerner's (1943, 1947) approach to government debt and deficits. The first law of functional finance states that the main financial responsibility of the government is to control the issuance of currency to where the supply of money in the economy is just sufficient to buy the whole of the output, at the full employment level, at current prices. In other words, there is no financial constraint on a government that is the monopoly issuer of its own currency to provide for both full employment and price stability. The ELR approach to full employment is a direct means of the government to maintain full employment (and issuing currency to do so) rather than providing fiscal stimulus and waiting for the multiplier to go into effect so that the private sector can provide jobs.

The second law of functional finance states that the government should sell bonds when it is desirable to reduce the money supply in order to maintain positive interest rates. The government debt is not really a "debt" in the conventional term; rather it can be considered the interest rate maintenance account (Wray 1990).

When the ELR employs workers from "off the bottom," there are obvious stimulus effects. Employment provides income for individuals to spend in the private sector. Lower-income groups have higher marginal propensity to consume, which will provide the necessary initial boost in demand for employers in the private sector to increase investment, and thus output, to satisfy the additional demand. Increased production in the private sector will then cause an increase in labor demand. Workers will then move from ELR employment to private sector employment (Murray2010b, 2012; Fullwiler 2007; Forstater 2000; Tcherneva and Wray 2005; Carlson and Mitchell 2002). The ELR program will move countercyclically to the business cycle. Government spending on an ELR program will also be countercyclical.

An ELR program is an improvement upon unemployment insurance. Instead of the government paying unemployed individuals to not work, it is paying them to work. Keeping this group of workers employed maintains their skill levels and social networks; reduces the social costs of unemployment, including health consequences, psychological stresses, and crime; and targets the disproportionally affected minority group thereby promoting racial equality while simultaneously alleviating insufficient effective demand (Wray and Forstater 2004, Forstater 2004).

Keeping workers trained in skills, and educated in fields that are demanded by the private sector, can increase productivity thus lowering costs to private sector production. It is a more comprehensive and direct-job-creation program. ELR also aligns with the American sense of democracy and social justice, because it encourages work rather than unemployment compensation, while still protecting the elders and the disabled.

Conclusion

The instrumental method requires Americans and our governing officials to decide which macroeconomic goals are worth pursuing. If the federal government is serious about the promotion of full employment, then a different methodology than what is offered by neoclassical economists is required. Policy makers should adopt an "instrumental methodology"; policy makers must articulate the policy goal first and then work with the private sector to achieve this goal. If deficiencies in pursuing full employment exist at the microeconomic level, then the federal government needs to step in and become involved in direct job creation. Government policy such as ELR is consistent with the existing US macroeconomic goals and contributes to the making of a good society.

Notes

1. It should be noted that New Keynesian sticky-wage and sticky-price models allow for the role of government intervention in the short run. New Keynesian theory is a branch of the neoclassical school and the methodological foundations are identical. There is nothing "new" or "Keynesian" with New Keynesian theory; it is merely a special case of neoclassical theory.
2. Heterodox economists would argue that economic decisions are rooted in, and guided by, their social and historical structure. Thus, none of production, distribution, or consumer behavior is isolated from their social environment. See J. H. Finch. "The Role of Grounded Theory in Developing Economic Theory," *Journal of Economic Methodology* 9, no. 2 (2002): 213–234.
3. On the other side of the methodological (and ideological) debate is heterodox economics. Heterodox economics diverges from the neoliberal tradition and is in stark opposition to contemporary neoliberal thought. Heterodox economic theory seems to hold steadfast to these principle tenets: (1) the economic system must be viewed as a non-ergodic historical process, (2) fundamental uncertainty is significant, (3) questions of production and distribution are important, (4) the workings of economic life do not take place in a vacuum, and (5) the economic process is a social process with social classes and

political institutions. Heterodox theory stems from a diverse collection of economists with differing and sometimes competing viewpoints; however, a survey of the heterodox literature seems to show that these five tenets remain fundamental. See for example see Holt 2007; Arestis 1996; Lawson 1994; and Hamouda and Harcourt 1990.

4. Traditional economic analysis is forward looking. Traditional economics forecasts a future state of the economic system from its initial state and from the postulated "laws of motion" of market-based economies.

Bibliography

Amundson, N. E., and W. A. Borgen. 1987. "Coping with Unemployment: What Helps and What Hinders." *Journal of Employment Counseling* 3: 97–106.

Arestis, P. 1996. "Post Keynesian Economics: Towards Coherence." *Cambridge Journal of Economics* 20: 111–135.

Barnes, C., and R. Kingsnorth. 1996. "Race, Drug, and Criminal Sentencing: Hidden Effects of the Criminal Law." *Journal of Criminal Justice* 24 (1): 39–55.

Baskoy, T. 2003. "Thorstein Veblen's Theory of Business Competition." *Journal of Economic Issues* 37 (4): 1121–1137.

Brenner, M. 1973. *Mental Illness and the Economy.* Cambridge, MA: Harvard University Press.

Browman, C., V. Hamilton, and W. Hoffman. 2001. *Stress and Distress among the Unemployed: Hard Times and Vulnerable People.* New York: Kluwer Academic/Plenum.

Bush, G. 2002. "Securing Freedom's Triumph." *New York Times*, September 1, A22.

Carlson, E. and W. Mitchell. 2002. *The Urgency of Full Employment.* Sydney: University of New South Wales Press.

Cohen, S. 2002. *Folk Devils and Moral Panics.* 3rd ed. New York: Routledge.

Feather, N. 1990. *The Psychological Impact of Unemployment.* New York: Springer-Verlag.

Fehl, U. 1994. "Spontaneous Order." In *The Elgar Companion to Austrian Economics*, edited by P. J. Boettke, 197–205. Cheltenham, UK: Edward Elgar.

Feld, S. 1997. "Structural Embeddedness and Stability of Interpersonal Relations." *Social Networks* 19 (1): 91–95.

Forstater, M. 2000. "Full Employment and Economic Flexibility." In *The Path to Full Employment,* edited by E. Carlson, and W. Mitchell, Sydney: The Economic and Labour Relations Review.

Forstater, M. 2003. "Must Spontaneous Order be Unintended?" In *The Evolution of Scientific Knowledge*, edited by H. Jensen, L. Richter, and M. T. Vendelo, 189–208. Cheltenham, UK: Edward Elgar.

———. 2004. "Notes on the Social and Economic Benefits of Job Creation in Kansas City's 3rd District." Special Report, 2004/1, Center for Full Employment and Price Stability.

Fulwiller, S. 2007. "Macroeconomic Stabilization Through an Employer of Last Resort." *Journal of Economic Issues,* 41: 93–134.

Granovetter, M. 1983. "The Strength of Weak Ties: A Network Theory Revisited." *Sociological Theory,* 1: 201–233.

Granovetter, M. 2005. "The Impact of Social Structure on Economic Outcomes." *Journal of Economic Perspectives* 19 (1): 33–50.

Hamouda, O., and G. Harcourt. 1990. "Post-Keynesianism: From Criticism to Coherence?" In *New Directions in Post-Keynesian Economics*, edited by J. Pheby, 1–37. Cheltenham, UK: Edward Elgar.

Harvey, D. 2005. *A Brief History of Neoliberalism.* Oxford, UK: Oxford University Press.

Hayek, F. 1973. *Law, Legislation, and Liberty.* Vol. 2. Chicago, IL: University of Chicago Press.

Holt, R. 2007. "What Is Post Keynesian Economics." In *Post Keynesian Macroeconomics: Essays in Honour of Ingrid Rima*, edited by M. Forstater, G. Mongiovi, and S. Pressman, 89–107. New York: Routledge.

Jahoda, M. 2002 [1933]. *Marienthal: The Sociography of an Unemployed Community.* New Brunswick, NJ: Transaction.

Kelvin, P., and J. E. Jarrett. 1985. *Unemployment, Its Social Psychological Effects.* Cambridge, UK: Cambridge University Press.

Keynes, J. M. 1964 [1936]. *The General Theory of Employment Interest and Money.* New York: Harcourt Brace.

———. 1988. *The Collected Writings of John Maynard Keynes.* Vol. 29. Cambridge, UK: Cambridge University Press.

Lawson, T. 1994. "The Nature of Post Keynesian and Its Links to Other Traditions: A Realist Perspective." *Journal of Post Keynesian Economics* 16 (4): 503–538.

Lee, F. S., and S. Keen. 2004. "The Incoherent Emperor: A Heterodox Critique of Neoclassical Microeconomic Theory." *Review of Social Economy* 62 (2) (June): 169–199.

Lerner, A. 1943. "Functional Finance and the Federal Debt." *Social Research* 10: 38–51.

———. 1947. "Money as a Creature of the State." *American Economic Review* 37(2): 312–317.

Lowe, A. 1942. "A Reconsideration of the Law of Supply and Demand." *Social Research* 5: 431–457.

———. 1951. "On the Mechanistic Approach in Economics." *Social Research* 18 (4): 403–434.

———. 1965. *On Economic Knowledge.* New York: Harper and Row.

———. 1976. *The Path of Economic Growth.* Cambridge, UK: Cambridge University Press.

———. 1987a. *Has Freedom a Future?* New York: Praeger.

Lowe, A. 1987b. "Toward a Science of Political Economics." In *Essays in Political Economics*, edited by O. Oakley, 157–192. New York: New York University Press.

———. 2003 [1935]. *Economics and Sociology*. London: Routledge.

Minsky, H. P. 1986. *Stabilizing an Unstable Economy*. New Haven: Yale University Press.

Murray, M. 2010a. "From Economic Freedom to Economic and Social Poverty: Institutional Approaches to the Business Enterprise, Structural Change, and the Role for Government." *Journal of Economic Issues* 44 (2) (June): 421–428.

———. 2010b. "An Instrumental Approach to Full Employment with Policy Implications." Manuscript, PhD Dissertation, University of Missouri, Kansas City.

———. 2012. "The Regional Benefits of the Employer of Last Resort Program." *Review of Radical Political Economy* 44 (3): 327–336.

Nell, E. J. 1998. The General Theory of Transformational Growth: Keynes after Sraffa. Cambridge, UK: Cambridge University Press.

Parada, J. 2008. "Post-Keynesian Theory of Business Enterprise and the Veblenian's Approach: Are There Commonalities?" *Revista Economia del Caribe* 2: 1–30.

Polonyi, K. 2001[1944]. *The Great Transformation*. Boston: Beacon.

Raphael, S., and R. Winter-Ebmer. 2001. "Identifying the Effect of Unemployment on Crime." *Journal of Law and Economics* 44: 259–283.

Spohn, C. 2001. "Thirty Years of Sentencing Reform: The Quest for a Racially Neutral Sentencing Process." In *Criminal Justice 2000*, edited by W. Reed and L. Winterfield, vol. 3, 501. Washington, DC: National Institute of Justice.

Spohn, C., and D. Holleran. 2000. "The Imprisonment Penalty Paid by Young, Unemployed Black and Hispanic Male Offenders." *Criminology* 38 (1): 281–306.

Steffensmeir, D., J. Ulmer, and J. Kramer. 1998. "The Interaction of Race, Gender, and Age in Criminal Sentencing: The Punishment Cost of Being Young, Black, and Male." *Criminology* 36 (4): 763–798.

Tcherneva, P. and L. R. Wray. 2005. "Can Basic Income and Job Gurarantees Deliver on their Promises?" Working Paper 42. Center for Full Employment and Price Stability.

Tcherneva, P. R. 2008. "Keynes's Approach to Full Employment: Aggregate or Targeted Demand?" Economics Working Paper 542, The Levy Economics Institute,.

Veblen, T. 1978 [1904]. *The Theory of Business Enterprise*. New Brunswick, NJ: Transaction.

Wallman, J., and A. Blumstein. 2005. "After the Crime Drop." In *The Crime Drop in America*, edited by J. Wallman and A. Blumstein, 2nd ed., 319–348. Cambridge, UK: Cambridge University Press.

Wray, L. R. 1990. *Money and Credit in Capitalist Economies*. Cheltenham, UK: Edward Elgar.

———. 1998. *Understanding Modern Money.* Cheltenham, UK: Edward Elgar.

———. 2000. "Public Service Employment Without Inflation." Working Paper 3, Center for Full Employment and Price Stability.

Wray L, and M. Forstater. 2004. "Full Employment and Social Justice." In *The Institutionalist Tradition in Labor Economics*, edited by D. P. Champlin and J. T. Knoedler, 253–272.Armonk, NY: M. E. Sharpe.

Part IV

Civic Institutions, Freedom, Time, and Good Society

Chapter 9

The Role of Nonprofit Organizations in the Good Society: The Case of Forsyth Futures, Forsyth County, North Carolina, USA

Jessica M. Bailey, Doris Páez, and Morteza Sadri

Introduction

Many sociologists have opined about the composition of good societies. Opinions tend either to be philosophical, abstract, and long-term or address specific, short-term social-change activities (e.g., passing a specific law, changing elected officials, influencing policy makers/authorities, etc.) Similarly, urban planners envision good societies as those with well–thought-out physical environments that seek to maximize safe and effective city spaces while minimizing under-used and deteriorated neighborhoods. For the urban planner, the look of the city, including such features as zoning and building locations, is the key element of the good society. Rarely are the opinions focused on the practical aspects of creating a good society in the present (i.e., strategies and resources that can add incremental progress toward the attainment of the good society today). There are limited descriptions of the role an organization that is an "honest broker" of community data and information, like Forsyth Futures, can play in making such a society a reality. Additionally, as urban and regional areas compete to maintain existing business and industrial entities in their locales and to attract new ones, the role of this honest broker of community data and information in the development of a working competitive advantage for any locality cannot be overemphasized.

Progress toward a good society today rests with the usage of community knowledge. Forsyth Futures assists the community in asking the right questions, collecting data, interpreting data, and using the resultant information to drive better policy-making and decision-making. There is also a crucial role played by Forsyth Futures in anticipating future trends affecting the competitive growth of urban and regional areas and in helping to shape a locality's competitive strategy. Overall, Forsyth Futures puts knowledge to work by providing a broad and objective view of local information, being a catalyst for change, serving as a liaison among individuals and groups with shared goals and objectives, and convening conversations to advance those goals and objectives. Succinctly, Forsyth Futures builds community knowledge and puts it to work. This chapter details ways in which pursuit of these activities adds directly and indirectly to the elements of a good society.

Elements of a Good Society

When one imagines a "good" society, the word *utopia* comes to mind. According to encyclopedic entries, utopia represents an ideal community, one in which there is a perfect balance of the political, legal, and social systems, resulting in ideal living conditions exemplified by conditions of peace and prosperity for the masses. The word itself denotes ambiguous meanings when examined from the perspective of its Greek origins—it can be interpreted as deriving from origins meaning both "good place" and "no place." This is particularly interesting, given that many sociologists have advanced the position that the purely good society possessing all of the characteristics of the ideal does not exist in reality.[1]

The well-known sociologist, Amitai Etzioni, argued that man, as a societal creature, is prone toward establishing bonds with others while protecting the rights of the individual. Equality among all members of any society may be an unrealistic goal, but the reduction of inequality is a realistic one. He also emphasized the important of adherence to moral values as a means of establishing a balance between social order and individual autonomy and advocated the need for dialogues that would enable people to discuss, debate, and build consensus around the mega issues that shape society.[2]

John Kenneth Galbraith, in his book of the same name, described the good society as one that would be the personification of the idea of liberalism—government intervention to support full employment, education, and regulation of businesses.[3] These concepts are intended to reduce inequality in the community. The Organisation of Economic Co-operation and Development (OECD) posited that good governance, which many would agree is an element of a good society, must include the following:

- Accountability, i.e. that government actions are based on objectives that are clearly-defined and agreed upon by the majority.
- Transparency, meaning that government actions are open to an appropriate level of scrutiny by others.
- Efficiency and effectiveness guiding the production of quality outputs at the best cost, while adhering to original intentions.
- Responsiveness of the government to societal changes, while taking into account the public interest.
- Forward vision, meaning that government anticipates problems based on current information and develops policies that anticipate changes.
- Rule of law, i.e. that the government enforces laws, regulations and codes that reflect transparency.[4]

Draper and Ramsay, drawing upon the work of Nobel Prize-winning economist Amartya Sen and philosopher Martha Nussbaum, suggest that a good society is composed of the following four elements: (1) meeting physical needs, (2) insuring physical safety, (3) making informed decisions, and (4) having civil and political rights. These elements are thought to constitute a good human life.[5]

In discussing freedom and virtue in a good society, Bradley Doucet postulated that the bases for achieving goodness were prosperity, peace, positivity, passion, and privacy, each of which are intuitively appealing as characteristic elements of any good society.[6] Prosperity, obviously, resounds as a characteristic because of its influence on so many aspects of human existence. Not only does it determine if one's family and oneself are adequately fed, but it also is the basis for adequate healthcare, education, transportation, relaxation, and recreation, as well as time for pursuit of personal, self-satisfying endeavors. Peace is also a crucial and necessary characteristic. Peace encompasses not only the absence of war but also the need and desire for personal safety due to lack of crime and assurance of protection for one's person and property. Positivity denotes having confidence in the future and a positive and hopeful outlook. This attitude is the underlying foundation of the can-do spirit that motivates creativity, ingenuity, and entrepreneurship. These motivational factors are, in and of themselves, necessary for the sustainability of a good society. The fourth element, according to Doucet, is passion, an indispensable quality that brings strong emotions to the community. Without passion, a society would be either dull or repressed, neither of which encourage all-out abandon in the pursuit of causes, principles, or ideas. A good society needs to have passion to accompany positivity to assure that the community's pursuits remain dedicated to the betterment of the masses and improvement of the lives of its citizens. The last element of a good society according to Doucet is privacy. Though one thinks, immediately, of this concept in relation to preventing intrusion of big brother into our personal domains, privacy as an element of a good society is also rooted in the concept of the need for the individual to achieve solitude so as to think, plan, and pray. Privacy permits an environment ideal for nurturing good, productive pursuits.

To these elements of a good society, Jordan has added the relations among people in the society. Good societies are strong communities, the strength resulting from people knowing their neighbors and being friendly and supportive of them. This, of necessity, calls for a respect for integration where personal relationships can develop and result in loving, committed unions nurturing of the raising of children and supportive of meaningful friendships.[7]

Urban Planning

Urban planning began as an offshoot of architecture, but it can be considered an element of a good society. It is the amalgam of a variety of disciplines, like engineering, landscape design, transportation, location analysis, law, and other social sciences, all focused on the preplanning of the ideal city setting—one that would avoid the pitfalls encountered by cities that sprawled as their populations grew. Instead, it seeks to guide the development of safe, well-organized, aesthetically pleasing living and working spaces. The urban planning concept of a good society places emphasis on the physical aspects of a metropolitan area, though cultural aspects such as the economic, social, and legal environments play a role in the overall framework.[8] There is a new framework for urban planning in the twenty-first century.[9] It is a paradigm that focuses on sustainability, less vulnerability to natural disasters, being proactive in favor of the poor inhabitants of cities, and enhancing the overall quality of life in metropolitan areas.

The development of a good society from an urban planning perspective benefits from the input of an honest broker of community knowledge. The role of information in this context can contribute to the decision-making that defines and supports living and working spaces in any metropolitan setting.

Developing a Competitive Advantage

The competitive nature of attracting new investment and employment opportunities to urban and regional areas, coupled with the necessity of developing a comprehensive future plan, is similar to the need of any business to identify a competitive advantage and develop a strategic management plan to capitalize on its competitive advantage. Driven by the idea of gaining, holding, and expanding its competitive advantage in order to continue existence and growth, entities strive to perform on a high level and in a superior fashion, well above the performance of their competitors. With that edge over its rivals, entities can sustain and improve upon what it is that they do best. For localities, an honest broker of data and information plays an irreplaceable role in preserving the competitive advantage of the community in attracting new investment and garnering employment opportunities for its citizens.[10]

Thompson, Strickland, and Gamble offers four strategic approaches available to any entity that can assist in its winning a competitive advantage:

1. *Low-cost provider.* Low-cost living areas can be developed which minimize the expenses related to housing, food, entertainment, healthcare, public services, and taxes.
2. *Differentiating features.* Any geographic locale can differentiate itself based on natural advantages, as well as manmade advantages such as safety, education, health, mobile and pedestrian congestion.
3. *Market niche.* A niche market can be exploited based on attracting tourists or being a destination for retirement.
4. *Best prices with features that match "higher–priced brands."* Offering the advantage of low-cost living, including low property taxes, sales taxes, various permits, and public utilities is another way that a community can establish a competitive advantage.[11]

Any such competitive advantage is sustained by taking an inventory of external and internal factors. This is where the role of an honest broker of data and information is most apparent. A community must be able to take advantage of the internal strengths while minimizing the effects of internal weaknesses. When dealing with the external environment, factors must be similarly weighed and acted upon as opportunities or threats. Being able to assist with these functions serves to support the strategic planning of any locality and makes a vital contribution to a successful future.

A Novel Approach to a Good Society

Forsyth Futures is a nonprofit organization that was established in Winston-Salem, North Carolina in 2006 and has become one of the leading providers of local data and research for use in the community. It is a new approach to moving the community toward a good society, because it is not an organization devoted to any one cause but a neutral agency of assistance to all government, businesses, and nonprofit organizations that are working toward the good of the community. In short, it is an entity that works with a collaborative of residents, organizations, and institutions who are all addressing critical community issues. Forsyth Futures' work is driven by a vision that is led by the principles of (1) improving equitable access, (2) addressing racial and other disparities, (3) valuing and nurturing diversity, (4) treating everyone with respect, (5) maximizing resources and minimizing duplication, (6) encouraging continuous improvement, (7) sharing ownership, and (8) being accountable. Forsyth Futures puts community knowledge to work by tracking issues indicators to identify community conditions, trends, and needs. Specifically, it examines the areas of economic self-sufficiency/development, engaged community, educational success, mental and physical health, safety, and sustainable environment.

Initiascapes, a community information tool developed by Forsyth Futures, documents the landscape of a community's initiatives by linking individuals, organizations, or groups working on an issue. This tool is both a process and a software solution that identifies and categorizes community resources (See Figure 9.1). This information is also used to create an illustration of resources and initiatives in the community (See Figure 9.2). It allows the community to then provide and/or apply this knowledge by leading or supporting initiatives that strategically address local issues. Forsyth Futures seeks to enhance the ability to expand community knowledge by coordinating and providing a platform for supporting all residents, organizations, and agencies with the defined community.

Via its databases and strategies for collecting community knowledge, Forsyth Futures has become the mechanism by which the governmental agencies, nonprofits, business, and public service entities located in the community can obtain synergy in confronting the relevant issues that are faced continuously, economic, self-sufficiency,

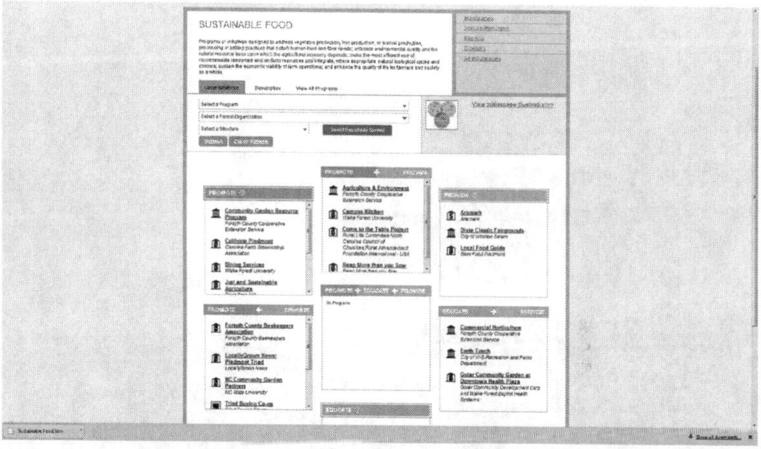

Figure 9.1 Categorization of sustainable foods programs and initiatives.

mental and physical health, environmental sustainability, safety, and community engagement. It identifies the players in each of the issue arenas, assists in formulating the correct questions to be invested in for community research, collects data and provides accurate interpretation and analysis, disseminates information for better policymaking and decision-making, and, when necessary, convenes conversations among key stakeholders to serve as a catalyst for in-depth discussion of issues.

Forsyth Futures has been able to reduce the amount of time that the community spends looking for local data and resources, to jump-start or link community conversations, to realize immediate improvements in quality and efficiencies of community initiatives, to focus community investments on key issues and strategies, and to spark entrepreneurism. Thus, the organization has been able to complete its goals of creating issues awareness, informing policy, and shaping paths for strategic communication actions.

Now that Forsyth Futures has established itself as a leader in the organization of local data, research, and community connections, it is considered by many to be experts in (1) designing and conducting local research; (2) evaluating strategies of local programs; (3) sharing data so as to add value to strategic and budgetary planning; (4) consulting with local organizations, funders, collaborators, and government entities; (5) specific data searches; (6) unique analyses of existing data; and (7) guiding a wide range of students in addressing community issues.

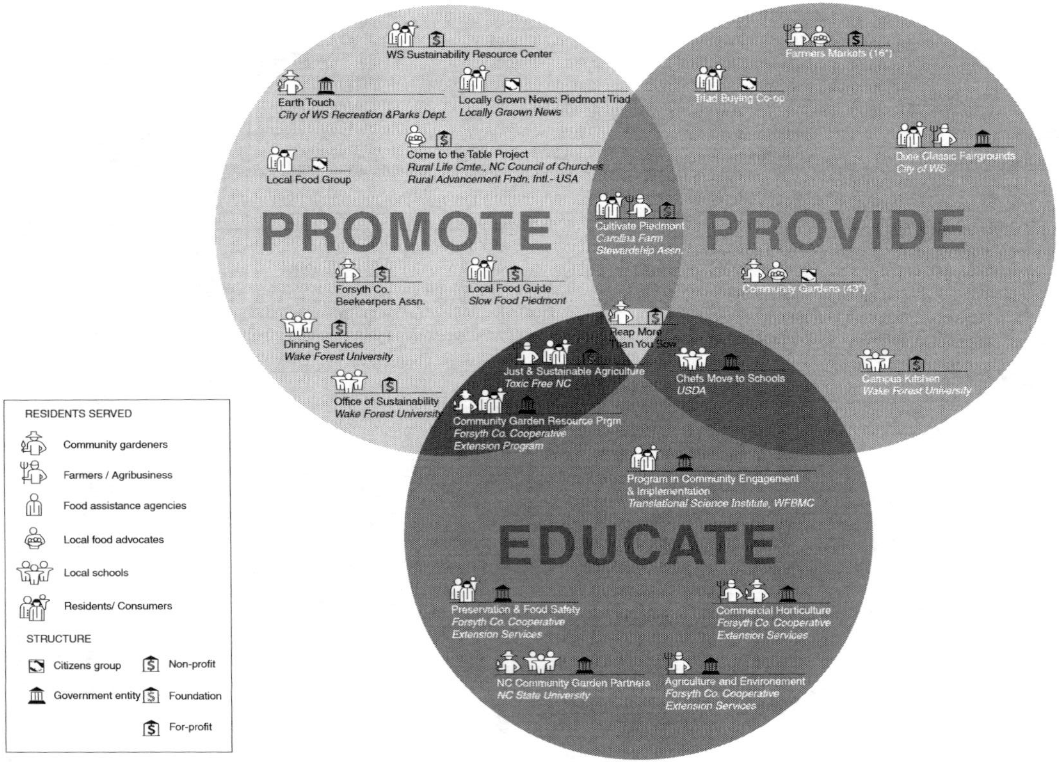

Figure 9.2 Forsyth county sustainable food Initiascapes.

Contributions to the Elements of a Good Society

The following discussion explains how the functions of Forsyth Futures contribute to the elements of the good society that were mentioned earlier.

Lessened Inequality

The data collection and information dissemination activities of Forsyth Futures are directly linked to the lessening of inequality in the community. It is a source of information for individuals, agencies, and organizations and is making a tremendous impact via its website, www.forsythfutures.org, as well as through its published reports and papers. As a result of the work of the organization, the county of Forsyth in North Carolina has the benefit of knowing all of the entities involved with a given issue, who are the leaders of that issue, how the community is performing over time, and trends on the horizon. In particular, data is categorized along various dimensions that identify the existence of inequalities. These data have become an indispensable tool for developing strategic initiatives that can address these imbalances.

Good Governance

While Forsyth Futures remains apolitical, the data it generates is useful in the development of public policy. Well-executed intervention by government to support full employment, education, and the regulation of business must be based upon objectives that are clearly defined and open to scrutiny. This is supported by the reports and papers generated by Forsyth Futures. To gauge the public interest and the extent to which recommendations achieve efficiency and effectiveness objectives, meaningful and objective information is needed. The Initiascapes work of Forsyth Futures has also been applied in an experimental analysis of a local government budgetary process for gauging tax dollar usage for community organizations. Again, the work of Forsyth Futures fulfills those goals of good governance, in additional to equipping the government to anticipate change and develop visions for the future.

Prosperity

In many ways, the efforts of Forsyth Futures contribute to the prosperity of the region. Since its vision is to build a community that contains economically self-sufficient residents, it defines economic self-sufficiency as those residents who can care for themselves and their families and are not dependent on government assistance. This includes those who are employable being employed and able to pay for life necessities.[12] Using this definition, it proceeds to investigate relevant indicators.

Affordable housing is investigated by examining local tax rates of residents of the region; the median prices of home sales in dollars for the local community, benchmarked against sales of the past year; and housing costs. This is important for moving the society toward prosperity because the goal of affordable housing is to have dwelling units available whose total costs are within reach of those earning at the median income level. The concept is applicable to both renters and purchasers in all income ranges. The lack of affordable housing has a negative effect on individual residents, families, and a community's overall health. Costs associated with housing may prevent residents from addressing other basic needs, such as nutrition and healthcare, or savings. From a community perspective, lack of affordable housing has been associated with decreases in the availability of low-cost labor, cultural and recreational activities, and civic participation. It also places additional burdens on social services and transportation systems.

To gauge income levels, specifically the percent of residents living at, below, and 200 percent below the poverty level, the economic indicators of poverty level, median income, average income, income per capita, number of persons receiving food and nutritional support, basic working family budgets, and household incomes are examined. The income level of residents is the primary measure of the community's economic success and potential growth. Income disparities are correlated with educational attainment, wealth accumulation, crime rates, availability and use of civic and cultural amenities, and community involvement.

Measures of the labor force include average commute time, number of paid employees or percent of paid employees, as well as the employment rate. This is a contributor to the attainment of a good society because the labor force size, wages, and employment rate are important indicators of the economic health and vitality of a community. It is also important to track the match between the labor force and the employers' needs.

Employers of the region are measured by investigating the occupational structure of the county, the number of paid employees of the county, and the average weekly wages among different agencies.

This is a contributor to the attainment of the good society because diversity of employment across several industries is a good indicator of a region's resilience to cyclical swings caused by the rise and fall of any particular industry. A diverse economy is much more capable of withstanding, and bouncing back from, a loss of a major employer or the closing of a large manufacturing facility.

Other important indicators of prosperity are those related to education. Measuring basic adult literacy is important because there is a strong link between poverty and, limited or non-literacy. Low levels of literacy are linked to lower wages, lower levels of employment, and more frequent spells of unemployment. A high percentage of people on public assistance have lower-than-average basic skills. Likewise, national research has shown that a child's academic performance in the third grade can accurately predict high school achievement. It has become clear that achievement gaps must be addressed early and effectively. Many children close developmental gaps during preschool particularly if they attend a quality preschool program. For the children with continued gaps, it is imperative that targeted support be initiated immediately upon entering kindergarten. High school completion rates can be an indicator of the condition of the school environment and the quality of school programs. Graduation rates reflect the community's support for and value of the process of education. Research has indicated that high school graduation is a reflection of higher lifetime earnings, which, in turn, are related to better healthcare and a higher quality of life. Since education is the foundation of the workforce, it is the basis for the community's well-being.

In addition to access to the data on community indicators described, Forsyth Futures also makes available a Resource Directory and eLearning platform, ForsythFutures. EDU, that are accessible to all residents via its website. These website elements are created as avenues for building and sharing knowledge among residents in an effort to inspire or support social (i.e., for the greater good) and for-profit entrepreneurship activities in the community. It is expected that these types of activities will also contribute to the prosperity of residents.

Peace

The work of Forsyth Futures contributes to the peace that is characteristic of a good society because it measures the degree to which residents of a defined locale are engaged in the community, that is, the degree to which residents demonstrate a sense of ownership and pride in their environment through such activities as voting, attendance at community events, volunteerism, and participation in community associations.[13] Voting and the degree to which people exercise that right measures how much individuals and groups influence policies and legislation. When rates of participation are high, residents are engaged in decision-making. When diversity of elected officials is apparent, varying perspectives are included in the decision-making process. Also, the rate at which residents are engaged in volunteer work is a reflection of the educational and civic health of the community and is related to a number of indicators of prosperity mentioned earlier. It is important to note that when residents are active participants in community associations, they harbor a greater sense of community. Inherent in these associations is the opportunity to discuss issues and the chance to work together to shape various aspects of the community. Thus, more cooperation leads to less discontent and evidence of that cooperation is what an honest information broker can provide.

Positivity

Having a positive outlook for the future is encouraged by the research of Forsyth Futures in the areas of healthcare, health coverage, and safety. These indicators are key to positivity because residents without health insurance coverage are more likely to have financial difficulties. Thus, measuring the degree to which individuals can secure regular, preventative medical care bodes well for a more positive future. Measuring mental health indicators are symbolic of residents' personal well-being, interpersonal relationships, and overall productivity within the community. Another indicator of positivity is the degree to which residents are free from criminal activity. In particular, the indicator of the number and proximity of emergency responders has been measured for the county. Fire, rescue, emergency medical, and low enforcement all shape residents' sense of security because their actions have a direct impact on the outcome of the emergency. Crime and prison entry statistics are also influential of the positivity of the community. Their interpretation can lead to perceptions of security and strategies to address active criminal populations.

Passion

This element of a good society is contributed to by Forsyth Futures via the community conversations that it conducts around relevant topics. On these occasions, community leaders, activists, participants, and other key individuals are invited to the "community table," a chance to dialogue and engage in spirited conversation. These community table events, which are usually attended by from 50 to 100 people, have raised the level of passion as residents have engaged in discussions of their feelings about selected topics, like healthcare and education, and shared in emotional interchanges with others. These strong emotions have fostered an environment that is anything but dull or repressed. The conversation sessions allow all to voice their opinions.

Relations between People

In addition to Forsyth Futures' influence on public policy decisions that, ultimately, may shape interpersonal relationships, the organization itself is engaged in activities that do so for its employees and other members of the community. The members of the board of the organization are drawn from various community participant organizations that interact with Forsyth Futures' staff on a regular basis. In addition, Forsyth Futures sponsors interns and AmericCorps VISTA workers who work within its facility and foster even more relationships within the community.

Urban Planning

Forsyth Futures contributes to the urban planning function by assisting governmental agencies in making zoning, infrastructure, and other decisions that shape the development of the municipality. The true value of an organization like Forsyth Futures is that it can contribute to the representation of all of the major and minor players in any nonprofit arena and assist multiple viewpoints to be given a voice.

Competitive Advantage

There is no better way to secure a competitive advantage for attracting direct investment in a community than by the use of empirical data and information that demonstrates the strength and economic vitality of the area. Information on the expenses related to the cost of living and usage rates of a variety of services and amenities are best handled by an honest broker of information for the community. An entity like Forsyth Futures can serve the function of market researcher and assist in establishing an advantage of niche for publicizing the location and attracting new investment for economic development. It can also orchestrate competitive analyses that can enable the community to differentiate itself by features or costs.

Impact on Forsyth County

Over the past six years, Forsyth Futures has evolved into a community leader in providing local data and research, as well as convening representatives from the community and serving as a catalyst for action. The support and results of Forsyth Futures' work offers evidence that the Forsyth County community is working toward being a good society, as well as developing into a better society by helping to attract employers who can provide employment for the citizens of the county. The organization increasingly is called upon to conduct, design, or provide an objective opinion on research or to conduct evaluations of programs addressing local issues and decision-making. Forsyth Futures' data and processes are also used in strategic or budget planning efforts being undertaken by organizations, funders, collaborative agencies, and governmental entities. Residents and community leaders now seek out more specific data or unique analyses of existing data before acting. Forsyth county students at all levels are being exposed to the role and application of objective and nonpartisan community knowledge to address critical community issues. Moreover, several times per year a broad cross section of residents come together to speak and to be impassioned at the organization's Community Table Conversations.

Conclusions

Elements of good society's postulates include lessened inequality, good governance, prosperity, peace, positivity, passion, relations among people, and the development of a competitive advantage. These features are typically described in terms that are philosophical, abstract, and long-term, or considered as part of addressing specific, short-term social change activities, such as passing a specific law, changing elected officials, or influencing policymakers/authorities. This discussion, however, demonstrates the advantages that can be gained by the use of an honest broker of data and information as a practical mechanism for creating a good society in the present. Community knowledge, when well developed and well disseminated can contribute not only to obviously desirable functions like good governance and prosperity but also to the more personally enriching functions of peace, positivity, passion, and stable and satisfying relations among people. It can even be useful in urban planning and in the definition and promotion of a competitive advantage for a locality. In this chapter, we have described Forsyth Futures, a nonprofit organization, which, as an "honest broker" of community knowledge, plays a role in making such a good society a reality today in Forsyth County, North Carolina.

Notes

1. Wikipedia, http://www.wikipedia.org/
2. Amitai Etzioni, *The New Golden Rule* (New York: Basic Books, 1966).
3. John Kenneth Galbraith, *The Good Society: The Humane Agenda* (New York: Houghton Mifflin, 1997).
4. http://www.oecd.org/document/32/0,3746,en_2649_33735_1814560_1_1_1_1,00.html.
5. Alan Draper and Ansel Ramsay, *The Good Society* (New York: Longman Publishers, 2008).
6. Bradley Doucet, "Freedom and Virtue in the Good Society," *The New Individualist: Challenging Both Left and Right* (2010) Winter.
7. http://www.une.edu.au/faculties/professions/Resources/goodsocietyframework.pdf.
8. http://www.wisegeek.com/what-is-urban-planning.htm.
9. Commonwealth Association of Planners, Reinventing Planning: a New Governance Paradigm for Managing Human Settlements, World Planners Congress, Vancouver June 17–20, 2006.
10. Arthur A. Thompson, Jr., A. J. Strickland III, and John E. Gamble, *Crafting and Executing Strategy: The Quest for Competitive Advantage, Concepts and Cases*, 18th ed. (New York: McGraw-Hill, Irwin, 2012), 5–6.
11. Ibid., 8–9.
12. Forsyth Futures, Making Progress 2009, Economic Overview.
13. Forsyth Futures, Making Progress 2009, Community Overview.

Chapter 10

The Acting Person: Reconstructing Economic Agency around a Living, Breathing, Existential Actuality

Edward J. O'Boyle

Joseph Berliner argues that four sets of arrangements constitute the core of an economic system and therefore of the good society: who gets what, who gets the available jobs, how economic activities are coordinated, and who owns capital (Berliner 1999, 17). Our understanding of economic affairs, however, inclines more toward William Waters who identifies the four parts of what now is called personalist economics: *person* as the basic unit of the economy, who acts freely but within certain limits, whose economic behavior is grounded in reason and faith, and who has a dignity beyond measure (Waters 1988, 114–120). Though not readily apparent, there is a powerful connection between these two perspectives. While Berliner is concerned about economic systems, Waters and this essay are concerned about economic agency. Simply put, it is the economic agent—the *acting person*—who sets the economic system in motion.

Our essay advances two propositions in support of a personalist reconstruction of the paradigm that informs our thinking about economic affairs. First, economic agency as represented in mainstream economics is outdated because it has oversimplified its representation of the economic agent as *homo economicus* in order to simplify economic analysis and produce empirical findings about which it can claim certitude. We propose instead the *acting person* who is more faithful to contemporary understanding of human nature and better aligned with human activity in current economic affairs. The result is greater complexity in economic theory that in turn demands more judgment in economic analysis. This proposition rests on the premise that certitude purchased at the price of oversimplification is an illusion.

Our second proposition is that economic agency constructed by mainstream economics on utility/profit maximization also misrepresents human nature. We propose instead that human beings routinely maximize what we call personalist capital in which certain good habits or virtues such as justice and courage are learned, practiced, and acquired and by which human beings become more fully human persons. Further, as human beings develop more fully as human persons, they become more effective and more highly valued as economic agents. This second proposition rests on the premise that the economic agent is inseparable from the human person.

These two propositions, which are presented in five main parts, set the foundations for a good society by acknowledging that most fundamentally the good society is built and sustained by the *active* involvement of ordinary human beings in everyday affairs. Thus, the origin of the *acting person*. The first part addresses the meaning of humanness and personhood. The second, examines the three levels of human action and what it means to *be* rather than to *become* a human person. In the third part the practice of virtues and vices that changes a human being into a *person in action* is examined. Personalist capital is taken up in the fourth part. The last part examines how human persons develop as economic agents—as *acting persons*—through consumption, work, and leisure.

Culture conditions how economic agents act, and this essay briefly calls attention to work in the Cajun shipyards of Louisiana. However, a limit on the length of essays in this volume precludes any extended treatment of the role of culture in economic affairs. Additionally, and most importantly, we do not herein address the critical role of the different modes of human communication—oral, script, and electronic—in the evolution of the economic agent from the passive homo economicus of mainstream economics to the active person of personalist economics (for more, see O'Boyle [2011], 91–118).

Humanness and Personhood

Fifty years ago, John Maurice Clark rejected the strict individuality of homo economicus as avowed by mainstream economics, affirming instead human duality.

> Man [sic] has a dual nature, individual and social; and however much individuals differ in their relative emphasis on these two sides, none is a whole man in whom either side is completely repressed. (Clark 1957, 118)

They are, as well, body and spirit, the one no less than the other. They are creatures whose nature demands that they be free to act, at times rationally, at other times emotionally. They are therefore self-determining and remain persons as long as they live. Crosby combines both principles in the following:

> Given the depth and intimacy of our embodiment, the only safe assumption is that a new human person begins to exist as soon as a new human body is formed, and continues in existence as long as the body is alive. (Crosby 2004, 124)

If we regard any human being as an object with only instrumental value, his/her personhood in a certain sense is denied. To illustrate, prostitutes are not persons because they have been reduced to sexual objects for strictly commercial purposes. Suicide bombers are not persons because they have rendered themselves into instruments of death and destruction. Even so, both cling to their basic personhood because as long as they are living they can be set free by human action. The prostitute can be convinced that sex is a gift not a commodity. The suicide bomber can be turned back by refusing to carry out the mission or by security forces.

Should humans be regarded as persons by virtue of who, what, and whose they are, that is in accordance with their nature, or by virtue of the value others attach to them, that is in accordance with the judgment of others? A norm of personhood and humanness that is based on human nature is an objective norm. However, a norm that is based on the value attached by others is a subjective norm. In the following, we propose that the proper norm of personhood and humanness is an objective norm.

Economic Agents are Persons: First Proposition.

Our argument that all economic agents are persons rests on two propositions. First, humanness and personhood are inseparably one. Second, *becoming* a person is not the same as *being* a person. As to the first proposition, humanness and personhood are one because they originate in a contingent being at the very first moment when that being is brought into existence. This is not to say that they are fully developed human persons when humanness and personhood first are present. Fullness comes later through the normal process of growth and development. Thus, even though economic agents are individuals and objects in the sense that economics views them in the workplace as inputs or human resources, they are first and foremost human persons.

Economic Agents are Persons: Second Proposition

The second proposition in defense of the personhood of the economic agent is that *becoming* a person is not the same as *being* a person. To illustrate, psychotherapist Rogers asserted repeatedly in *On Becoming a Person* that a human being literally becomes a person, implying that he/she though fully a human being at times might not be a person. Giavanola also seems to be caught in some confusion as well in using similar language though her intent is to flesh out the meaning of personhood by adding "human richness"—" an internal multidimensionality and plurality which intrinsically characterizes each person and that every society should guarantee or at least promote" (Giavanola 2005, 250). Notice the similarities in their language.

> A person is a fluid process, not a fixed and static entity; a flowing river of change, not a block of solid material; a continually changing constellation of potentialities, not a fixed quantity of traits. (Rogers 1961, 122)
>
> Such an anthropological richness... allows us to think of human beings in a dynamic frame in which they are constantly involved in the process of "becoming" themselves and realizing themselves. (Giavanola 2005, 215)

Grisez and Shaw however understand personhood not as a matter of *becoming* a person but one of *being* a person and insist on the distinction. To appreciate their argument one must first examine what they mean by the three levels of action and how each level is associated with a different type of freedom.

Human Action and Being a Human Person

At the first level, which is associated with physical freedom, the action taken leads naturally to a specific outcome provided there is no physical constraint in place. The retriever has been trained and predictably fetches the downed duck unless the dog is physically restrained. The newborn baby naturally takes to its mother's breast provided it is not physically separated from her. At the first level, the action undertaken is very simple. For that reason, both animals and humans are capable of action at this level.

At the second level, which is associated with freedom to do as one pleases, the action is undertaken to achieve a specific end. At this level, two conditions must be in place: (1) the end must be desired and (2) the means employed must be sufficient to achieve the desired end. Thus, a farmer plants corn in order to feed to his cows and when it is harvested the corn becomes available to feed them. Often the kind of freedom involved in action at the second level clashes with a requirement imposed by society that limits the freedom to do as one pleases. A woman is free to marry whomever she pleases but not someone who is a close relative. A man is free to marry whomever he pleases but not to beat his wife or abuse his children. Human beings are free to do as they please, provided they act responsibly. Because intentionality is required, only humans are capable of action at the second level.

At the third level, which is associated with self-determination, the significance of the action derives from the good that it produces in the person participating in the action. Fishing for the purpose of catching fish for dinner is purposeful and foresighted and therefore is action on the second level. Fishing with another person in order to enjoy and strengthen a friendship is action at the third level.

> Persons are persons; the question for them is how to be what they already are. If the problem were how to *become* a person, it would mean that "personhood" was some sort of definite goal or objective toward which one could work by action at the second level. But this is clearly not the case. We already possess personhood. We are not working toward the goal of becoming persons; we are instead coping constantly with the difficult but fascinating problem of how to *be persons.*
>
> ...Persons are faced with the constant necessity of making choices and, in doing so, of determining themselves. How to use their freedom of self-determination-how, in other words, to *be persons*-is the challenge which continually confronts them. (Grisez and Shaw 1974, 14; emphasis in the original)

How then does a human being grow and develop more fully as the person he/she already is? The answer is that growth and development take place through the choices made at the third level of action in which the actor does not achieve the good or purpose intended but instead participates in it, and this participation occurs over the entire period the action is undertaken. Action at the second level means looking into the future. Action at the third level means acting in a consequential way in the present. It is action at this level that affords the opportunity to grow and develop more fully as a human person (Grisez and Shaw 1974, 17, 21).

The child grows and develops as a person according to the potentialities present from the very beginning that empower him/her to act, and by acting, the child unfolds as a unique person. To illustrate, some are endowed with special mental faculties and years later become teachers, inventors, researchers. Others with physical talents become athletes, structural iron workers, ballet dancers. Still others have a gift for evoking what is best in others and become orchestra conductors, supervisors, coaches. Others are endowed with a caring nature and become nurses, ministers, nannies. Every human being, every economic agent, is different, but all are alike in that all are persons.

Personhood can be affirmed or denied, granted or taken away, conditional or unconditional. By representing the economic agent as an instrumentality, as a means to an end with a fundamental worth that derives from the contribution made to economic affairs, mainstream economics in effect makes the personhood of the economic agent conditional. In sharp contrast, while acknowledging that different economic agents make different contributions to economic affairs, personalist economics insists that every human being is endowed with a sacred dignity that is separate and distinct from his/her instrumentality, a dignity that cannot be denied, taken away, or rendered subordinate to instrumental value. The personhood of the economic agent is unconditional.

Virtues, Vices, and the Acting Person

As long as the child acts only at the first or second level, he/she remains an *innocent* person. Once he/she begins acting at the third-level, the child becomes a *person in action*. This unfolding of one's own personhood is a continuous process that takes place throughout one's lifetime. The child may become an evil person or a good person according to how he/she acts over a lifetime. The child becomes an evil person by embracing vices (acting unjustly, maliciously), a good person by acquiring virtues (acting courageously, justly).

> The Good of man is the active exercise of his soul's faculties in conformity with excellence or virtue, or if there be several human excellences or virtues, in conformity with the best and most perfect among them. (Rackham 1934, 33)
>
> The Noble is that which is both desirable for its own sake and also worthy of praise; or what is both good and also pleasant because it is

> good. If this is a true definition of the Noble, it follows that virtue must be noble, since it is both a good thing and also praiseworthy. (Roberts 2007, Chapter 9)

> Moral excellence comes about as a result of habit. We become just by doing just acts, temperate by doing temperate acts, brave by doing brave acts. (Aristotle, unsourced)[1]

A child becomes a weak or indifferent person by doing little or nothing, by not acting. Whether the child acts righteously, wickedly, or indifferently, he/she remains a person throughout, just as changes in weight and height, cognitive abilities, and other human skills and talents over the child's development as a teenager and later as an adult do not alter the essential reality that he/she is a person from the beginning of life to the end. Development from an *innocent* person to an *acting person* is a two-stage process.

> All free males are born with the potential to become ethically virtuous and practically wise, but to achieve these goals they must go through two stages: during their childhood, they must develop the proper habits; and then, when their reason is fully developed, they must acquire practical reason (*phronêsis*). (Kraut 2001, 4–5)

> Although we must be fortunate enough to have parents and fellow citizens who help us become virtuous, we ourselves share much of the responsibility for acquiring and exercising the virtues. (Kraut 2001, 3)

The rate at which this transformation from *innocent* person to *acting person* varies from person to person because each one is unique with a unique disposition to acquire this virtue or that vice (Rickaby 1918, 2).

Our attention is drawn to the four virtues commonly referred to as cardinal or practical virtues: justice, courage, moderation, and prudence. Justice is rendering to others that which is owed. Courage is firmness in the face of difficulty and constancy in the pursuit of the good. Moderation restricts the attractiveness of pleasures and provides balance in the use of created goods. Prudence prompts one to select the best means to achieve a good end.

Following Aristotle, justice is the mid-ground between rendering too much to others and rendering too little, between favoritism for example and ripping off. Courage is the golden mean between the vices of cowardice (too little) and rashness or recklessness (too much). Moderation is the mean between gluttony and extreme self-denial, between workaholism and sloth. Prudence helps us discern excess and deficiency in other areas, enabling us to locate the mean though not activating us toward that mean. Thus, prudence is fundamental to the other virtues (Rickaby 1918, 5–8; Kraut 2001, 5–7).

We refer to the four as *practical* virtues because they relate not to thought or truth but to practical human action. Moderation and courage are always inward-directed, toward self; justice is outward-directed, toward others (Schall 2004, 410, 414–415). Prudence is not rational self-interest unless it is tempered by justice and friendship or love (Finnis 2005, 20). It involves both the end sought and the means to attain that end, calls for reason rather than impulse, and takes counsel from others in the selection process (Elmendorf 1892, 4). Prudence therefore is both inward- and outward-directed.

Justice is "a very cold virtue," "the most terrible of the virtues." Strictly speaking, justice results in a condition wherein no one *owes* anything to anyone else. Schall describes this condition as an "isolated hell" (Schall 2004, 409, 412, 419). The remedy is found in the virtues of gratitude, benevolence, and charity.

> Relationships of justice, by themselves, are quintessentially impersonal. We get what is due—no more, no less. This indifference to the person to whom we are just or who is unjust to us is what I meant earlier in suggesting that gratitude, benevolence, and charity are needed in addition to justice. We must be just even to our enemies, to those who hate us, to those we do not know or care to know. (Schall 2004, 419)

The virtue of forgiveness is another remedy for what is lacking in the virtue of justice. In economic affairs, forgiveness is the golden mean between enabling irresponsible financial behavior and crushing the human spirit under an unbearable load of debt. Forgiveness by definition must be given freely by the one who holds the debt claim. The physician who does not charge an impoverished patient for care that is rendered and the landlord who allows a single mother who has lost her job and cannot pay the rent to remain in her apartment with her children exemplify the true meaning of forgiveness. In every instance, forgiveness involves a need that otherwise would not be met.

In economic affairs, justice, courage, moderation, and prudence operate in the limiting mode. Justice limits ill-gotten gain (in a routine exchange one agent gets too little because the other agent takes too much). Courage limits evil from occurring when a person knows what do to in a difficult situation and is willing to confront that difficulty. Moderation limits excess in work, consumption, and leisure. Prudence limits recklessness in allocating resources toward some given good. All four virtues are learned either from others or on one's own and therefore can be taught to others.

We conclude this part with some extended remarks on the virtue of justice because it plays such an important role in economic affairs. Every exchange between economic agents necessarily involves economic gain for both parties. What is gotten must be greater than what is given up. Otherwise, exchange collapses. However, limits on the amount of economic gain are necessary to prevent one party from taking advantage of another and to assure that market exchange serves everyone fairly and effectively. Those limits derive from the duties that economic agents owe one another under the principles of equivalence, distributive justice, and contributive justice.

The principle of equivalence limits ill-gotten or excessive gain because what is gotten and what is given up in the exchange are what were freely and openly agreed to before the exchange took place. For example, the ill-gotten gain for the employer who operates a sweatshop is the added profits from denying his/her workers what is due them.

The principle of distributive justice limits ill-gotten gain because the superior assures that what is gotten and what is given up are the same for everyone in the same or similar circumstances. To illustrate, the ill-gotten gain for the employer who pays some workers less than others for the same work is the added profits gotten through discrimination.

The principle of contributive justice limits excessive gain because each member gives up (contributes) what is necessary to maintain the group provided what is gotten by that member is the same or similar to what is gotten by the other members of the group. The ill-gotten gain for the inside trader comes at the expense of persons who sell shares that the inside trader knows are undervalued or who buy shares that the insider knows are overvalued.

Justice, courage, moderation, and prudence are essential to an efficient, orderly, and peaceful economy. Mainstream economics asserts that these matters are addressed through the "invisible hand of the market." Personalist economics argues that the "invisible hand" fails whenever economic agents have not learned and acquired the practical human virtues and do not practice them faithfully. Clark among others asserted a similar view.

> In a modern economy it has become impossible to trust an "invisible hand" to turn crude self-interest into an efficient engine for meeting every social need. We must have a sensitive awareness of what our social needs are, and what the economic machine is doing to them; and we must work with conscious purpose to make that economy meet those needs. (Clark 1957, 180–181)

Personalist and Other Forms of Capital

Forms of capital other than physical, financial, and human are being recognized at least at the margins of mainstream economics. Most notable among them is social capital that commonly is defined in terms of human networks, human interactions, and human sociality and that contributes to economic development.

Because the very concept of social capital is controversial and lacking in clear specificity (Knorringa and van Staveren 2007, 1–9), we prefer in the following to use "personalist capital," which though it has greater specificity, should not be taken as either radically different than social capital on the one hand or its replacement on the other.

Personalist capital refers to a human development process in which certain good habits or virtues are learned, practiced, and acquired and by which a human being becomes more fully a human person. Similarly, personalist capital can depreciate and human development can be arrested and even reversed through the learning, practicing, and acquiring of certain bad habits or vices by which a human being deteriorates as a human person. The virtuous person accumulates personalist capital in a way that parallels the accumulation of physical and human capital—by investing in good habits. The wicked person destroys personalist capital by investing in bad habits.

The *person in action* refers to a human being who chooses to act either virtuously or viciously, who is functioning at the third level of action. In economic affairs, the *person in action* by definition is the economic agent who accumulates personalist capital by acting virtuously and who destroys it by acting viciously.[2] The *innocent* person refers to a human being who has not yet begun to engage in action at the third level and therefore has no stock of personalist capital.

This emphasis on the role of virtue in economic affairs is not new. In his *Moral Sentiments*, Smith repeatedly calls attention to the importance of sympathy, generosity, and benevolence. Notice as well that the virtues of thrift and diligence are accepted in mainstream economics though perhaps not with the same emphasis. In the following we restrict ourselves mainly to the four practical virtues and the vices, the extremes, which those virtues seek to avoid.

Personalist capital and person are constructed around the central concept of limit. Plainly, no employer wants a worker who cannot limit his drinking or who steals. No one wants to work for an employer who sweats his labor or with others who shirk their responsibilities. No consumer respects a merchant who deliberately misrepresents the quality of the goods for sale or does not fully disclose interest charges on credit purchases. No merchant wants a customer who promises to pay the balance owed later but doesn't follow through or insists on being served before everyone else.

As with physical capital and human capital, there is a distinct return to personalist capital. In general, employers prefer the diligent worker to the lazy worker. Buyers favor the merchant who is always honest to one who is devious. These preferences are expressed and the personalist capital of a specific economic agent is rewarded (imperfectly because economic agents are not perfect human persons) through routine exchanges in the product market and the resource market. Notice, for example, the employment difficulties encountered by convicts following their release from prison, public announcements from the Better Business Bureau and Federal Trade Commission identifying business practices and in some cases specific enterprises that are scamming the public, the complete collapse of Arthur Anderson following the public disclosure that it had been "cooking the books" for Enron. Malthus appears to be saying that personalist capital is more important than human capital.

> Talents, indeed, though undoubtedly a very prominent and fine feature of mind, can by no means be considered as constituting the whole of it. There are many minds which have not been exposed to those excitements that usually form talents, that have yet been vivified to a high degree by the excitements of social sympathy. In every rank of life, in the lowest as frequently as in the highest, characters are to be found overflowing with the milk of human kindness, breathing love towards God and man, and though without those peculiar powers of mind called talents, evidently holding a higher rank in the scale of beings than many who possess them. Evangelical charity, meekness, piety, and all that class of virtues distinguished particularly by the name of Christian virtues do not seem necessarily to include abilities, yet a soul possessed of those amiable qualities, a soul awakened and vivified by these delightful sympathies, seems to hold a higher commerce with the skies than mere acuteness of intellect. (Malthus 1959, 131)

Personalist capital is not transferable in the same sense that physical capital, which is a thing that is distinct and separate from its owner and therefore can be bought and sold, is transferable. As with human capital, personalist capital is embedded in a human being, cannot be detached from that human being, and therefore cannot be bought or sold. There is nothing inappropriate in referring to acts of virtue or vice as contributing to the accumulation or loss of personalist capital just because this kind of capital is lacking in materiality.

Materiality has everything to do with physical capital, it has nothing to do with personalist capital. However, both are real assets in economic affairs insofar as both are valued in the market system. Physical capital that has no value is junk. Personalist capital that has no value is inconsequential.

Personalist capital also resides in communities of persons as social beings, but it must first reside in persons as distinct individuals. To illustrate, "Cajun engineering" refers to a pride of workmanship in certain Louisiana shipyards where Cajuns with limited formal educational backgrounds assert with pride that "if you can draw it, we can build it." Cajun engineering is a form of personalist capital that is embedded in the culture and is passed from person to person, from generation to generation. If all of the children of the Cajuns working in these shipyards were to seek their fortunes in other lines of work, the shipyard might survive with workers drawn from different cultural backgrounds, but Cajun engineering would not.

These two aspects of personalist capital—embedded in persons (the individual dimension) and residing in communities of persons (the social dimension)—approximate in a very real sense the relationship between physical capital and the public infrastructure in that physical capital is owned by individual beings and the infrastructure belongs to the community. Put differently, there is no personalist capital in its social dimension and no public infrastructure when human beings act strictly as individual beings.

In the mid-1990s Becker used "personal capital"[3] that along with social capital he sees as forming part of human capital. Using a utility-function approach, Becker argues that utility maximization depends not only on preferences based on current but also on past and future consumption activity. He recommends expanding the concept of individual preferences to include "personal habits and addictions, peer pressure, parental influences on the tastes of children, advertising, love and sympathy, and other neglected behavior" (Becker 1996, 3–12).

By personal capital (P) Becker refers to the impact of the agent's own experiences and past consumption on current and future utilities. By social capital (S) he refers to the impact on the agent's preferences from actions undertaken by others in the past. Becker's expanded utility function is $u_t = (x_t, y_t, z_t, P_t, S_t)$, where x, y, and z refer to different goods consumed. Utility maximization remains the rule.

By defining personal capital and social capital as he does, Becker in effect affirms that humans are both individual beings and social beings, and rejects the strictly autonomous individual dimension of homo economicus. Our conceptualization of personalist capital and Becker's conceptualization of personal capital are alike in that both incorporate good habits and bad habits. Becker, for example, extends economic analysis to include such good habits as honesty, sympathy, and caring, and bad habits such as lying, envying, and drinking or smoking excessively (Becker 1996, 7–12).

However, the differences between Becker's personal capital and ours are more significant than the similarities. First, we do not accept the utility-function approach[4] because Becker's personal capital is based on second-level action—consumption is undertaken for the utility that is gotten—whereas personalist capital is based on third-level action. Second, Becker defines a good habit as one in which greater current consumption increases future utility. With a bad habit, however, greater current consumption decreases future utility. Third, though affirming the duality of human nature, Becker does not differentiate person from individual or personalism from individualism and does not argue that good habits and bad habits make a human being more fully or less fully a human person and thereby more effective, more highly valued or alternatively less effective, less highly valued as an economic agent (Becker 1996,119).

Fourth, Becker in substance rejects Aristotle's golden mean to the effect that certain good habits such as moderation *limit* consumption in order to protect human well-being. It is necessary for Becker to do this in order to preserve the utility-maximization rule. Fifth, Becker says the individual acquires social capital by the impact on his/her own preferences through action taken by others. We argue instead that action taken by others influences action taken by the individual, thereby influencing his/her own personalist capital, for better or worse.

As with all mainstream economists, Becker in the end asserts that an economy functions best when it maximizes utility, when it achieves Pareto optimality. Libertarians are likely to argue that an economy functions best when it maximizes human freedom. *Personalist economics, in contrast, claims than an economy functions best when it maximizes personalist capital thereby enhancing a human being as a human person and rendering that person more effective and more highly valued as an economic agent.*

The personalist perspective for sure is a major departure from the mainstream economics way of thinking. In 2003, however, John Deere CEO Robert Land affirmed these ideas.

> The remarkable, although imperfect, performance of vigorous pro-market capitalism is one that can and must be expanded. This will

> permit great corporations, large and small, *those which practice the four cardinal virtues*, to create value on an enduring basis, to be utilized as the means they can be in solving global problems, and to contribute to the greater good of human flourishing. (Lane 2003, 4; emphasis added)

Consumption, Work, and Leisure: Personalist Economics vs. Mainstream Economics

Mainstream economics regards consumption as satisfying human wants and the prudent consumer as one who maximizes the utility gotten from the available income. The concept of need is disregarded except when poverty is addressed and only when it is separated from consumer behavior. Whatever the consumer does with the goods and services purchased is strictly his/her own business because no one knows better than the consumer what will best satisfy his/her wants. For that reason, even when the food bought and consumed is virtually the same, there is no difference between having Thanksgiving dinner alone or spending it with family and friends. No difference between shopping for a suit, dress, or pair of shoes alone or in the company of another. No concept in the mainstream way of thinking that alone may mean loneliness and loneliness in turn can have a negative effect on the human spirit.

This disregard for the human spirit derives from the premise of mainstream economics that the economic agent is an autonomous, utility-maximizing individual functioning mechanically as an embodied creature in a material, physical world where pleasure and pain are measured and compared in a decision-making process that is essentially passive. Anything relating to the human spirit is not economics even when it is tied closely to working or consuming.

Personalist economics holds fast to the view that consumers are beings with a body and a spirit and that they meet the needs and satisfy the wants of the body and spirit through the goods and services they buy and consume in a decision-making process that is essentially active precisely because they are living, breathing, existential actualities, not utility-calculating machines. They truly are *acting persons*. For better or worse, the action undertaken often changes the person who acts. Routinely eating too much diminishes a person who in the extreme becomes a glutton. Regularly sharing the same food with others enhances a person who becomes a friend. Though personalist economics admits there are many difficulties in measuring the effects of consumption on the human spirit, those effects are every bit as real as the effects on the human body.

Personalist economics does not dismiss human need and separate poverty from consumer behavior. Rather, consumption not only satisfies human wants but also meets human needs. Since need is a normative concept, meeting need through consumption invariably involves judgments as to what constitutes need. Thus there will be differences between researchers regarding how to define and measure the specific dimensions of need, and for that reason, researchers are well advised to state their specifics as clearly as possible. The disadvantage in doing economic analysis is that these differences make for differences in empirical findings and therefore some uncertainty in the conclusions drawn from those findings. The advantage is that consumer behavior is construed in a way that makes sense to the typical consumer who instinctively knows the difference between his/her own personal needs and wants, and factors both into the decision-making process. Further, combining needs and wants links consumer behavior to poverty by raising the question as to what society should do for those without sufficient income to meet their material needs.

Personalist economics views work as having two effects on the working person. First, it provides income to purchase the goods and services that are needed or desired. Second, it provides opportunities to (1) associate with others and develop a sense of belonging to a group with shared aims and (2) apply and enhance creative talents and energies. Mainstream economics regards the first but not the second as within the domain of the discipline because the first effect is objective in nature representing what the worker contributes to the production of goods and services whereas the second effect is subjective representing what the work itself does to the person of the one who works.

The objective side of work demands a human body. Put differently, virtually no work can be accomplished by anyone other than an embodied human. In that regard there is little to choose between mainstream economics and personalist economics. The subjective side of work responds to the needs of the human spirit but the spirit first must be embodied because without the body no work can be done and therefore no subjective effect can be brought forth. Here personalist economics departs from mainstream economics.

The second effect can be positive or negative. To illustrate, discriminating in pay and promotion and assigning a person to work for which he/she is overqualified turn the subjective effect negative. Designing and implementing a pay and promotion scheme based on performance and finding the best match between the work to be done and the skills and talents of the worker turn the subjective effect positive. The objective effect of work is tied ultimately to the goods and services produced. The subjective effect is linked to the human spirit and for that reason has an impact on the development of the worker as a person. Anyone who works knows the difference between a good day at work and a bad day, and that difference often is reflected in their performance and physical appearance.

Mainstream economics sees leisure as time spent not working and considers it outside the domain of economics. This unfortunate definition tells us nothing about leisure. Personalist economics, however, sees leisure in terms of both the human body and human spirit and as crucial to personal development. A coffee break and a power-nap at work reenergize the body. Similarly, a good night's sleep allows the body to handle the demands of the following day. A week in the mountains or at the seashore can infuse the human spirit with the beauty of the natural environment. An afternoon at a professional baseball game with grandfather can instill in a youngster dreams of one day succeeding on the same field of play.

Leisure can be taken quite seriously as the continuation into adulthood of the play activity that is so vital to the development of children and what they are urged to do every day. In the end, leisure means setting aside time to care for the human body and spirit in ways other than the ones that are available through work and consumption.

Consumption, work, and leisure can be separated analytically, but in practice, they frequently are intertwined as three sets of pairs and a fourth set involving all three activities at once. The working lunch combines work and consumption. The three-day holiday weekend mingles consumption and leisure. Working after hours at home and at the same time watching a college football game merges working and recreating. The working vacation brings together all three. These three economic activities have two things in common: (1) they involve both the human body and the human spirit and (2) they are subject to limits.

Certain limits inhere in economic affairs and others must be imposed because humans are embodied spirits. Human materiality assures certain physical limits regarding consumption and work. The human body can consume only so much in one sitting and can work continuously only for some fixed number of hours without rest. Further, without other limits on what and how much we consume, on how long and how hard we work, and on how much we allow for or indulge in revitalizing leisure activities, limits deriving from moderation that reside quietly in the human spirit, our development as human persons is arrested or misdirected. Disregard those limits and consumption becomes gluttony and obesity, work transforms into obsession and exhaustion, and leisure changes into escape and boredom. The practical virtues, especially moderation, provide useful and effective limits on consumption, work, and leisure, and their faithful practice contributes to the realization of the full potential of the human person.

To John Paul, materiality matters importantly to human nature, and material means are necessary to meet human material needs. To a large extent, mainstream economics and modern culture agree. However, John Paul warns that material means will not satisfy the nonmaterial needs of humans and condemns the "consumerism" of Western economies for perpetuating that false and dangerous value. Consumption is good, he says, unless it leads to a life spent in the enjoyment of material things as ends in themselves (John Paul 1991, § 36). In mainstream economics, human wants are regarded as unlimited and *having more* is taken as essentially good. In personalist economics, *having more* matters less than *being more*. Acquiring more of the goods of the world is less important than developing more fully as a human person.

The subjective dimension of human work, according to John Paul and affirmed by personalist economics, is more important than the objective dimension. Further, human work to John Paul is the continuation of God's Act of Creation that lasted six days and was followed by a day of rest (John Paul 1981, § 25). In like fashion, humans require a seventh day of rest to consider what they have done and what they ought to be doing. In other words, humans require both work and leisure to become more fully the person they were meant to be and leisure has the positive connotation of input to that development. To the modern world of mainstream economics, leisure has only the negative connotation of time spent not working.

Because in personalist economics human beings are more important than mere things, labor is more important than capital. Indeed, humans alone have rights because they are persons, because they are endowed with an intelligence and free will that differentiate them from all other creatures. In the world of economic affairs and mainstream economics, intentionally and otherwise, humans often are reduced from persons to things, objectified more and more in both the workplace and the marketplace.

Human beings are "embodied spirits" and as workers are resources to be applied to the production of goods and services. However, humans have worth not because they are useful toward some economic purpose though this kind of valuing has its own practical application in wage and salary administration and for that reason cannot be dismissed out of hand. Rather, each one has a dignity and worth beyond human measure. In mainstream economics and modern economic affairs, human value commonly is determined instrumentally. One's own worth is determined by the value attached to one's work. In personalist economics, this kind of valuing is superseded by the sacred dignity of every living, breathing human person.

Workers have rights in order to assure the preservation of their fundamental dignity as human persons and access to the means necessary for their material survival, such as the right to associate, to strike, to a safe workplace, to a day of rest. To some extent, mainstream economics and others engaged in economic affairs also affirm these rights but as *legal* rights, as flowing from the hand of government and therefore contingent. Personalist economics sees them as *natural* rights flowing from the hand of the Creator, and therefore inalienable.

Humans are more than the one-dimensional, self-interested, self-absorbed, and passive individuals of mainstream economics and contemporary Western culture. They are the two-dimensional, active persons of personalist economics with an identity as separate and unique human beings, never to be taken simply as a cog in a machine or as totally subordinate to the whole, but at the same time united in solidarity with family, company, neighborhood, region, nation, and all humankind. Human existence *always* is coexistence.

In Conclusion

In mainstream thinking, homo economicus is subject to change in that the economic agent is capable of acquiring or losing the human capital that is embedded in his/her nature. Further, mainstream economics acknowledges that at times homo economicus acts altruistically, in accordance with the needs and desires of others. Mainstream economics reconciles this kind of behavior with the self-centeredness of homo economicus by labeling it "enlightened self-interest." Even so, homo economicus overwhelmingly is never changing because that (over-) simplifying proposition assures a predictability of behavior in economic affairs and in turn empirical findings from economic analysis about which there is greater (apparent) certainty.

For some time we referred to the economic agent of personalist economics as *homo socioeconomicus* (O'Boyle 1994, 286–313). We are replacing that term with the *acting person*—the *person in action*—for two reasons. First, the literature has become cluttered with similar terms such as *homo reciprocans, homo politicus, homo sociologicus, homo darwinianus,* and others that mainstream economics has not taken seriously. Using *the acting person,* we hope, avoids the problem of being thrown together with those terms and then being thrown out with them. Second, *the acting person/person in action* connects economic agency to human action in economic affairs, notably work, consumption, and leisure, that unmistakably changes the economic agent who in acting virtuously or viciously accumulates or depletes personalist capital, and thereby is more effective and more highly valued as an agent or less effective and less highly valued.

Finally, mainstream economics asserts that in the end homo economicus maximizes utility and profit, and the economy functions best when it reaches Pareto optimality. Maximizing utility and profit are based on the proposition that the good invariably consists in *having* more. Personalist economics, in contrast, claims that most fundamentally the economy functions best when the *acting person* maximizes personalist capital thereby enhancing him/herself as a human person and rendering him/herself more effective and more highly valued as an economic agent. Maximizing personalist capital rests on the assertion that the good always inheres in *being* more.

The mainstream paradigm claims that the good society consists in everyone having more of the good things that the economy produces. The personalist paradigm replies that it consists in everyone becoming better persons by the good they do in everyday economic affairs.

Notes

1. See http://quotationsbook.com/quote/27256/. Accessed January 8, 2013.
2. Elmendorf (1892, 1–2) claims that "as habits [virtues and vices] are generated and increased by acts, so ceasing from action diminishes them and sometimes totally destroys them."
3. In 1888, Ingram used "personal capital" to mean that "in agriculture nature labours along with man, whilst in manufactures nature does nothing, man does all" (Ingram 1888, 105).
4. Van Staveren and Knorringa (2007, 109) state that the utility-function approach is one of the three ways by which social capital is integrated into economic analysis.

Bibliography

Becker, Gary S. 1996. *Accounting for Tastes.* Cambridge: Harvard University Press.

Berliner, Joseph S. 1999. *The Economics of the Good Society.* Malden: Blackwell.

Clark, John Maurice. 1957. *Economic Institutions and Human Welfare*. New York: Alfred A. Knopf.

Crosby, John F. 2004. *Personalist Papers*. Washington, DC: Catholic University of America Press.

Elmendorf, John J. 1892. "Chapter V. On Virtues." *Elements of Moral Theology*. http://maritain.nd.edu/jmc/etext/emt.htm. Accessed June 7, 2007.

Finnis, John. 2005. "Aquinas' Moral, Political, and Legal Philosophy." *The Stanford Encyclopedia*. http://plato.stanford.edu/entries/aquinas-moral-politcal/#Vir. Accessed June 7, 2007.

Giavanola, Benedetta. 2005. "Personhood and Human Richness: Good and Well-Being in the Capability Approach and Beyond." *Review of Social Economy* 63: 249–267.

Grisez, Germain, and Russell Shaw. 1974. *Beyond the New Morality: The Responsibilities of Freedom*. Notre Dame: Notre Dame University Press.

Ingram, John. 1888. *History of Political Economy*. Edinburgh: Adam and Charles Black.

John Paul II. 1981. *Laborem Exercens*. Boston: St. Paul Editions.

———. 1991. *Centesimus Annus*. http://www.vatican.va/holy_father/john_paul_ii/encyclicals/documents/hf_jp_iI_enc_01051991_centesimus-annus_en.html. Accessed October 28, 2010.

Knorringa, Peter, and Irene van Staveren. 2007. "Beyond Social Capital: A Critical Approach." *Review of Social Economy* 65: 1–9.

Kraut, Richard. 2001. "Aristotle's Ethics." *Stanford Encyclopedia of Philosophy*. Revised June 3, 2005. http://plato.stanford.edu/entries/aristotle~ethics/. Accessed February 12, 2007.

Lane, Robert W. 2003. "The Great Corporation: Vigorous Competition, Cardinal Virtues, Value Creation." Lecture presented at Augustana College, Illinois on October 23. http://www.deere.com/en_US/compinfo/speeches/2003/031028augustana.html. Accessed January 26, 2007.

Malthus, Thomas R. 1959. *Population: The First Essay*. Ann Arbor: University of Michigan Press.

O'Boyle, Edward J. 1994. "*Homo Socio-Economicus*: Foundational to Social Economics and the Social Economy." *Review of Social Economy* 52: 286–313.

———. 2011. "From Individual to Person: An Evolutionary Process Grounded in Human Communication." In *Looking Beyond the Individualism and* Homo Economicus *of Neoclassical Economics*, edited by Edward J. O'Boyle, 91–118. Milwaukee, WI: Marquette University Press.

Rackham, H. 1934. *Nicomachean Ethics*. Translated by H. Rackham. Book 1, chapter 7, section 15. http://www.bartleby.com/73/567.html. Accessed January 9, 2013.

Rickaby, Joseph. 1918. "Chapter V: Of Habits and Virtues." *Moral Philosophy: Ethics, Deontology and Natural Law*. London: Longmans, Green. http://www2.nd.edu/Departments//Maritain/etext/moral105.htm. Accessed

December 10, 2006.

Roberts, W. Rhys. 2007. *Rhetoric*. Translated by W. Rhys Roberts. Book 1, chapter 9. http://theOphrastus.typepad.com/noncontradiction/2007/09/rhetoric-transl.html. Accessed July 26, 2011.

Rogers, Carl R. 1961. *On Becoming a Person: A Therapist View of Psychotherapy*. Boston: Houghton Mifflin.

Schall, James V. 2004. "Justice: The Most Terrible of the Virtues." *Journal of Markets and Morality* 7: 409–422.

Smith, Adam. 1976. *The Theory of Moral Sentiments*. Edited by D. D. Raphael and A. L. Macfie. Oxford: Oxford University Press.

United States Supreme Court. 1973. *Roe* v. *Wade*. http://supreme.justia.com/us/410/113/case.html. Accessed May 12, 2010.

Van Staveren, Irene, and Peter Knorringa. 2007. "Unpacking Social Capital in Economic Development: How Social Relations Matter." *Review of Social Economy* 65: 107–135.

Waters, William R. 1988. "Social Economics: A Solidarist Perspective." *Review of Social Economy* 46: 113–143.

Chapter 11

Time on the Ledger: Social Accounting for the Good Society

Tom Walker

The characteristics of a good society are typically itemized by abstract nouns such as "justice," "compassion," "liberty," "prosperity," or "security." Those nominalizations imply a concrete sequence of actions, a narrative. Take, for example, the narrative in Matthew 25, 35–36 from the New Testament: "For I was hungry and you gave me something to eat, I was thirsty and you gave me something to drink, I was a stranger and you invited me in, I needed clothes and you clothed me, I was sick and you looked after me, I was in prison and you came to visit me."

In the biblical passage, the actions (done for "one of the least of these brothers and sisters of mine") certify the worthiness of those who perform them for entry into the kingdom of heaven—a metaphor for the good society if ever there was one. The New Testament might thus define a good society as a *charitable* one in which citizens come to the aid of their needful neighbors, regardless of wealth or status. That society ultimately reflects the moral qualities of its individuals.

Since the Enlightenment, this episodic, individualistic kernel has been supplemented with the idea of secular progress. As a society's knowledge and productive powers increase, its capacity for doing good also grows. Goodness, then, would translate expanded capacity into action—even to the extent of institutionalizing the prevention of deprivation and distress, rather than relying on personal charity.

When we think about how society might be improved, we usually also have in mind some sort of metric or political arithmetic—the calculation either of an aggregate sum of some descriptive ratio, a distribution or of a per capita allotment. Such arithmetic takes double-entry bookkeeping as its model. It indicates the capacity to act and changes in that capacity. Adam Smith (1790) highlighted the "distribution of the necessaries of life." Franklin, 1839) pondered the computation "by some political arithmetician" of a four-hour working day. Thomas Jefferson's friend, the Marquis de Chastellux (1969), proposed a formula for calculating public happiness.

Would an alternative vision of the good society display a similar fascination with numbers and methods for deriving them? I will argue that it would indeed. An outline for the kind of reckoning required—of the curtailment of unwarranted toil—was hinted at already in speculations by Chastellux, and Franklin, and has been a recurrent, if subterranean, theme in political economy since the earliest days. Even Smith upheld "ease of body and peace of mind" as "what constitutes the real happiness of human life."

How does one measure "ease of body and peace of mind?" We will get to the question of *how* later, but first I would like to explain why it is crucial to calculate the objective and not merely to commend it.

Accounting vs. Double Counting

Werner Sombart (1952) described the concept of capital as something that "did not exist before double-entry book-keeping." "Capital," he wrote, "can be defined as that amount of wealth which is used in making profits and which enters into the accounts." Rob Bryer (2006) identified a capitalist "mentality" that uses accounting information to control the labor process "by holding the collective worker accountable for the rate of return on capital" (592). Such control from the bottom line is central, not incidental, both to the domination of the labor process by capital and to the evolving ways domination has been implemented through successive waves of technology. An alternative to domination requires the development of a counter-mentality that "turns the capitalist development of calculation and accountability to other ends" (593).

Bryer defined such counter-mentality as socialist but I would amend that to a "social-accounting mentality" to enlist and implicate an existing social-accounting tradition as well as to differentiate the alternative mentality from advocacy of state socialism. Ownership of the means of production may be beside the point, or suitable forms of ownership may be more eclectic than traditional socialism assumes. It is not private ownership per se that is onerous but the domination over the labor process that capital decrees and a one-dimensional accounting mentality that it enforces.

Social accounting is simply the kind of accounting that needs to be done when two or more accounting entities are aggregated. It differs from the accounting of a single enterprise in the way that interactions between the constituent parts are treated. Great care needs to be taken in defining the boundaries between parties to avoid the double-counting errors that are pervasive in exercises of social accounting.

When bookkeeping practices are naïvely transferred to social accounting problems, including collective bargaining, they produce confusion and error. Today, national income accounting, the Gross Domestic Product (GDP), is the most prominent example of social accounting. Although economists acknowledge that GDP is flawed as a measure of welfare, they nevertheless promote GDP growth as an imperative for achieving full employment or some other normative goal, citing correlations between GDP and the other, more appropriate, measures of welfare. Critics of this growth imperative suggest those correlations are misleading.

When the US Commerce Department released its first comprehensive report of national income and product accounts in 1947, the national priority of maximizing production was manifest in their methodology. Simon Kuznets, who in the 1930s had led the NBER national income measurement project, was asked by *The Review of Economics and Statistics* to review the Commerce Department's report. His critique was scathing. Kuznets (1948) objected that the Commerce Department's report lacked a clear definition of the end goal of economic activity and thus counted the activity itself rather than the *product* of that activity.

Technically, the issue was one of distinguishing final consumer goods from intermediate goods, the inclusion of which would constitute duplication or "double counting." Most pointedly, Kuznets objected to the inclusion of all goods purchased by the government as final products, arguing that a great deal of government activity—particularly during wartime—adds nothing to final utility but only measures the auxiliary costs of maintaining society at large.

In reply, Commerce Department economists (Gilbert et al. 1948) defended their methodology on the grounds of expediency and the excessive cumbersomeness and subjectivity of examining each purchase to determine whether it was a final or intermediate good. Besides, they claimed their approach avoided "moralistic" judgments and its focus on material production served important national concerns arising out of the Depression and wartime mobilization. The Commerce economists had a strong case regarding feasibility and relevance to urgent priorities of the recent past. As to moralistic judgments, though, they overlooked the irony that to abstain from judgment is itself a moralistic judgment.

More recently, Roefie Hueting (2010) adapted Kuznets's analysis of duplication to the issues of social and environmental externalities, introducing the term "asymmetrical entering" as a more inclusive description than double counting for the type of accounting error that occurs. Asymmetrical entering refers to the costs of repairing or substituting for an environmental or social free good after it has been damaged or destroyed. Because there is no monetary exchange involved, there is no subtraction from the GDP for the original damage to the environment or social wellbeing. But this creates an asymmetry when the cost of repair is counted in GDP. Even the calculation of net domestic product (NDP), which subtracts estimated capital depreciation from GDP, ignores the environmental and social impacts. Stefano Bartolini (2006) has made a related point about what he terms negative externality or negative endogenous growth (NEGs). This describes a vicious cycle in which the products required to substitute for the free goods of nature and society destroyed by the negative externalities of industrial activity count as growth even as they too are generating additional negative externalities, which then lead to more substitution, more growth, and so on.

A Case Study: The Newcastle Engineers' Strike

On May 29, 1871, engineers in Newcastle, England, went on strike for a nine-hour working day. The strike lasted for four and a half months and ended when employers conceded to the workers' demand to reduce the workweek from 59 hours to 54 hours. In the wake of the strike's successful conclusion, agitation for the nine-hour day quickly spread throughout England, meeting with singular success.

The climax to the strike revolved around an exchange of letters to the editor of the *Times of London* between Sir William Armstrong, spokesman for the employers, and John Burnett, president of the Newcastle Nine Hours League. In one of his letters, Armstrong presented a cost calculation whose error was disarmingly subtle and a lesson in the allure of double counting. Armstrong reckoned that the move from a 59-hour week to a 54-hour week, at the same weekly pay, would result in an 8-percent hourly wage gain for the workers (actually it would be over 9 percent). Estimating the cost to the employer was more difficult, Armstrong maintained. The workers' gain, he assumed, would register as a corresponding loss, of the same percentage, to the employer. In addition to this increased wage cost, however, the employer would also face a loss of revenue due to the diminished output during the shorter week. Armstrong estimated that this indirect cost would amount to roughly the same as the direct loss from the higher wages.

Armstrong's double-counting mistake was not easy to detect. Burnett appears to have overlooked it in his reply, although he did challenge Armstrong's assumption that output would decline in proportion to the reduction in hours. In retrospect, Armstrong's assumption of a proportionate decline could be viewed as "naïve" (Robbins 1929), but it was less egregious than his double-counting error, which arose from mixing up hourly wage *rates* and weekly output.

Assuming, as Armstrong did, that output would change in direct proportion to hours worked, hourly output would remain constant after the change to the shorter workweek while hourly wages increased by 9 percent. Meanwhile, weekly wages would remain constant while weekly output would decrease by nearly 8.5 percent. Each of these accounts sums up the full effect of the change viewed from the two different accounting periods. What Armstrong did, though, was to add together the percentage *hourly* increase in wage costs and the percentage *weekly* decrease in output (and resulting revenue), thus counting the same effect twice.

In the nineteenth century, Newcastle was synonymous with coal. "To carry coals to Newcastle," remains a proverb signifying a useless, redundant activity. Coal was literally and figuratively the bedrock of the industrial revolution. In his presidential address to the British Association for the Advancement of Science in 1863, Sir William Armstrong asked whether England would one day run out of coal, and if so, what would be the consequences.

William Stanley Jevons (1865) undertook to answer Armstrong in The Coal Question, best known today for its perspective—known as the Jevons paradox or rebound effect—regarding the perverse effects of efficiency improvements on the conservation of coal resources. That paradox challenges expectations of technological optimists that efficiency improvements alone can solve either supply limitations or the threat to climate stability from carbon emissions. Jevons's argument was not novel. As he explained, it applied "a principle recognized in many parallel instances." The principle is most familiar in connection with the introduction of machinery, where the economizing of labor, "for the moment, throws labourers out of employment. But such is the increased demand for the cheapened products, that eventually the sphere of employment is greatly widened" (140).

Jevons contended that this same principle applied, "with even greater force and distinctness, to the use of such a general agent as coal." Whether it applies with greater force is an empirical question, depending on the relative elasticities of demand for labor and energy resources. The evidence is not encouraging, though. For example, the energy intensity of employment in the United States, measured in BTUs consumed per employed person, increased by 60 percent from 1949 to 1973. From 1973 to 1986, consumption per employed person decreased by a little over 20 percent, but since 1986 it has remained virtually level. Overall, it took about 20 percent more energy consumed to employ each person in 2009 than it did 60 years earlier. Comparable global statistics are harder to come by but they are likely to be even less encouraging because of the shift of high energy using manufacturing industries overseas from the United States.

On the day engineers and employers in Newcastle settled the strike, the London correspondent for the *New York Times* filed a dispatch with the untimely assessment that no resolution of the strike was in sight (FHJ 1871). The *Times* correspondent concluded his report with a peculiar allegation. Although he conceded the reasonableness of the strikers' announced aims and a respectable third party—A. J. Mundella, MP—attested to the sincerity of those objectives, the *Times* correspondent wasn't having any of it.

"I find it very hard to take this view," he objected to the suggestion that the union was sincere in its motives. Instead, the London correspondent alleged "some ulterior design," underpinning the workers' long and determined struggle. "The League," he asserted, "is only an offshoot of the Unions, and the great object of the Unions is to surround production with all manner of restraints and restrictions, so that it shall not be accomplished too fast or by a small number of workmen." Allegedly underlying this obstructionism was a fallacious belief "that the amount of work to be done is a fixed quantity, and that in the interest of the operatives, it is necessary to spread it thin in order to make it go far."

There was a context for the London correspondent's suspicious outburst, but it had little to do with the Newcastle strike itself. The claim about a belief in a fixed amount of work to be done would congeal some 20 years later into what is now known as the lump-of-labor fallacy. It then drifted into introductory economics textbooks where it remained a staple for much of the twentieth century, appearing in each edition of Paul Samuelson's *Economics* from 1948 to 2009.

Paul Krugman (2003) recited the fallacy claim in his *New York Times* column:

> Economists call it the "lump of labor fallacy." It's the idea that there is a fixed amount of work to be done in the world, so any increase in the amount each worker can produce reduces the number of available jobs... As the derisive name suggests, it's an idea economists view with contempt, yet the fallacy makes a comeback whenever the economy is sluggish.

While economists may indeed view the idea with contempt, it is not clear who actually believes in it. Economists present no evidence in support of their attribution of the idea to unions or workers; advocates of shorter hours have repeatedly repudiated the alleged belief. So where exactly did this elusive idea that economists, and the London correspondent for the *New York Times,* view with such contempt come from?

The clue to the alleged fallacy's origin is contained in the correspondent's allegations about the unions' objective "to surround production with all manner of restraints and restrictions" and in his suspicion of an "ulterior design." These two indictments were staples of antiunion rhetoric in England since the 1830s. The locus classicus for these allegations, as they applied to the hours of work, would most certainly be the heavily promoted pamphlet, *Character, Object and Effects of Trades' Unionism* by the assistant commissioner of Poor Laws and examiner for the 1833 Royal Commission on Employment of Children in Factories, Edward Carleton Tufnell (1834).

During the 1833 Royal Commission inquiry, Tufnell asked Manchester cotton manufacturer, Peter Ewart, what he supposed was the chief motive of the cotton spinners' union in advocating the ten-hours factory bill. Ewart's reply was a speculation from a political opponent of the union and of the factory legislation, quite possibly influenced by the novelized popular political economy of Harriet Martineau whose best-selling novel, *A Manchester Strike,* "made considerable use of the wages fund analysis [of classical political economy] to argue that strikes are futile" (Vint 2007). Tufnell appropriated the gist of Ewart's commission testimony, embellished it with a tone of indignation, and presented it as blunt fact in his anonymously published pamphlet:

> The Union calculated, that had the Ten-hour Bill passed, and all the present factories worked one-sixth less time, one-sixth more mills

> would have been built to supply the deficient production. The effect of this, as they fancied, would have been to cause a fresh demand for workmen; and hence, those out of employ would have been prevented from draining the pockets of those now in work, which would render their wages really as well as nominally high. Here we have the secret source of nine-tenths of the clamour for the Ten-hour Factory Bill, and we assert, with the most unlimited confidence in the accuracy of our statement, that the advocacy of that Bill amongst the workmen, was neither more nor less than a trick to raise wages—a trick, too, of the clumsiest description; since it is quite plain, that no legislative enactment, whether of ten or any other number of hours could possibly save it from signal failure.

Thirty-seven years later, the Newcastle strikers stated unequivocally that what they wanted was to work fewer hours so they could have time to advance their education and thereby improve their skills and usefulness. They wanted the shorter day so that they might have more energy left at the end of the day to devote to their studies. They sought the health benefits of spending less time breathing factory air and having more time for physical recreation and sport.

Toward a Republic of Leisure

The prospect of a perpetually expanding amount of work runs up against both human and natural limits. Even if there is always more work, there is not an unlimited amount of coal, fossil fuels, or atmosphere to absorb their greenhouse gas emissions. Those limits may not immediately halt exploitation but may at first divert it into a feedback loop of growing negative externalities whose cost of repair perversely counts as economic growth. Within conventional economic theory, a possible solution would be to price the externalities and ensure that their costs are taken fully into account through taxation, for example. The alternative presented here may best be considered as an implementation of that solution, which, however, relies on popular initiative rather than government regulation and technocratic expertise. It involves two main components, one institutional and the other statistical.

The institutional innovation envisions a nonmarket, nongovernmental constituency I call the "labor commons union." The statistics needed to guide the union's decision-making are produced within a social accounting framework that, unlike the current GDP and traditional enterprise bookkeeping, explicitly recognizes the costs of unemployment and the value of free time. I begin with the labor commons union.

The Labor Commons Union

In "Foundations for Environmental Political Economy," John Dryzek (1996) explored the prospects for an environmentalist economic subject, *Homo ecologicus,* as an alternative to the traditional rational actor or economic man. Dryzek criticized previous efforts at positing an ethical, environmentalist subject, saying they were flawed by wishful thinking and reductionism. The alternative Dryzek proposed instead was based on his interpretation of Elinor Ostrom's (1990) case study work on managing common pool resources.

The new political economy, Dryzek argued, would be one that not only can account for instrumental rationality—even deploy it in its proper place—but that can also point to alternatives grounded in something firmer than wishful thinking. Dryzek's alternative not only would rely exclusively on subjectivity but would also take into account communication between people (other than purely economic exchange). Such a communicative model of economic behavior already exists in Ostrom's work. Communication and interaction between individuals distinguished the successful resource management regimes she studied from the unsuccessful ones. In successful common pool resource management institutions, participants learned to distinguish whom to trust, discern the effects their actions will have on others and on the shared resource, behave more straightforwardly toward each other, and build institutional arrangements for resolving conflicts.

Ostrom's framework for distinguishing different types of goods and services classifies them as having either high or low subtractability (also referred to as rival goods)—meaning that one person's use of a resource leaves less available for others—and as either more or less excludable, depending on how difficult or costly it is to exclude people from access to the good (Ostrom 2009). Taken together, those two pairs constitute a matrix, shown in Table 11.1, that specifies four ideal types of goods. These characteristics are not binary, and therefore many types of goods can shift from one category to another depending on changes in demand, supply, technology, or administration. Private goods are subtractable and excludable (that is it is not difficult to exclude beneficiaries). Examples would include food and clothing. Public goods, such as lighthouse services, for example, are neither highly subtractable nor excludable. The remaining sectors are common pool resources, such as fisheries and forests, which are subtractable but difficult to exclude, and toll goods, such as golf courses or swimming pools, which have low subtractability but are not difficult to exclude people from.

Table 11.1 Ideal types of goods

		Subtractability of Use	
		High	Low
Difficulty of Excluding Potential Beneficiaries	High	Common pool resources	Public goods
	Low	Private goods	Toll goods

Source: "Beyond Markets and States." Elinor Ostrom (2009).

Employment as a Good

Labor demand is commonly treated by economists as a commodity the employer purchases with a wage or salary. On the supply side, the canonical model alleges a subjective choice for the worker between income and leisure. This model has consistently "been refuted by evidence" (Pencavel 1986). An alternative way to view a job position, with its income, status, and promotional opportunities, would be as a composite good that the worker, in part, purchases with his or her time, relevant skill, and credentials and search activity. From the perspective of the job seeker, job positions would arguably rank within Ostrom's analytical grid as both highly subtractable and difficult to exclude potential competitors from. Employment thus could count as a common pool resource in that framework.

The labor commons union is proposed here as an experimental institution that would treat employment as a common pool resource. Such an undertaking has various precedents. The traditional workers' ethic of the craft guilds viewed the work available as something akin to a common resource. Guild principles included the practice of dividing up the custom equitably among the available tradesmen. In addition there are worker co-ops, works councils, syndicalism, and the movement unionism such as the eight-hour leagues and nine-hour leagues in the United States, Canada, and the UK in the nineteenth century.

As an ethical proposition, sharing work is the reciprocal gesture—like the gift—expressing and reinforcing cooperative working arrangements. John Maurice Clark's (1923) analysis of social overhead costs, discussed below, suggests that the notion *also* makes economic sense, given an appropriate social accounting framework. Collectively, working people would be better off if they joined in refusing to compete in a race to the bottom. By collectively conserving work effort, the workers acting cooperatively might achieve higher levels of productivity than otherwise, as well as build greater social solidarity and job security.

The potential for reduced hours to result in higher productivity—in some cases, even higher total output—is explicit in Sydney Chapman's theory of the hours of labor, discussed in the next section. In his theory, Chapman documented market failure in the allocation of hours of work, often resulting in hours of work that were too long from the standpoint of both worker welfare and optimal output.

Are today's labor unions up to the challenge? In the UK, the United States, and Canada, unions have long abandoned their traditional strategies of prioritizing the demand for shorter hours, especially in response to unemployment. Instead, the preferred employment strategy has been to call for fiscal stimulus through increased government spending. How, then, would the labor commons union come into existence? How might it be organized and governed? What principles would it uphold and tactics would it employ? These important details must be left for future elaboration, not least because they differ from case to case and in many instances would involve the reorientation of and transition from established institutions. One particular, however, can be specified, that is the analytical model for guiding decision-making within the union.

The Hours and Output Spreadsheet

In the early 1960s, Edward Denison (1962) estimated that roughly one-tenth of the economic growth that occurred between 1909 and 1957 in the United State could be attributed to the "effect of shorter hours on quality of a man-hour's work." A few years earlier, labor economist Joseph Zeisel (1958) called the long-term decline in the industrial workweek, "one of the most persistent and significant trends in the American economy in the past century." That is, it *had* been a persistent and significant trend up until around 1940. After a brief spike during World War II, however, the length of the average workweek in manufacturing quickly subsided to prewar levels and then remained virtually flat for the next 65 years (see Figure 11.1). By March 2010, the average manufacturing workweek lasted six minutes longer than had the average workweek in August 1945.

In the broader economy, annual hours of work continued to decline after World War II but at a slower rate than they had previously (see Figure 11.2). Part of that decline, however, can be attributed to the increased participation of women and students in the labor force, often as part-time workers, and to a sectoral shift of employment away from manufacturing and toward services. Annual hours for full-time workers and for adult, nonstudent men showed less movement.

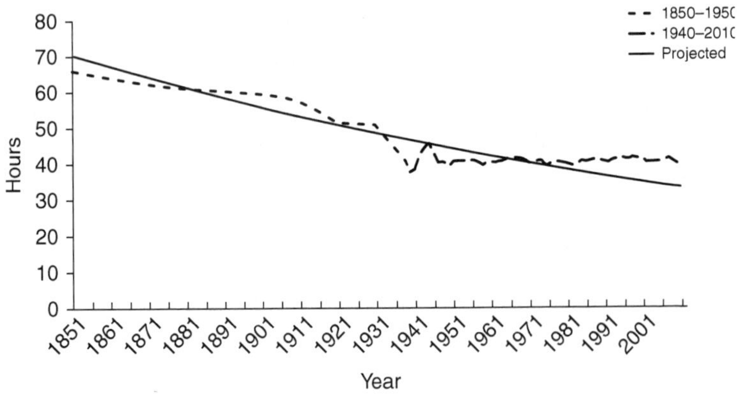

Figure 11.1 US weekly hours (industrial) 1850–2010.

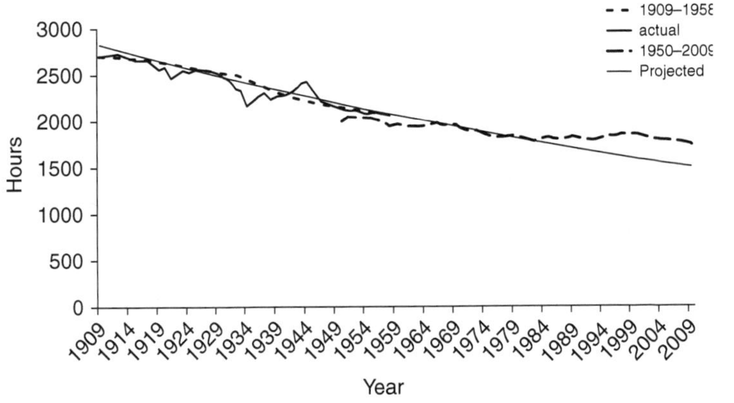

Figure 11.2 US annual hours worked 1909–2009.

Nevertheless, had the annual hours of work continued to decline at the rate that prevailed from 1909 to 1958, average annual hours in 2009 would have been nearly 14 percent lower than they were—an annual average of around 1,500 hours instead of 1,742.

What might the effect of shorter hours have been on job creation? Intuitively, it is tempting to take the total number of hours worked in 2009 (approximately 250 billion hours) and divide by the lower annual average per worker. This calculation would yield an additional 22.6 million jobs (net) created between 1980 and 2009 if hours had continued to decline in accord with the long-term trend. But wouldn't the productivity gains from shorter hours be expected to offset some or even most of that hypothetical job creation? With increased productivity, the given amount of total output produced in 2009 could simply have been produced in fewer total hours. But who says total output would have remained the same if average hours had changed and if the change in average hours resulted in higher productivity? Economists often claim that faster productivity growth leads to higher employment in the long run.

University of California economist Carl Walsh (2004) summarized this view: "There is little debate among economists about the long-run effect of productivity on employment.... In the long run, faster productivity growth should translate into an increase in the overall demand for labor in the economy." There are two ways the salutary effect can occur. The lower cost of production may so enlarge the demand for a product that it more than offsets the increased output per worker. Otherwise, technology frees workers for employment producing new products or services that were previously unavailable.

Denison deplored the surprising lack of attention given to the relationship between hours and output in published projections of economic growth—especially given the "virtual unanimity of opinion among economists" that shorter hours had in the past contributed substantially to higher output. To begin to address these issues, I have developed a spreadsheet model to evaluate the effects of shorter working time on productivity and employment. The spreadsheet model can serve as a navigational tool or "management information system" for the labor commons union. It takes empirical cues from Denison and Zeisel but analytically relies on the economics of fatigue and productivity pioneered by Sydney J. Chapman (1909).

In Chapman's theory, the output during a working day—or any other duration of work—has a discernible pattern. Setting aside the immediate effect of breaks and interruptions in the flow of work, work usually requires some set up and settling in period after which the pace of work increases until it reaches a peak or plateau—which may last several hours—after which it then declines as fatigue sets in toward the end of the day. This pace of work or rate of productivity can be ideally represented as a sine curve that first rises and then falls. The cumulative output that occurs over the course of the day can be evaluated as the area under the curve up to any given length of time.

The amplitude and period of the sine curve (its height and length) are determined by the current state of technology and the characteristics of the worker—such as health, skill, and motivation. Over the longer run, there can be established an optimal length of the working day for maximizing total output. Through the accumulation of fatigue, the worker's health and motivation act on total output as a kind of feedback mechanism. For any given optimal length of the working day, the long-term effect of extending the usual working day beyond that optimum risks the accumulation of fatigue and the resulting depression of total output—not just hourly productivity—below what could have been achieved in fewer hours of work. The occasional brief stint of overtime work would probably have little or no effect on total output or perhaps even boost it a bit. But a persistent regime of scheduled overtime will tend to detract from total output because the worker will gradually adjust his or her work pace downward to offset the fatigue from the longer days. Or, if the pace isn't adjusted, the increased fatigue may result in more absenteeism, accidents, deterioration in the quality of work, and so on.

Most significantly, Chapman's theory demonstrated market failure in the determination of the hours of work. The counter-intuitive finding of his theory was that the profit-maximizing behavior of firms in a competitive market led them to seek hours of work that are longer than optimal for output. Leading British economists of the 1920s and 1930s—including (emphatically) Cecil Pigou (1952), Lionel Robbins (1929), and John R. Hicks (1932)—accepted that analysis as canonical. Hicks summarized the historical behavior of the firm as follows:

> The long hours worked in the early days of the Industrial Revolution are notorious; they were reduced, it is well known, mainly by State regulation and Trade Union action. It was found, after they had been reduced, that the output of eleven hours' work might be greater than that of twelve. Employers had been working at more than the output optimum, without realising it.
>
> Probably it had never entered the heads of most employers that it was at all conceivable that hours could be shortened and output maintained. (Hicks 1932, 107)

This conclusion of market failure remains unchallenged. Instead, it was bypassed when Hicks added a further assumption that union bargaining power could *impose* hours of work that were optimal for output. "A very modest degree of rationality on the part of employers will thus lead them to reduce hours to the output optimum *as soon as Trade Unionism has to be reckoned with at all seriously*" (218; emphasis added).

The standard assumption about the hours of labor is not, as may be supposed, a straightforward story about efficient allocation through competitive markets. Instead, it is a convoluted tale of market failure and then imagined correction in response to union strike threat. Given the erosion of union density and the near total eclipse of work time reduction as a union priority, threat is less plausible today than it may have been either in the 1930s when Hicks proposed it or in the 1950s when it became generally accepted (see Nyland [1989], Walker [2007a]).

Given the total quantity of output in an economy, the number of workers employed, the total hours worked and assuming that the average annual (or daily or weekly) hours of work per employee are optimal, one can construct a generic Chapman work curve for that economy. Alternatively, a counter-factual baseline model can be built by projecting the "persistent and significant" trend in the hours of work, which prevailed in the United States from the mid-nineteenth century to the mid-twentieth century. Using that baseline model, we can then estimate the effect on total output of deviations from that trend. Such a hypothetical projection is undoubtedly controversial but it can be justified by reference to specific historical conditions, such as abandonment of a shorter hours strategy by unions, pursuit of demand management policies by governments, increased proportion of per-employee benefit payroll costs, ideological opposition of economists and policy makers to working time policy, and so on.

There is no sure-fire formula for translating the resulting estimate of, in this case, expanded output into an estimate of associated employment gains. A procedure sometimes used by economic forecasters is simply to apply a ratio from the empirical observation (or rule of thumb) known as "Okun's Law," which describes a relationship between the rate of economic growth and changes in the unemployment rate. Such an estimate may be suspect on theoretical grounds. The justification for relying on Okun's Law as a rule of thumb is admittedly crude: "Everybody does it." But all we are trying to do here is rationalize moderating our estimate of the quantity of employment that may be created by a trend optimization of working time. Recall that we began by discounting the simple "redistribution" of a given number of total hours among a much larger number (22.6 million) of workers. Here, we are shying away from the assertion that a given increase in output will generate a *proportionate* increase in employment. After all, some unspecified portion of that increase in output must already be accounted for in the productivity gain. Okun's Law may not be the right tool but it is the only tool we have—for now.

A final objection to these calculations would have to do with how a given reduction in hours was implemented. If a government mandate imposed a one-size-fits-all regulation, it might cause inefficiencies that would impede employment creation. The institutional arrangement of the labor commons union was designed expressly to circumvent such pitfalls of implementation.

With all those caveats, it needs to be repeated that the purpose of the exercise is not to predict precisely how many jobs would be created through a reduction of the workweek but to show that the potential for job creation is not based on an exclusive presumption of redistributing a given amount of employment.

A Hypothetical Example: Five Million Jobs?

To give an example of the kind of calculation this model enables, I have estimated the job-creating potential of a workweek conforming to the historical trend in average annual hours prevailing from 1909 to 1958. This model assumes that the average length of the workweek in 1909, 52 hours, was optimal for the level of technology that existed in 1909 and that the 1958 average of 39.6 hours was also optimal, given the technology of 1958 (see Figure 11.3). The underlying hypothesis is that the long-term trend in hours—at least in the period from 1909 to 1958—reflected an underlying technological dynamic and that deviation from that trend, especially after 1980, also represents a deviation away from the path of optimal output.

These are, of course, only assumptions. They differ from the standard assumption that the given hours of work are optimal for an explicit theoretical reason—Sydney Chapman's analysis demonstrated the tendency of the hours bargain in a competitive market to lead to longer than optimal hours, unless checked by government, trade union, or other *noneconomic* action. The standard assumption of optimal hours gets around that implication of Chapman's theory by tacitly, and probably unknowingly, making the additional assumption of substantial trade union strike threat. My model makes the latter assumption explicit and then rejects it as implausible.

Projecting the 1909–1958 trend suggests that by 2009 the optimal workweek would have averaged to 29 hours, for example, a 32-hour workweek with five weeks annual vacation (see Figure 11.4). *By definition*, a workweek longer than that of optimum would reduce output below its potential. The spreadsheet model estimates that compared to the baseline projection, excessive hours of work resulted in the loss of about 6.5 percent of total potential output or about 8 percent of growth since 1958. This compares with Denison's estimate of 10 percent growth attributable to higher productivity from shorter hours

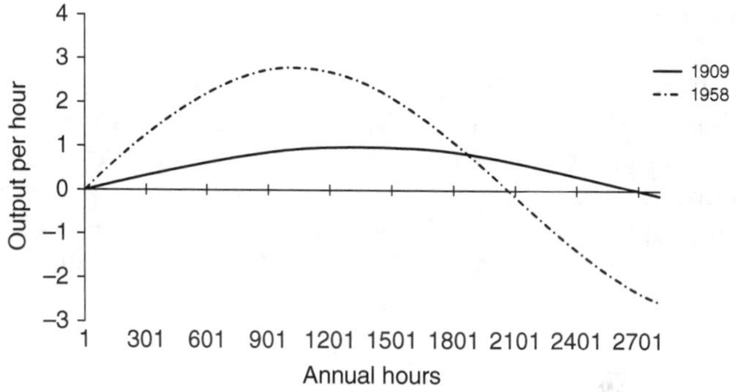

Figure 11.3 Work curves, 1909 and 1958.

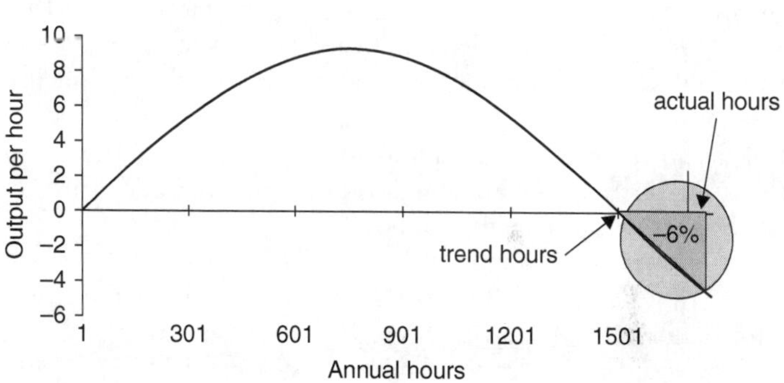

Figure 11.4 Work curve, 2009.

between 1909 and 1957. Translated into jobs lost, this could represents over five million jobs if we assume a 1 percentage point increase in unemployment for every 2 percentage point drop in output. There are many unspecified variables that could upset this estimate. For example, how would the trend in optimal hours have been affected by the variation in the pace of technological change? We don't, and probably can't, know what the "true counter-factual" is. That's beside the point. The objective is to develop a new way of looking at the issue of hours of work, not to establish the optimality of a 1,500 hour annual average or to ascertain the exact number of jobs actually foregone by failure to achieve that standard.

However, I've used some fairly conservative benchmarks to anchor the trend line. If I had chosen 1940 instead of 1958 as the endpoint, then the trend would have indicated an optimal working year of 1,400 hours—around 11 million potential jobs foregone. Whether the additional economic growth would be a good thing is another matter. This model doesn't itself demonstrate the job-creating potential of work time reduction in the absence of economic growth, but it does suggest the job-creating contribution that work time reduction can make in an expanding economy. Actual results would depend crucially on how policies were implemented but there is arguably a case for some experimentation—and for jettisoning economists' lump-of-labor contempt for work time reduction (Walker 2000, 2007b).

Accounting for Labor and the Environment

Not only can employment be regarded as yet another common pool resource among others, but it can also be argued that it is the common pool resource *par excellance*—the paragon that stands as the single most far-reaching and democratically vital instance of a common pool resource. Donald Stabile (1993) alluded to something in this vein when he noted that "human labor is also the primary constituent of the society whose values must be part of any criterion of social evaluation. The appropriate starting point in any policy directed at social costs is with those imposed on labor."

In *Studies in the Economics of Overhead Costs,* Clark (1923) offered the following parable to illustrate his argument about the overhead costs of labor: "If all industry were integrated and owned by workers, what would be the relation of constant to variable expense?...it would be clear to worker-owners that the real costs of labor could not be materially reduced by unemployment." After all, the cost of maintaining the worker and his or her family in good stead has to be borne by someone whether or not that worker is employed. If those costs are not met, the ability of the worker to contribute to society will deteriorate. Meanwhile, the time spent out of work will amount to a dead weight loss both to the worker and to the society as a whole. This is not to say that all industry necessarily *should* or *must* be integrated into a single, worker-owned enterprise in order to achieve full employment. But what is imperative is that if all industry isn't so organized, there still needs to be an appropriate accounting framework that acknowledges the worker's fixed costs as readily as the double-entry bookkeeping does the firm's. It is not only an ethical question but also a matter of basic accounting integrity.

In "Accountants and the Price System: The Problem of Social Costs," Stabile (1993) focused on the perspective introduced by Clark. Stabile criticized abortive efforts by accountants in the 1970s to change the way social costs were evaluated on the corporate account books. To explain why they had failed, Stabile cited analyses by Clark and K. William Kapp (1950) that viewed the social costs of labor as central to any more general process of social evaluation. Such an outlook was missing from the works of social cost accountants of the 1970s. "Market values are a weak thread from which to hang a whole system of value," Stabile argued, "but accountants cling to it doggedly. Without an alteration of this basic tenet of accounting, social cost accounting cannot develop into a criterion of social value."

Returning again to Clark's thought experiment of the hypothetical state where all industry is integrated and owned by workers, we can see that it stands as an example of a nonmarket process of social evaluation whose results can be worked out with little hesitation. Involuntary unemployment would be regarded as sheer waste rather than as a regrettable but necessary expedient for containing labor costs. Social accounting for unemployment would come to a very different assessment of economic efficiency than would an asymmetrical, pseudo-social accounting relying exclusively on the metaphor of the firm. Gains in desired disposable time (as opposed to idleness) would need to be valued as *economic* gains and losses of free time as *economic* losses (see Walker [2011]).

Conclusion

The above outline of a social accounting framework for disposable time is only a preliminary sketch. Much refinement can go into its data handling, such as breaking down the analysis into occupational and industrial classifications. Such refinement might produce a very different trend analysis. Different assumptions could be tested about the macroeconomic effects of work time reduction on consumption and the multipliers that might apply to different scenarios. I also haven't talked about the applicability of this kind of analysis to national income and product accounting, but a hint of its applicability may be taken from two of the pillars of my argument, John Maurice Clark and Edward F. Denison, both of whom were pioneers of national income accounting. Over a century ago, Sydney J. Chapman, prize-winning pupil of Alfred Marshall and future chief economic adviser to the British government wrote: "The ideal working day of the future cannot be eight hours, for it must be essentially a progressive ideal. As a community advances, agitation for shorter hours will be constantly breaking out anew." A new outbreak of agitation for shorter hours is long overdue.

Bibliography

Bartolini, S. 2006. "Beyond Accumulation and Technical Progress: Negative Externalities as an Engine of Economic Growth." In *Environment, Inequality and Collective Action*, edited by M. Basili, M. Franzini and A. Vercelli, 52–71. London and New York: Routledge.

Bryer, R. 2006. "Accounting and Control of the Labour Process." *Critical Perspectives on Accounting* 17: 367–397.

Burnett, J. 1872. *Nine Hours' Movement. A History of the Engineers' Strike in Newcastle and Gateshead.* Newcastle-upon-Tyne: John W. Swanston.

Chapman, S. J. 1909. "Hours of Labour." *Economic Journal* 19: 353–373.

Chastellux, F. J. 1969 [1774]. *An Essay on Public Happiness.* New York: Augustus M. Kelley.

Clark, J. M. 1923. *Studies in the Economics of Overhead Costs.* Chicago: University of Chicago Press.

Denison, E. F. 1962. *The Sources of Economic Growth in the United States and the Alternatives Before Us.* New York: Committee for Economic Development.

Dryzek, J. S. 1996. "Foundations for Environmental Political Economy: The Search for *Homo Ecologicus*?" *New Political Economy* 1: 27–40.

FHJ. 1871. "English Affairs. The Labor Question—The Newcastle Strike—Influence of the International—The Masters and the League—Imported Labor—The Masters' View—The Real Question at Issue." *New York Times*, October 19.

Franklin, B. 1839. *Memoirs of Benjamin Franklin.* Vol. II. New York: Harper and Brothers.

Gilbert, M., G. Jaszi, E. F. Denison, and C. F. Schwartz. 1948. "Objectives of National Income Measurement: A Reply to Professor Kuznets." *Review of Economics and Statistics* 30: 179–195.

Hicks, J. R. 1932. *The Theory of Wages.* London: Macmillan.

Hueting, R. 2010. "Why Environmental Sustainability Can Most Probably Not Be Attained with Growing Production." *Journal of Cleaner Production* 18: 525–530.

Jaszi, G. 1958. "The Conceptual Basis of the Accounts: A Re-examination." In *A Critique of the United States Income and Product Accounts.* Princeton, NJ: Princeton University Press.

Jevons, W. S. 1865. *The Coal Question.* London and Cambridge: Macmillan.

Kapp, K. W. 1950. *The Social Costs of Private Enterprise.* Cambridge, MA: Harvard University Press.

Krugman, P. 2003. "Lumps of Labor." *New York Times,* October 7.

Kuznets, S. 1948. "National Income: A New Version." *Review of Economics and Statistics* 30 (3): 151–179.

Nyland, C. 1989. *Reduced Worktime and the Management of Production.* Cambridge: Cambridge University Press.

Ostrom, E. 1990. *Governing the Commons: The Evolution of Institutions for Collective Action.* Cambridge: Cambridge University Press.

———. 2009. *Beyond Markets and States: Polycentric Governance of Complex Economic Systems.* Nobel Prize Lecture. http://nobelprize.org/nobel_prizes/economics/laureates/2009/ostrom_lecture.pdf. Accessed January 23, 2011.

Pencavel, J. 1986. "Labor Supply of Men: A Survey." In *Handbook of Labor Economics,* edited by O. Ashenfelter and R. Layard, 3–102. Amsterdam: North Holland.

Pigou, A. C. 1952. *The Economics of Welfare.* 4th ed. London: Macmillan.

Robbins, L. 1929. "The Economic Effects of Variations of Hours of Labour." *Economic Journal* 39: 25–40.

Smith, A. 1790. *The Theory of Moral Sentiments.* London: A. Millar.

Sombart, W. 1952. "Medieval and Modern Commercial Enterprise." In *Enterprise and Secular Change,* edited by F. C. Lane and J. C. Riemersma, 25–40. London: Allen & Unwin.

Stabile, D. R. 1993. "Accountants and the Price System: The Problem of Social Costs." *Journal of Economic Issues* 27: 171–188.

Tufnell, E. C. 1834. *Character, Object and Effects of Trades' Unionism.* London: James Ridgway and Sons.

Vint, J. 2007. "Harriet Martineau and Industrial Strife: From Theory into Fiction into Melodrama." Discussion papers in Economics 2007–2, Manchester: Manchester Metropolitan University—Department of Economics.

Walker, T. 2000. "The 'Lump-of-Labor' Case against Work-Sharing: Populist Fallacy or Marginalist Throwback?" In *Working Time: International Trends, Theory and Policy Perspectives,* edited by L Golden and DM Figart, 196–211. London and New York: Routledge.

———. 2007a. "Missing: The Strange Disappearance of Sydney j. Chapman's Theory of the Hours of Labour." Conference presentation, World Congress for Social Economics, Amsterdam. http://papers.ssrn.com/sol3/papers.cfm?abstract_id=1125543.

———. 2007b. "Why Do Economists Dislike a Lump of Labor?" *Review of Social Economy* 65 (3): 279–291.

———. 2011. "The Hours of Labour and the Problem of Social Cost." *Marshall Studies Bulletin* 12. http://www.dse.unifi.it/CMpro-v-p-141.html.

Walsh, C. 2004. "The Productivity and Jobs Connection: The Long and the Short Run of It." *RBSF Economic Letter* 2004–18. http://www.frbsf.org/publications/economics/letter/2004/el2004-18.pdf. Accessed January 23, 2011.

Zeisel, J., 1958. "The Workweek in American Industry 1850–1956." *Monthly Labor Review* 81: 23–29.

Contributors

Jessica M. Bailey received her doctorate in Marketing from the University of Missouri-Columbia in 1983. She is presently the dean of the School of Business and Economics at Winston-Salem State University in North Carolina. Dr. Bailey serves in leadership roles with various organizations devoted to economic development and change in the Piedmont region of North Carolina. During the last 25 years, she has held senior/executive positions with various universities in the United States. Dr. Bailey has coedited the book *Modern Competitiveness in the Twenty-first Century: Global Experiences* (2011) and has authored and coauthored a number of book chapters, journal articles, and scholarly works in the fields of marketing and international business. Her research interests include international business and educational administration.

Paula M. Cole is lecturer of economics at the University of Denver in Denver, Colorado. Her research examines the essential role of care in the economy from a feminist, institutionalist, and economic perspective. Paula's current work explores how an inclusive and sustainable economy can be socially constructed.

Nikolaos Karagiannis obtained his PhD from the University of Leeds, England, in 1996. He is currently teaching Economics at Winston-Salem State University, North Carolina. Dr. Karagiannis is the research coordinator of the School of Business and Economics at Winston-Salem State University and the managing editor of the journal *American Review of Political Economy* (ARPE). He has authored, coauthored, and coedited 14 books; and has published widely in scholarly journals and in edited books in the areas of economic development, public sector economics, and macroeconomic policy analysis. He is particularly interested in developmental state theory and policy, and his research has focused extensively on the applicability of this interventionist view in different contexts such as EU countries,

Caribbean small island economies, North African countries, and the United States.

Valerie K. Kepner is assistant professor of Economics at King's College in Wilkes-Barre, Pennsylvania. Her dissertation researched the influence of social capital on the migration decisions of the financially disadvantaged. More generally, her research interests lie within the heterodox, and more specifically institutionalist, schools of economic thought. Her current work focuses on the incompatibility of capitalism, consumerism, and environmental sustainability.

John Marangos is associate professor of Political Economy at the Department of Economics, University of Crete, Greece, and a visiting scholar at the School of Business and Economics, Winston-Salem State University, North Carolina. The focal points for Dr. Marangos's research include economic transition processes in the Balkans, Eastern Europe, in the former Soviet Union, and in Asia; international development; and innovative methodologies for teaching economics. His publications or those in process of being published include six books, eight book chapters, thirteen entries in encyclopedias, and over sixty refereed journal articles. Dr. Marangos's latest publication is an edited book titled *Alternative Perspectives of a Good Society* (2012). His most recent project is a textbook in Comparative Economic Systems titled *Consistency and Viability of Economic Systems*, to be published by the end of the year. Dr. Marangos was the editor in chief of the *Forum of Social Economics* and section editor for the *Global Business and Economic Review*.

Danièle Meulders is Full Professor at the Université Libre de Bruxelles (ULB) and codirector of the pluri-disciplinary international research network on Labour Market and Gender in Europe (Marché du travail et genre en Europe—MAGE). At the ULB, she directs the research team on labor economics at the Département d'Economie Appliquée (DULBEA). Her main research interests are in the fields of labor economics (evaluation of employment policies, effects of training on employment, women in the labor market [professional segregation, atypical employment, wage gaps], the European Employment Strategy, and the European policies for social protection and inclusion), public economics (tax competition, the redistributive and macroeconomic consequences of European integration on social protection, comparison of social protection and tax systems across Europe), and income (re)distribution and poverty analysis. Her research has also involved evaluating family policies across Europe.

Michael J. Murray is assistant professor of Economics at Bemidji State University, Minnesota, and a research associate with the Center for Full Employment and Price Stability. He received his PhD from the University of Missouri, Kansas City. His current research focuses on simulations of various Employer of Last Resort proposals, heterodox price and production modeling, and the economics of Adolph Lowe. He is coeditor of *The Job Guarantee: Toward True Full Employment* and *Employment Guarantee Schemes*; has published in the *Review of Radical Political Economy* and *Journal of Economic Issues*; and has contributed to edited collections.

Edward J. O'Boyle, PhD, is senior research associate affiliated with the Mayo Research Institute. He specializes in personalist economics that centers on persons as economic agents in which he replaces the individual and individualism of mainstream economics, which are rooted in the Enlightenment and the script stage of human communication, with the person and personalism that spring from the electronic stage of human communication. He has published in *Monthly Labor Review*, *Pediatrics*, *Linacre Quarterly*, *Journal of Markets and Morality*, *International Journal of Social Economics*, *Business Insights*, *Review of Social Economy*, *Journal of Business Ethics*, *Logos*, *Ethics and Information Technology*, *Forum for Social Economics*, *Catholic Social Science Review*, and *American Review of Political Economy*. He is a past president of the Association for Social Economics. Publications sponsored by the Mayo Research Institute are accessible at www.mayoresearch.org.

Síle O'Dorchai has been researcher at the Département d'Economie Appliquée of the Université Libre de Bruxelles (DULBEA) since 2001. In 1997, she obtained a master's degree in Slavic Studies at the Katholieke Universiteit Leuven; in 2001, one in Economics at the Université Libre de Bruxelles; and in 2007, she finished her doctoral thesis titled "Family, Work and Welfare States in Europe: Women's Juggling with Multiple Roles." Her main research interests are in the fields of labor economics, gender economics (with a particular interest in gender gaps in employment and wages), and household and population economics. Her research addresses the issue of the individualization of income and poverty measures, that of decision-taking, and the sharing of tasks and responsibilities within households. She also analyses the influence of public policies on the work-life balance. In her teaching she focuses on the social economy and the nonprofit sector. Besides numerous research reports, she has published scientific articles in the *Journal of Comparative Policy Analysis*, *Feminist*

Economics, Journal of Income Distribution, International Journal of Manpower, and others.

Doris Páez earned a BA in Psychology from the University of South Florida (USF) in Tampa, Florida. She also earned an MA and EdS from the USF. In 1992, she was awarded a PhD from the University of Florida in Gainesville, Florida. Páez is a graduate of the inaugural class of the Liberty Fellowship, a two-year fellowship for the state of South Carolina's most prominent leaders (aged 25–45 years). She is currently the executive director of Forsyth Futures, a nonprofit research organization in Winston-Salem, North Carolina. She was recruited to join Forsyth Futures in 2009 after a successful career working in higher education administration and teaching, as well as a practicing psychologist. Prior to moving to North Carolina, she held the position of executive director of the Metropolitan Studies Institute at the University of South Carolina-Upstate. In addition to her work in community indicators, throughout her career, Páez has participated, led, and evaluated national, state, and local initiatives addressing educational and mental health issues of culturally and linguistically diverse children and families, as well as community-based initiatives. She is the author of 80 publications and has conducted over 600 national, state, and local presentations. She has served on the faculties of North Carolina State University, Winston-Salem State University, University of Florida, Medical University of South Carolina, Furman University, New Mexico State University, and Florida International University. She is a recipient of the National Association of School Psychologists' Presidential Award for her work in culturally responsive education and mental health.

Denise Pearson, PhD, has worked in the higher education community for more than 20 years. She is currently employed at Winston-Salem State University as assistant provost for Faculty Affairs and professor of Education. Prior to joining Winston-Salem State University, Pearson worked at the University of Denver, School of Continuing and Professional Studies, as associate dean. In this capacity she served as the chief academic affairs leader for master's, graduate certificate, and degree completion programs, and established external advisory boards comprising community leaders in public, private, and nonprofit sectors to guide the development of new programs and serve as a link to the larger community. Pearson's research interests involve issues related to organizational leadership and conflict management, with an emphasis on higher education and historically black colleges and universities (HBCUs). In 2006, she was hosted as a visiting professor in the Conflict Management Program at the Nelson Mandela Metropolitan University in Port Elizabeth, South Africa. She also worked collaboratively on a US Department of Education grant between the University of Denver and the University of the West Indies to build conflict-resolution capacity in Trinidad & Tobago communities. Pearson received a PhD in Administration & Supervision of Education from Marquette University, MA in Conflict Resolution from the University of Denver, MS in Education Administration from Concordia University, and BA in Human Services from Pace University.

K. Maeve Powlick is an economist living in the Hudson Valley of New York. She works with rural and urban communities of concentrated poverty to combine theory and practice of economic development at the community level, with youth at the center. Her work includes original mixed-methods research, program evaluation, grant writing, and consulting. Dr. Powlick works to include youth as equal partners in the knowledge-creation process, and has led Participatory Action Research (PAR) projects with youth at Harvey Milk High School in New York City and as part of the federally-funded Promise Neighborhoods project in Hudson, NY. She earned her PhD in Economics at the University of Massachusetts, Amherst, in September 2011, and completed her undergraduate education at Wells College. She is mother to two young children, Isaac and Grace, who remind her every day that children are active agents of change.

Morteza Sadri received his doctorate in Urban Planning from the University of Washington in 1985. He is the president and founder of Liaison International, Inc., an international trade and business consulting firm specializing in market research and international market development, with representation in the United States and abroad. Dr. Sadri has taught a wide variety of courses in marketing, management, and international business in the United States and overseas.

Janet Spitz received her PhD from Stanford University Business School in 1991, MBA from Cornell University in 1985, and BA from Cornell University in 1973. From dissertation research on productivity and wage relations in economic theory and labor markets, Dr. Spitz's focus has now shifted to business globalization: its driving ideologies, behaviors, and consequences. She has published widely, including in the *American Journal of Economics and Sociology*, *New Political Science*, and the *Forum for Social Economics*. Dr. Spitz serves as a reviewer for the *Forum for Social Economics*, the *Bulletin of*

Political Economy, *Sage Open Forum*, and *Wiley Press*. She is a member of the American Economic Association Committee on the Status of Women in the Economics Profession; the International Association of Feminist Economists; the Association for Social Economics; the Center for Citizenship, Race, and Ethnicity Studies and is employed at the College of Saint Rose in Albany, NY, as associate professor of Business. Dr. Spitz spent her last sabbatical at the University of Queensland in Brisbane, Australia, where she extended her work on ideological drivers of business globalization. This chapter stems from that most recent work.

Shann Turnbull obtained an MBA from Harvard in 1963 and became a part-time teacher at Australia's first business school while being a serial entrepreneur. He founded many enterprises with three of them becoming traded on the Australian stock exchange. From 1967 to 1974 he was a partner in a private equity firm that acquired and reorganized a dozen publicly traded companies. He became chair/CEO/director of public companies and initiated the first educational qualification in the world for company directors. This was launched in 1975 with his first book on *Democratising the Wealth of Nations*. The novel ideas in his book led to consulting assignments for multinational corporations, United Nations, World Bank, and governments, including, in 1991, the People's Republic of China and Czechoslovakia. Dr. Turnbull is a prolific writer on reforming the theories and practices of capitalism archived at http://ssrn.com/author=26239. He is a coauthor of *Building Sustainable Communities: Tools and Concepts for Self-reliant Change*. In 2000 two of his articles were published with the seminal contributions of leading scholars in the Corporate Governance volume of *The History of Management Thought*. His 2001 PhD thesis established the science of governance. This provided the basis for creating an MBA course at Macquarie University, Sydney, for governance architects in public, private, and nonprofit organizations. It also provided the theoretical basis for writing *A New Way to Govern: Organizations and Society after Enron*. In 2011 Dr. Turnbull founded in the UK the Green/Sustainable Money Working Group to provide alternative types of money in the event of another financial crisis.

Tom Walker teaches courses in Labour and the Environment and Collective Bargaining in the Labour Studies Program at Simon Fraser University, Burnaby, Vancouver, BC, Canada. He has been a peace and social justice activist since the 1960s. With an MA in Education from Simon Fraser University, he has over 20 years of experience as an educator and social policy research consultant to unions, community organizations, and local governments. Since 1995, Walker has immersed himself in research on shorter working time. His articles on the history of the debate around working time have been published in the *Marshall Studies Bulletin*, the *Review of Social Economics,* and in *Working Time: Trends, Theory and Policy Perspectives,* edited by Lonnie Golden and Deb Figart.

Robert B. Williams teaches Economics at Guilford College, North Carolina. He has recently published a book on ecological economics, titled *Greening the Economy: Integrating Economics and Ecology to Make Effective Change* (2010). He is currently working on a new book that examines how systems of privilege explain the rising concentration of wealth and the declining economic mobility among US households. When not found teaching in the classroom or writing in his office, Dr. Williams can be located either on the basketball court or in his garden harvesting fruits, vegetables, and flowers. He currently lives in Greensboro, NC, with his partner, artist, and educator, Mary Beth Boone.

Index

Printed in the United States of America